WINE DOGS USA

2

more dogs from North American wineries

Craig McGill and Susan Elliott

A Giant Dog book

WINE DOGS USA 2
MORE DOGS FROM NORTH AMERICAN WINERIES

ISBN 978-1-921336-10-2

COPYRIGHT © GIANT DOG, FIRST EDITION 2008
WINE DOGS ® IS A REGISTERED TRADEMARK

DESIGNED BY SUSAN ELLIOTT, COPYRIGHT © McGILL DESIGN GROUP PTY LTD, 2008
ALL ILLUSTRATIONS COPYRIGHT © CRAIG McGILL, McGILL DESIGN GROUP PTY LTD, 2008
ALL TEXT NOT ATTRIBUTED, COPYRIGHT © CRAIG McGILL, McGILL DESIGN GROUP PTY LTD, 2008

ALL PHOTOGRAPHY © CRAIG McGILL, 2008

PRINTED BY APOL BOOKBUILDERS, CHINA
PROOFREADING AND EDITING BY VICKY FISHER

PUBLISHED BY GIANT DOG, ABN 27 110 894 178. PO BOX 964, ROZELLE NSW 2039 AUSTRALIA
TELEPHONE: (+612) 9555 4077   FACSIMILE: (+612) 9555 5985   INFO@WINEDOGS.COM
WEB: WWW.WINEDOGS.COM

FOR ORDERS: ORDERS@WINEDOGS.COM

OTHER TITLES BY CRAIG McGILL AND SUSAN ELLIOTT INCLUDE:
WINE DOGS AUSTRALIA – MORE DOGS FROM AUSTRALIAN WINERIES ISBN 978-1-921336-02-7
WINE DOGS DELUXE EDITION – THE DOGS OF AUSTRALASIAN WINERIES ISBN 0-9580856-2-5
WINE DOGS: USA EDITION – THE DOGS OF NORTH AMERICAN WINERIES ISBN 0-9580856-6-8
WINE DOGS ITALY / I CANI DEL VINO – I CANI DELLE AZIENDE VINICOLE ITALIANE ISBN 978-1-921336-11-9
WINE DOGS NEW ZEALAND – THE DOGS FROM NEW ZEALAND WINERIES ISBN 978-1-921336-12-6

HEALTH WARNING: VETERINARY ASSOCIATIONS ADVISE THAT EATING GRAPES, SULTANAS OR RAISINS CAN MAKE
A DOG EXTREMELY ILL AND COULD POSSIBLY RESULT IN FATAL KIDNEY FAILURE. IN THE INTERESTS OF CANINE
HEALTH AND WELLBEING, DO NOT FEED YOUR DOGS GRAPES OR ANY GRAPE BY-PRODUCT.

for Tok

28 FEBRUARY 1993 – 4 MARCH 2008

TOOTSIE 9-YEAR-OLD IRISH WOLFHOUND X, MALOY O'NEILL VINEYARDS, PASO ROBLES CA

CONTENTS

FOREWORD *BY ROBERT M. PARKER JR*   7

HARRY THE SOMMELIER DOG *BY JENNIFER ROSEN*   37

AURORA THE GOATHERD *BY LARRY OATES*   61

THE STORY OF PORT *BY ERIC DUNHAM*   85

ROVER, BORDEAUX COLLIE *BY LORI CRANTFORD*   117

LIFE WITH OUR JACK RUSSELLS *BY GAREN STAGLIN*   129

MIDNIGHT IN THE WINERY OF GOOD AND EVIL *BY MAT GARRETSON*   133

WOLF *BY ADAM LECHMERE*   155

BITCH... *BY ZOE WILLIAMS*   171

A GRAND DAY OUT *BY HEIDI BARRETT*   207

TOOTSIE TO THE RESCUE *BY SHANNON O'NEILL*   231

OF WINE AND DOGS *BY JOHN POTTER*   245

WINERY AND VINEYARD MANAGEMENT *BY HANK KELLEY*   251

PUPINOT *BY BRIAN DOYLE*   289

HARMONY, CHI AND THE NATURAL ENERGY OF THE WINE DOG *BY KRIS CURRAN*   311

A DOG NAMED ANDRE *BY SUSAN SOKOL BLOSSER*   331

THE WOOF STREET TIMES *BY ZAR AND ELENA BROOKS*   383

CANINES, PARKER AND ME *BY ELIN McCOY*   455

STATS, FACTS AND MORE LIES... *BY CRAIG McGILL*   531

WINERY AND VINEYARD LISTINGS   536

WINE DOGS BREED INDEX   557

BUDDY 4-YEAR-OLD ENGLISH BULLDOG, ROBERT AND PAT PARKER

FOREWORD
by Robert M. Parker Jr

FIRST AND FOREMOST, what a pleasure it has been to share in the great success Craig McGill and Susan Elliott have had with the first edition of Wine Dogs, USA. *Moreover, how gracious it is of them to ask me to write a brief introduction about the importance of our canine companions.*

Few pleasures in life can equal the extraordinary companionship and adoration our dogs extend to us every waking moment. I count my blessings for having been raised with dogs since my earliest memories. As I have said many times, I will go to my grave with dogs as my companions, making sure that my last will and testament provides for their proper care long after my passing. The loyalty, limitless devotion, love, and fidelity dogs display is unequaled by any other species – human or animal. Looking into a dog's eyes, you know that you are never judged except as their loving friend, and that all they expect is a friendly pat, scratch, and a decent meal.

In return, we have full-time therapists, psychiatrists, lovers, confidants, pals, and companions that, through their own systems of sounds and barks, are fully able to communicate their desires, pleasures, and on rare occasions, their frustrations and anger. They live for no other purpose than to serve us, and they ask so little in return.

This book is another homage to these extraordinary companions. Their eagerness to please and their sunny, happy dispositions displayed in the following marvelous photographs need no further explanation. I am convinced that all dogs go to heaven, for certainly they deserve a place there as much as any human being. And if, for reasons beyond my comprehension, they don't go to heaven, then I want to be where they are when I die.

ROBERT M. PARKER JR WAS BORN IN BALTIMORE, MARYLAND AND INITIALLY PURSUED A CAREER IN LAW. HIS INTEREST IN WINE BEGAN IN 1967 AND IT WASN'T LONG BEFORE ROBERT HAD STARTED TO CARVE OUT A SPECTACULAR CAREER IN WINE WRITING THAT NOW SPANS OVER 28 YEARS. HE IS THE FOUNDER OF *THE WINE ADVOCATE* AND IS THE CONTRIBUTING EDITOR FOR *FOOD AND WINE* MAGAZINE. HE ALSO PERIODICALLY CONTRIBUTES TO OTHER MAGAZINES INCLUDING *THE FIELD* AND FRANCE'S *L'EXPRESS*. HE IS THE AUTHOR OF MANY BEST-SELLING AND AWARDED WINE BOOKS INCLUDING *BORDEAUX, BURGUNDY, PARKER'S WINE BUYER'S GUIDE* AND *THE WINES OF THE RHONE VALLEY AND PROVENCE*. ROBERT'S BULLDOG GEORGE WON THE COVETED "PALME DOG" PRIZE AT THE CANNES FILM FESTIVAL FOR BEST CANINE PERFORMANCE IN A FILM FOR HIS CAMEO IN THE DOCUMENTARY *MONDOVINO*.

CHLOE

OBSESSION: DRIED LAMB LUNG
PET PEEVE: GETTING KICKED OFF MOM'S BED
FAVORITE PASTIMES: SWIMMING IN THE POND
AT HER HOUSE AND CHASING THE DUCKS
FAVORITE TOY: RIPPING THE GUTS OUT OF STUFFED ANIMALS
KNOWN ACCOMPLICES: THE LABRADORS AT WINWARD WINERY

FOUR VINES WINERY TEMPLETON, CA | HEELER X, 1 | OWNER: SUSAN A. MAHLER

FAVORITE TOY: STUFFED CIGAR
PET PEEVE: THE NEIGHBOR'S CAT
FAVORITE PASTIME: SOAKING UP THE SUN
OBSESSION: GETTING THE NEXT TREAT
FAVORITE FOOD: ANYTHING OUT OF THE GARBAGE CAN
NAUGHTIEST DEED: JUMPING ON THE TABLE AND EATING PIZZA

CAESAR

MOOSE

FAVORITE FOOD: BABY CARROTS
PET PEEVE: PEOPLE EATING IN FRONT OF HIM
OBSESSION: GOING FOR A RIDE IN THE WOODY WAGON WITH BRUCE
NAUGHTIEST DEED: PASSING GAS AND CLEARING OUT THE ROOM
FAVORITE PASTIMES: HANGING WITH BRUCE AND MIXING
THE SOUND BOARD AT DOOBIE BROTHERS RECORDING SESSIONS

OBSESSION: FOOD
PET PEEVE: BEING ALONE
KNOWN ACCOMPLICE: MARY JANE
FAVORITE TOY: SQUEAKY HAMBURGER
FAVORITE FOODS: FRUIT AND VEGETABLES
NAUGHTIEST DEED: POOPING ON THE CARPET
FAVORITE PASTIME: FOLLOWING PHYLLIS EVERYWHERE

SKETCHER

LUPO

FAVORITE FOOD: BEEF
FAVORITE TOY: STICKS
KNOWN ACCOMPLICE: YANA
FAVORITE PASTIMES: CHASING STICKS
AND HANGING OUT WITH DARYL
PET PEEVE: BEING LEFT BY HIMSELF

PET PEEVE: SHARING
FAVORITE TOY: RUBBER CHICKEN
NAUGHTIEST DEED: UNSTUFFING THE COUCH CUSHION
OBSESSION: PRUNING PLANTS IN THE VINEYARD
KNOWN ACCOMPLICES: JOE, BODOG AND LUCY
FAVORITE PASTIME: EATING ICE CUBES
FAVORITE FOODS: PEACH YOGHURT
AND CHOCOLATE SLIMFAST

DELILAH

OWNER: BARB SPELLETICH | BOSTON TERRIER, 14 WEEKS | **SPELLETICH CELLARS** NAPA, CA
13

SKY

FAVORITE PASTIME:
PLAYING WITH DIEGO AND FIONA

KNOWN ACCOMPLICES: FIONA, DIEGO
AND THE CHICKENS

OBSESSION: GUARDING THE CHICKENS

PORTER CREEK VINEYARDS HEALDSBURG, CA | COLLIE X, 1 | OWNER: ALEX DAVIS

PET PEEVE: CATS
KNOWN ACCOMPLICE: SKY
OBSESSION: PLAYING IN WATER
FAVORITE TOY: IRRIGATION SYSTEMS
NAUGHTIEST DEED: EATING A TIBETAN RUG

DIEGO

OWNER: GEORGE DAVIS | GREAT PYRENEES, 3 | **PORTER CREEK VINEYARDS** HEALDSBURG, CA | 15

PAPPI

OBSESSION: FOLLOWING HIS HUMANS

NAUGHTIEST DEED: EATING AN
ENTIRE ROAST CHICKEN WHEN LEFT
IN CAR WITH IT FOR 15 MINUTES

PET PEEVE: CATS IN HIS HOUSE

FAVORITE PASTIME: TRAVELING

FAVORITE TOYS: HUMANS

FAVORITE FOOD: STEAK

Joseph Swan Vineyards

Produced and Bottled by Joseph Swan Vineyards
Forestville, California, Alcohol 14.5% by Volume

PET PEEVE: CATS
FAVORITE PASTIME: LAYING ON
THE COUCH AND CHEWING
ON HER AARDVARK
FAVORITE FOODS: CAT FOOD AND
ANY TABLE FOOD SHE CAN SCAM
NAUGHTIEST DEED: CHEWING
THE FEET OFF ALL HER TOYS

ANNIE

DIMITRI

NAUGHTIEST DEED: ESCAPING
FAVORITE TOYS: OTHER DOGS
PET PEEVE: BEING GIVEN A BATH
FAVORITE FOOD: LEFTOVER HARVEST DINNER
OBSESSIONS: TREATS AND CURLING UP IN A LITTLE BALL

FAVORITE TOYS: PEOPLE
PET PEEVE: BEING TOLD 'NO'
FAVORITE FOODS: HAPPY HOUND DOG
TREATS AND YOGHURT CONTAINERS
FAVORITE PASTIME: RUNNING FAR AND WIDE
OBSESSION: SLEEPING WITH DIMITRI IN THE WINTER

PET PEEVE: TAKING BATHS
FAVORITE TOY: TENNIS BALLS
FAVORITE PASTIME: CHASING SALAMANDERS
KNOWN ACCOMPLICE: ANYONE WHO HAS TREATS
FAVORITE FOODS: FILET MIGNON AND KOBE BURGERS
NAUGHTIEST DEED: EATING PEOPLE'S FOOD FROM THE PICNIC TABLE

KIRBY

KALI

NAUGHTIEST DEED: HERDING
THE PG&E MAN AND THE HORSES
FAVORITE FOOD: ANYTHING YOU'RE EATING
FAVORITE PASTIMES: RACING AND CHASING ANYTHING
PET PEEVE: HIS BROTHER MAC GETTING THE ATTENTION
KNOWN ACCOMPLICES: BONNIE AND MAC

PET PEEVE: TAKING A BATH
FAVORITE PASTIME: PLAYING BALL
KNOWN ACCOMPLICES: BONNIE AND KALI
FAVORITE FOODS: CORN CHIPS AND HAMBURGERS
NAUGHTIEST DEED: LIFTING HIS LEG ON THE VET'S RECEPTION CHAIR

MAC

PET PEEVE: TAKING A BATH
FAVORITE PASTIME: PLAYING BALL
KNOWN ACCOMPLICES: BONNIE AND KALI
FAVORITE FOODS: CORN CHIPS AND HAMBURGERS
NAUGHTIEST DEED: LIFTING HIS LEG
ON THE VET'S RECEPTION CHAIR

NAUGHTIEST DEED: HERDING
THE PG&E MAN AND THE HORSES
FAVORITE FOOD: ANYTHING YOU'RE EATING
FAVORITE PASTIMES: RACING AND CHASING ANYTHING
PET PEEVE: HIS BROTHER MAC GETTING THE ATTENTION
KNOWN ACCOMPLICES: BONNIE AND MAC

MAC

PET PEEVE: KITTIES
FAVORITE PASTIME: SWIMMING
FAVORITE FOOD: FILET ROAST
FAVORITE TOY: TENNIS BALL
OBSESSION: CHASING STICKS
KNOWN ACCOMPLICES:
SPITFIRE AND SIR LLOYD OF ROSS
NAUGHTIEST DEED: CHASING THE FEDEX TRUCK

BRUNO

FAVORITE PASTIMES: WRESTLING WITH LARRY THE CAT AND RUNNING IN CIRCLES
KNOWN ACCOMPLICES: LARRY AND SADIE
NAUGHTIEST DEED: HUMPING HIS BLANKIE
PET PEEVE: BIG DOGS THAT SURPRISE ATTACK
FAVORITE TOY: PIGGIE THE SMALL STUFFED PIG
FAVORITE FOOD: TRADER JOE'S BEEF LIVER TREATS

JACK

OWNERS: DOUG AND DARCI HILL | BICHON FRISE, 2 | **HILL FAMILY ESTATE** YOUNTVILLE, CA

25

HALLIE

NAUGHTIEST DEED: THIEVING
FAVORITE FOOD: RAWHIDE BONES
PET PEEVE: HAVING HER PAWS TOUCHED
FAVORITE TOY: A SILICON WINE BARREL BUNG
FAVORITE PASTIME: RIDING IN THE PICKUP TRUCK

PLUMPJACK WINERY OAKVILLE, CA | SPRINGER SPANIEL, 7 | OWNER: JOHN CONOVER

FAVORITE TOY: TENNIS BALL
PET PEEVE: BEING LEFT AT HOME
OBSESSIONS: WATER AND SQUIRRELS
FAVORITE PASTIMES: FINDING
WATER AND SWIMMING
KNOWN ACCOMPLICES: HALLIE, LILLY,
MILES THE CAT AND HARPER

REGGIE

BETTY BOOP

FAVORITE TOY:
SQUEAKY ROOSTER

OBSESSION: RETRIEVING
STICKS FROM THE LAKE

NAUGHTIEST DEED:
SHAKING WATER ON THE CAMERA

BETTY BOOP

FAVORITE PASTIMES:
PLAYING BALL AND SWIMMING
FAVORITE FOOD: SCIENCE DIET
PET PEEVE: HOT AIR BALLOONS
KNOWN ACCOMPLICE: BLACKY THE CAT

TIFFANY

OBSESSION: BELLY RUBBING
FAVORITE TOY: A PLASTIC WATER BOTTLE
FAVORITE PASTIMES: SLEEPING AND EATING
FAVORITE FOOD: ANYTHING AND EVERYTHING
NAUGHTIEST DEED: PASSING GAS IN THE TASTING ROOM
PET PEEVE: GETTING STUCK WITH LUCY'S SMALL DOG BED
KNOWN ACCOMPLICES: MOOKY, KELLY AND PEANUT

WHALEBONE WINERY PASO ROBLES, CA | ENGLISH BULLDOG, 10 MONTHS | OWNERS: BOB AND JANALYN SIMPS

KNOWN ACCOMPLICES: THE KELHAM TRIBE
FAVORITE FOOD: FRESHLY CAUGHT NAPA VALLEY RABBIT
FAVORITE TOY: RUTHERFORD GRILL PRIME RIB BONES
NAUGHTIEST DEED: SHREDDING LOUIS VUITTON SLIPPERS
PET PEEVE: RON'S BROTHER HAMILTON AND THE SWIMMING POOL
FAVORITE PASTIMES: CHASING RABBITS AND SLEEPOVERS WITH FRIENDS

MISS ELLIE

OWNER: RON NICE

MOOSE

PET PEEVE: GUESTS THAT IGNORE HIM
FAVORITE TOY: HIS TOY HEDGEHOG, HEDGIE
OBSESSION: HEDGIE
NAUGHTIEST DEED: BEGGING FROM PICNICKERS
FAVORITE FOODS: FRESH FRUIT AND VEGETABLES
KNOWN ACCOMPLICES: TONA, EGAN AND GRANDPA
FAVORITE PASTIME: HAVING PICNICS WITH WINERY VISITORS

HARRY THE SOMMELIER DOG

by Jennifer Rosen

AS A TEENAGER, I lived for a few years on a large farm owned by my Great Aunt Laura. She was what was once known as a spinster and an heiress, but people caught up in her whirlwind just called her unique.

In place of family, she had a stable full of horses, and a large pack of dogs. Breeds went in and out, but the leashes, chains and collars that were an integral part of her fashion statement stayed the same.

A short, stylish woman, Aunt Laura stood ramrod straight and walked very fast with an odd toe-to-heel placement that was considered healthful at the time. Late afternoons would find her striding for miles across her land, clinking with chains, whips and leashes and surrounded by a pack of what looked like a dozen wolves. Woe to the trespasser who got within range. "Who are you?" my aunt would demand as the hapless fellow cowered up a tree, "And what do you think you're doing here?" After she was quite certain the guy had wet his pants she'd begin talking to him about shark fossils in the stream, or wild mushrooms in the woods and pretty soon he'd have an open invitation to visit.

By the time I arrived the pack was mostly German Weimeraners, the long-haired kind. If you've never seen these, imagine a large golden retriever with a muddy-grey coat and yellow-green eyes. Aunt Laura was wild about both these colors, as one look at her car, house and clothes would tell you. Unfortunately for my opportunity to own exquisite designer hand-me-downs, I happen to look deathly in those colors. But that's another story.

Now, due to some accident of breeding, in the midst of all this fur was one short-hair named Harry. Harry was the most elegant dog I've ever seen. He moved with a suspended, gravity-defying trot, and stood with what Irish horse-traders call "a leg at each corner." His soulful, wide-set eyes and high head carriage struck a note between noble and haughty.

Harry had a special set of rain gear, made to measure for him in Scotland; a beautiful trench coat with epaulettes and tartan lining plus a matching hat and boots, although these never stayed on long because for some reason, Harry couldn't stand to have his paws touched. You could run your finger over the top of his foot and he'd snatch it right up. We never knew why, but it only added to his fastidious air.

All in all, he reminded me of the head-butler in a grand English country house, or the kind of sommelier who wears a silver tastevin on a chain and makes you quake when it's your turn to taste and pronounce judgment on that first pour.

There was one chink in Harry's armor. He had fixed his amorous attentions upon a psychedelic purple paisley Superball, about the size of your fist. He kept it in his mouth all day, sometimes chewing, sometimes just holding it in his jaw and mouthing it lovingly. He would only drop it when it was time to eat. But of course when you drop a Superball it rebounds all over the place, like into all the other dogs busy wolfing down their dinner. Harry would go through this agonizing choice of whether to rescue his beloved or defend his kibble.

This would have been more of a wine story except that Aunt Laura didn't really drink. Unless you want to count those few special occasions when she'd "take" a tiny glass of Lillet. But admirers and former trespassers who didn't know this would often show up bearing a bottle, which would be promptly locked in the liquor closet, a small cubby under the stairs.

As I got older and began learning about wine, it began to irk me that not only were the bottles kept in a space that could go over 90 degrees on a summer night, but, worse, they were all kept standing up. In those pre-screwcap days, that meant a lot of dried-up corks and spoiled wine. So one day I sat down in front of the closet and carefully lay all the bottles down on their sides. A few days later, Aunt Laura went noodling through the house and stood them all back up.

I explained all about corks and seals, but she thought the bottles looked messy on the floor. Over and over I'd sneak in and set them down, and she'd find out and stand them all up again.

Then one day – I wasn't there, and my aunt told me about this later – she came upon Harry standing at the door to the liquor closet, scratching the floor, sniffing the door and whining. Figuring he must smell a mouse or a rat, she unlocked the closet and as she did, Harry plunged his head in and KO'd a number of bottles before my aunt could grab his collar and haul him back.

Harry continued to paw and whine, straining against his collar. Then, he reached out one paw and with a kind of fastidious punch, he flattened a bottle of Chateauneuf-du-Pape. Curious, my aunt gave him a little more leeway with which he proceeded to knock down bottles like they were bowling pins. Finally, with a great lunge, he broke free of my aunt's grasp, thrust his head all the way into the closet, and felled the bottles left standing. Then he backed up, turned around, walked away, and sat down like nothing had happened, quietly chewing in his usual noble way.

"I had no idea what it all meant" my aunt told me later, "but he seemed so satisfied. And I couldn't help wondering if maybe he agreed with you about storing wine bottles on their sides." And from then on, not only did she leave the bottles lying, but eventually let me move them down to the cellar, where the cool temperatures were far more suitable to an aging bottle.

When she died, decades later, she left a large cellar of these gift bottles, along with a secret stash of pre-prohibition wine, all in good shape, all on its side.

At the time, though, I was just grateful to sommelier-dog Harry. So much so, in fact, that I vowed never to hide his Superball in the closet again

JENNIFER ROSEN IS THE AUTHOR OF *WAITER, THERE'S A HORSE IN MY WINE, THE CORK JESTER'S GUIDE TO WINE* AND A NEW GAME, *CORK JESTER'S WINE TEASERS*. SHE WRITES A WEEKLY WINE COLUMN FOR THE *ROCKY MOUNTAIN NEWS* AND ARTICLES FOR MAGAZINES AND PAPERS AROUND THE WORLD. JENNIFER SPEAKS FRENCH AND ITALIAN, MANGLES GERMAN, SPANISH AND ARABIC, AND WORKS OFF THE JOB PERKS WITH BELLY DANCE, TIGHTROPE AND TRAPEZE. WWW.CORKJESTER.COM

JAMES

FAVORITE PASTIME: HIKING
FAVORITE TOY: RUBBER SQUIRREL
OBSESSIONS: BALLS AND STICKS
NAUGHTIEST DEED: CHEWING ON RUGS
PET PEEVE: STAYING HOME FROM WORK
FAVORITE FOOD: AMERICAN CHEESE SLICES
KNOWN ACCOMPLICE: BOWIE FROM ARNOT-ROBERTS

OBSESSION: SLEEPING
FAVORITE TOY: ANY TOY JAMES HAS
PET PEEVE: COMING IN THE HOUSE
FAVORITE FOOD: AMERICAN CHEESE SLICES
NAUGHTIEST DEED: CHEWING ON SHOES

FAVORITE PASTIME: CHASING BUNGS
FAVORITE TOY: SOCKS OF ANY KIND
FAVORITE FOOD: AMERICAN CHEESE SLICES
PET PEEVE: GOING ANYWHERE IN THE CAR
NAUGHTIEST DEED: CHEWING JEANS AND SUNGLASSES

LUCQUE

MORA

FAVORITE TOY: CATTLE
OBSESSION: BARKING
AT FLYING VULTURES
FAVORITE FOOD:
SMOKED STEELHEAD TROUT
KNOWN ACCOMPLICE: NADIE
NAUGHTIEST DEED: STEALING RIB EYES AT BBQS
PET PEEVE: STAYING AT HOME WHEN DOUGLAS GOES TO WORK
FAVORITE PASTIMES: CHASING JACK RABBITS AND CLIMBING TREES

OBSESSION: FOOD
FAVORITE FOOD: CHEESE
FAVORITE TOY: CHEW TOY
PET PEEVE: DISRESPECT
KNOWN ACCOMPLICE: BUBBA
NAUGHTIEST DEED: PLAYING "KEEP AWAY"

KADO

MINNIE

FAVORITE FOOD: QUESO
PET PEEVE: WILLIE NELSON
FAVORITE PASTIME: CHEWING UP CORKS
FAVORITE TOYS: BABY PACIFIER AND CORKS
OBSESSIONS: PATROLLING THE PERIMETER
AND PROTECTING THE HOMESTEAD
KNOWN ACCOMPLICE: WILLIE NELSON

PET PEEVE: MINNIE
FAVORITE FOOD: BACON
FAVORITE TOYS: MINNIE AND BARREL BUNGS
FAVORITE PASTIME: CHASING BIRDS IN THE VINEYARD
NAUGHTIEST DEED: EATING A QUART OF PORK DRIPPINGS
KNOWN ACCOMPLICES: MINNIE AND MAGGIE FROM THE LANGE WINERY

WILLIE NELSON

OWNER: EMILY STOLLER SMITH | LABRADOR X, 4 | THE EYRIE VINEYARDS McMINNVILLE, OR 45

ROYAL

OBSESSION: BIRDS
PET PEEVE: THE GOOSE
FAVORITE TOY: HER IMAGINATION
FAVORITE PASTIME: RUNNING FLAT OUT
FAVORITE FOOD: ANYTHING HER NUMEROUS
ADMIRERS CARE TO CONTRIBUTE
NAUGHTIEST DEED: INAPPROPRIATE PEEING
KNOWN ACCOMPLICES: BELLA AND ROGER

PET PEEVE: *BEING ALONE*
FAVORITE PASTIME: *CHASING OTHER DOGS*
FAVORITE FOOD: *ORGANIC DOG FOOD*
FAVORITE TOY: *GEORGE BUSH CHEW TOY*
OBSESSION: *HUNTING MOUNTAIN LIONS*
NAUGHTIEST DEED: *CHEWING COW PIES*
KNOWN ACCOMPLICES: *ROYAL AND JASPER*

BELLA

WNERS: *CHRIS, BRADLEY AND JASPER JAMES* | *RHODESIAN RIDGEBACK, 3* | **MEDLOCK AMES** *HEALDSBURG, CA*

FAVORITE PASTIME: SLEEPING
FAVORITE TOY: A SQUEAKY RABBIT
NAUGHTIEST DEED: EATING KLEENEX
PET PEEVE: BEING LEFT HOME ALONE
KNOWN ACCOMPLICES: STEVE AND MURPHY
OBSESSIONS: TREATS AND WANTING HIS OWNERS
FAVORITE FOOD: ANYTHING HIS OWNERS ARE EATING

MAX

FAVORITE TOY: BARREL BUNGS
PET PEEVE: BEING LEFT AT HOME BY HERSELF
OBSESSION: SNIFFING EVERYTHING AND EVERYONE
NAUGHTIEST DEEDS: CHASING THE CAT AND TERRORIZING SQUIRRELS
FAVORITE PASTIMES: PLAYING AT DOG PARK AND GREETING WINERY VISITORS

ROSIE

OWNER: MACK OWEN | SHAR-PEI X · 3 | O.S WINERY SEATTLE, WA | 49

PUA KEA

FAVORITE FOOD: APPLES
FAVORITE TOY: SQUIRREL-TAILED TENNIS BALL
OBSESSIONS: BROOMS AND THE TAPE MEASURE
PET PEEVE: BEING BOTHERED WHILE SLEEPING
FAVORITE PASTIMES: PLAYING WITH OTHER DOGS AND RIDING IN THE CAR
NAUGHTIEST DEEDS: COUNTER-SURFING AND ALMOST SETTING HOUSE ON FIRE

PET PEEVE: CHICKENS
FAVORITE FOOD: PASTA
KNOWN ACCOMPLICE: MAX THE BULL-MASTIFF
FAVORITE TOY: STONES ALMOST TOO BIG TO CARRY
NAUGHTIEST DEED: THROWING COUCH PILLOWS EVERYWHERE WHEN UPSET
FAVORITE PASTIMES: JUMPING FOR TREATS AND STARRING IN "A TASTE OF LUDWIG"

LUDWIG

LUCE

FAVORITE FOOD: CHICKEN
FAVORITE TOY: A PLUSH MOLE
KNOWN ACCOMPLICE: MARGRIT
PET PEEVES: DARKNESS AND RAIN
FAVORITE PASTIME: PLAYING WITH MALBEC
NAUGHTIEST DEED: DIGGING INTO SHEETS AND PILLOWS

FAVORITE FOOD: ICE CUBES
FAVORITE TOY: YELLOW DUCK TOY
FAVORITE PASTIMES: GOING ANYWHERE
CAROLYN GOES AND FROLICKING IN THE SNOW
NAUGHTIEST DEED: GIVING UNSOLICITED KISSES
PET PEEVES: HARSH WORDS AND SHOUTING
KNOWN ACCOMPLICES: BEN AND BAILEY

TRUDIE

BOUCHON "BOU"

FAVORITE TOYS: CORKS
FAVORITE FOODS: COOKIES,
POULET ROTI AND PINOT NOIR
OBSESSIONS: STUFFED ANIMALS,
RUNNING IN CIRCLES AND BARKING
PET PEEVES: HIGH HEELS AND BEING ALONE
FAVORITE PASTIMES: BUBBLE BATHS AND BEING HELD
NAUGHTIEST DEED: CHASING ANYTHING WITH A TAIL!
KNOWN ACCOMPLICES: TUFF AND FANNY PURRBRIGHT

PET PEEVE: THIEVING CHIPMUNKS
FAVORITE PASTIME: BIRD HUNTING
KNOWN ACCOMPLICES: JEFF AND BOU
FAVORITE TOYS: TENNIS BALLS AND BOU
FAVORITE FOOD: ANYTHING FROM THE GRILL
OBSESSION: SWIMMING, SWIMMING, SWIMMING
NAUGHTIEST DEED: GETTING SPRAYED BY SKUNKS (FOUR TIMES!)

TUFF

TASER

OBSESSION: CATS
FAVORITE FOOD: BANANA
PET PEEVES: SKUNKS AND CATS
FAVORITE TOY: STUFFED MONKEY
KNOWN ACCOMPLICE: COOKIE THE BULLDOG
NAUGHTIEST DEED: EATING 50 MANY
GRAPES HE HAD AN "EXPLOSION"
FAVORITE PASTIME: SITTING ON THE COUCH
AND WATCHING ANIMAL PLANET

OBSESSION: FOOD
FAVORITE TOY: TASER
PET PEEVES: WIND AND THUNDER
FAVORITE FOODS: BANANAS AND BELL PEPPERS
FAVORITE PASTIMES: HIKING AND ANNOYING TASER
NAUGHTIEST DEED: EATING SEVERAL REMOTE CONTROLS

TALLULAH

OBSESSION: RUNNING
FAVORITE FOOD: LONGHORN CHEESE
NAUGHTIEST DEED: STEALING CHEESE
KNOWN ACCOMPLICE: HIS SISTER MYFE
PET PEEVE: NOT HAVING HIS
FAVORITE SPOT TO SLEEP IN
FAVORITE PASTIMES: SNOOZING
AND CHASING EVERYTHING THAT RUNS

MITCH

OBSESSION: RUNNING
FAVORITE FOOD: WINE CRACKERS
PET PEEVE: BEING LEFT IN HER PEN
KNOWN ACCOMPLICE: HER BROTHER MITCH
NAUGHTIEST DEED: EATING THE OWNER'S CHEESEBURGER
FAVORITE PASTIMES: CHASING EVERYTHING THAT RUNS AND SNOOZING

MYFE

AURORA

FAVORITE TOY: SYRAH THE WINERY CAT
NAUGHTIEST DEED: CROTCH SNIFFING
PET PEEVE: NOT GETTING TO GO ON EVERY TRIP
FAVORITE PASTIME: WALKS, WALKS AND MORE WALKS
FAVORITE FOOD: TRADER JOE'S PEANUT BUTTER COOKIES
OBSESSION: TRYING TO HERD THE NEIGHBOR'S GOATS
KNOWN ACCOMPLICES: SYRAH, RUGBY, BO, LARRY AND JOYCE

AURORA THE GOATHERD

IT WAS PRETTY APPARENT from the git-go that Aurora had a fair amount of herding instinct. Because she is a rescue dog, it is hard to say with certainty just exactly where these tendencies come from, but her behavior has provided enough evidence to point to shepherd somewhere in the mix. When we wander trout streams, go for walks, cross country ski, or otherwise are out and about, and the "pack" is spread out over a distance, she is in constant motion checking in on everyone to be sure that no one gets lost. When guests arrive at the winery, she greets them at their car and guides them to the appropriate entrance. Her great frustration, however, lies with the goats next door, which are penned in a fenced pasture and not accessible for bringing together.

From the little that we do know, Aurora spent her formative year with a suburban family in the company of children and other dogs. When she came to live with us in rural Washington State, it was quite a different setting. First there were the peacocks to drive from the property – this is not Versailles so we have no reason to tolerate their whitewash on everything. The goats presented a wonderful opportunity to exhibit her talent at herding, if only there was not that obnoxious (and electrified) fence in the way. Not to be deterred, she waits until they approach the lower pasture and charges directly at them veering off at the last minute and driving them back to the upper reaches of their enclosed domain. This provides hours of amusement for Aurora (as well as us), along with a convenient exercise program.

This bit of entertainment seemed to have the potential to turn tragic one morning when Aurora was let out the front door and charged across the yard in a bee-line towards the pasture. Following her intended trajectory, I saw that a goat was grazing at the edge of the pasture with its head projecting through one of the fence panels, oblivious to the oncoming canine torpedo. As Aurora approached, the goat became aware of her advance and attempted to retract its head, only to have its horns catch on the heavy wire.

The goat's struggle was palpable as Aurora closed the distance at a high rate of speed, its neck muscles straining against the fence, while instinct created a vision of its pending fate. Aurora was oblivious to my calls and continued headlong in response to her own instincts, closing in on the doomed creature with all possible speed. As she braked her rapid approach and skidded into her target, her jaws opened and – she proceeded to bath the terrified goat's face with licks.

Eventually, the unnerved goat extricated its by now thoroughly marinated head from the fence and staggered back to safety, as well as to assess just what had happened to it. If goats have an oral history, I suspect that this adventure will be passed down from generation to generation. Unless, of course, the individual who was the target of this "attack" spends the rest of its life in therapy.

LARRY AND JOYCE OATES OVERSEE THE ANTICS OF AURORA AT SLEEPING DOG WINES IN THE YAKIMA VALLEY OF WASHINGTON STATE. LARRY ADOPTED THE MANTLE OF "ALPHA VINTNER" IN 2002 AFTER LONG PRACTICE AS A HOBBY WINEMAKER AND THE DESIRE TO SEE A TANGIBLE PRODUCT AFTER YEARS OF WORKING IN THE ENVIRONMENTAL FIELD.

OBSESSION: *BEES*
PET PEEVE: *BEING STUNG BY BEES*
KNOWN ACCOMPLICE: *FRITZ*
FAVORITE TOY: *JASPER THE CAT*
NAUGHTIEST DEED: *CHASING JASPER*
FAVORITE FOOD: *SOMEBODY ELSE'S*
FAVORITE PASTIME: *WANDERING IN THE VINEYARD*

PATZIE

HARRY

FAVORITE FOOD: CHEESE
FAVORITE PASTIME: RUNNING
FAVORITE TOY: STUFFED TOY PHEASANT
OBSESSION: TRYING TO CONTROL HIS LEASH
NAUGHTIEST DEED: CHEWING ON THE KITCHEN CABINET
KNOWN ACCOMPLICE: THEO, HIS GERMAN SHEPHERD PAL

BROADLEY VINEYARDS MONROE, OR | GOLDEN RETRIEVER ? | OWNER: CLAUDIA BROADLEY

FAVORITE FOOD: CARROTS
KNOWN ACCOMPLICE: KEELY THE CAT
PET PEEVE: TOO MANY HUGS IN A ROW
FAVORITE TOY: OVERSIZED STUFFED SHEEP
NAUGHTIEST DEED: LEARNING HOW TO UNLATCH
THE GATE AND TAKE HIMSELF FOR A WALK
FAVORITE PASTIME: ANYTHING TO DO WITH ODORS:
SMELLING THEM, COLLECTING THEM AND CREATING THEM

BARLEY

ROCKY

FAVORITE TOY: RILEY
OBSESSION: PHIL THE CAT
FAVORITE PASTIME: RUNNING
FAVORITE FOOD: STOLEN MUFFINS
NAUGHTIEST DEED: RUNNING AWAY
PET PEEVE: BEING SEPARATED FROM RILEY
KNOWN ACCOMPLICES: RILEY AND NORMAN

OBSESSION: BIRDS
FAVORITE PASTIME: DRAGGING HIS BED
AROUND IN THE MIDDLE OF THE NIGHT
FAVORITE TOY: WHATEVER ROCKY HAS
PET PEEVE: HAVING HIS PAWS WIPED
KNOWN ACCOMPLICES: ROCKY AND NORMAN
NAUGHTIEST DEED: RUNNING AWAY TO SEE THE NEIGHBOR'S DOG

OBSESSION: ELIZABETH
PET PEEVE: BEING LEFT ALONE
FAVORITE TOY: SQUEAKY SANTA
KNOWN ACCOMPLICES: ROCKY AND RILEY
NAUGHTIEST DEED: DESTROYING DOG BEDS
FAVORITE FOODS: PEANUT BUTTER AND BANANAS
FAVORITE PASTIME: SLEEPING ON THE HEATER VENT

NORMAN

PHOEBE

FAVORITE TOY: SARAH
OBSESSION: TRACTORS
KNOWN ACCOMPLICE: SARAH
PET PEEVE: GETTING IN THE CAR
NAUGHTIEST DEED: EATING A PEACOCK
FAVORITE PASTIMES: HERDING TRACTORS AND CHASING CHICKENS

OBSESSION: FOOD
FAVORITE TOY: GARDEN HOSE
KNOWN ACCOMPLICE: PHOEBE
NAUGHTIEST DEED: RUNNING INTO A CAR
FAVORITE PASTIME: RUNNING AFTER THE QUAD BIKE
PET PEEVE: NOT BEING ABLE TO GO EVERYWHERE

SARAH

BUCKY AKA WINO

PET PEEVE: BEING LEFT ALONE
FAVORITE TOY: GRAPE VINE CUTTINGS
NAUGHTIEST DEED: SWIMMING IN THE POND
FAVORITE PASTIME: RIDING ON THE JOHN DEERE TRACTOR
FAVORITE FOODS: CHICKEN JERKY AND OREO COOKIES
OBSESSIONS: CHASING HIS TAIL AND GOING ANYWHERE WITH DAD
KNOWN ACCOMPLICES: MATEO, ACE, HIS GIRLFRIEND JULIE AND TUCKER

FAVORITE PASTIME:
PLAYING WITH CHILDREN
OBSESSIONS: CHEWING AND
RUNNING IN THE VINEYARD
FAVORITE FOOD: FURNITURE
FAVORITE TOY: ANYTHING THROWN
KNOWN ACCOMPLICES: BUCKY AND KODIAC

MATEO

CARLEY

FAVORITE TOY: DUCKY
FAVORITE FOOD: CHICKEN
KNOWN ACCOMPLICE: DUKE
FAVORITE PASTIME: CHASING MAGNUM
NAUGHTIEST DEED: EATING THE CAT'S FOOD
PET PEEVE: WHEN DUCKS LAND IN THE POOL
OBSESSION: CHASING BIRDS OUT OF THE VINEYARD

PET PEEVE: AGGRESSIVE MEN
FAVORITE TOY: SQUEAKY PUPPY
OBSESSION: CHASING THE CATS
FAVORITE FOOD: BEEF RIB BONES
NAUGHTIEST DEED: SLEEPING ON THE BED WITH MARIE
KNOWN ACCOMPLICE: ASHLEY (THE ONE CAT THAT ISN'T AFRAID)
FAVORITE PASTIME: CHASING CARLEY UP AND DOWN THE VINEYARD ROWS

MAGNUM

INDICA

PET PEEVE: GETTING STITCHES
FAVORITE TOY: FUZZY OCTOPUS
FAVORITE FOOD: DYNAMITE DOG FOOD
FAVORITE PASTIME: FOLLOWING THE
GOLF CART AROUND THE VINEYARD
NAUGHTIEST DEED: EATING A WHOLE
STICK OF BUTTER OFF THE COUNTER

FAVORITE PASTIMES: EATING, SLEEPING AND CHASING RABBITS
FAVORITE TOYS: BALLS AND RABBITS
NAUGHTIEST DEED: EATING HALF A HAM OFF THE COUNTER FOR BREAKFAST
PET PEEVE: NOT BEING FED ON TIME
KNOWN ACCOMPLICES: MAX AND ROSA

SAMSON

LLOYD

FAVORITE FOOD: RIBS
FAVORITE TOY: HIS MONKEY
FAVORITE PASTIMES: GOING TO LAKE TAHOE
AND RUNNING THROUGH WINERY CAVES
PET PEEVE: PEOPLE WHO COME TO THE
HOUSE AND INVADE HIS TERRITORY
NAUGHTIEST DEED: CHEWING REMOTE CONTROLS
KNOWN ACCOMPLICES: LANDER, CHEYENNE AND STORM

LADERA VINEYARDS ANGWIN, CA | LABRADOODLE, 3 | OWNER: NICOLE DUNCAN

NAUGHTIEST DEED: STEALING FOOD
FROM THE CATERERS WHEN
THEY ARE DOING EVENTS
FAVORITE TOY: LLOYD
PET PEEVE: NOT BEING FED
FAVORITE FOOD: STOLEN TIDBITS
FAVORITE PASTIME: CHASING RABBITS
THROUGH THE VINEYARDS

KAYA

CHILI

FAVORITE FOOD: STEAK
OBSESSIONS: CUDDLING, PEOPLE AND FOOD
FAVORITE TOYS: TENNIS BALL AND FRISBEE
FAVORITE PASTIME: FETCHING TENNIS BALLS
KNOWN ACCOMPLICES: ISAAC (RIP), BOGEY,
DUNCAN, ABU, BABETTE, DAPHNIE AND BRODEY
PET PEEVES: BATHS AND THE MAILMAN'S UNIFORM

FAVORITE PASTIME: FETCH
FAVORITE FOOD: MEXICAN
PET PEEVE: BEING LEFT BEHIND
FAVORITE TOYS: ANY BALL OR STICK
KNOWN ACCOMPLICES: BODHI AND SKYLLA
OBSESSION: CHASING ERIC ON THE QUAD BIKE
NAUGHTIEST DEED: EATING THE KIDS' DINNER OFF THE TABLE

CHARLOTTE

OWNERS: ERIC JF

FRANCOISE

FAVORITE FOODS:
HOTDOGS AND GREENIES

OBSESSION: "WOOING" HIS OVER-SIZED STUFFED
EASTER EGG (WHICH HE THINKS IS HIS GIRLFRIEND)

NAUGHTIEST DEED: USING HIS PETITE SIZE
TO CHARM HIS WAY INTO RESTAURANTS TO BEG

PET PEEVE: NOT GETTING ENOUGH RESPECT DUE TO HIS SIZE

FAVORITE PASTIME: BARKING AT THE COYOTES AND MOUNTAIN LIONS

PET PEEVE: BEING BITTEN BY RATTLESNAKES
FAVORITE FOOD: PORK BELLY LEFTOVERS
FROM 'DEBORAH'S ROOM' RESTAURANT
FAVORITE TOY: HIS DINNER BOWL WHICH
HE CARRIES WITH HIM EVERYWHERE
NAUGHTIEST DEED: SWIMMING WITH
GUESTS IN THE POOL AT THE JUST INN

SUNNY

OWNERS: JUSTIN AND DEBORAH BALDWIN | LABRADOR 12 | JUSTIN WINERY PASO ROBLES CA | 81

CHURCHILL

FAVORITE FOOD: TACOS
FAVORITE TOY: RUBBER DUCKY CHEW TOY
PET PEEVE: HAVING HIS EARS STEPPED ON
NAUGHTIEST DEED: BITING THE HEELS OF
TASTING ROOM VISITORS TO GET ATTENTION
OBSESSION: RISING ABOVE HIS NAPOLEON COMPLEX
FAVORITE PASTIME: TAKING A WALK WITH HIS POWERFUL
NOSE WHICH OFTEN GETS HIM INTO TROUBLE

FAVORITE FOOD: BREAD
OBSESSION: TENNIS BALLS
FAVORITE TOY: TENNIS BALLS
FAVORITE PASTIME: GAMES OF CATCH WITH A
TENNIS BALL STOLEN FROM NEARBY TENNIS COURT
NAUGHTIEST DEEDS: NIBBLING ON CONTRACTORS'
BOOTS AND BEING CRANKY AT NIGHT
PET PEEVES: WINDSTORMS AND LOUD SNEEZING
KNOWN ACCOMPLICE: HER STEPSISTER, MAYSY

KONNIE

MUNCH

FAVORITE PASTIME: PLAYING WITH MAYSY AND PORT
FAVORITE FOOD: HANDMADE VENETIAN MASKS
NAUGHTIEST DEED: SEE FAVORITE FOOD...
FAVORITE TOY: LE LANI, THE GIANT GREAT PYRENEES
OBSESSION: HIS THREE-LEGGED FRIEND, PORT
PET PEEVE: NOT SITTING IN THE DRIVER'S SEAT

THE STORY OF PORT

1994 – 2008

IT WAS A SUNNY DAY in the summer of '94 when I met Port. Outside, I heard the distinct sound of an animal in distress. It took only moments to realize what was happening across the field from my house – a very small animal had fallen into harm's way and was being attacked by a Pit Bull.

I ran to the scene, broke up the fight and found that the small animal was a puppy that was very badly injured. Instinctively, I wrapped him up and took him to the veterinarian. I agreed to pay for the emergency surgery and recovery.

The puppy had lost a leg, but found a home. With only three legs – two on the port side – I named him Port, and he was my best friend.

STORY BY ERIC DUNHAM — DIRECTOR OF WINE, DUNHAM CELLARS, WALLA WALLA, WA.

SALTY

FAVORITE FOOD: BBQ
KNOWN ACCOMPLICE: NIGEL
OBSESSION: SQUIRREL HOLES
PET PEEVE: VACUUM CLEANERS
FAVORITE PASTIME: CHASING BUNGS
FAVORITE TOY: STUFFED TOY LOBSTER
NAUGHTIEST DEED: SHOE CHEWING

MINASSIAN-YOUNG VINEYARDS PASO ROBLES, CA | RED HEELER X, 2 | OWNER: KATE JONES

PET PEEVE: BIRDS
FAVORITE FOOD: TRI-TIP
KNOWN ACCOMPLICE: SALTY
OBSESSION: MILK BONE TREATS
FAVORITE TOY: STUFFED SNOWMAN
NAUGHTIEST DEED: CHASING DEER
FAVORITE PASTIME: CHECKING VINEYARDS

NIGEL

PINOT

FAVORITE TOY: BLUE DOG TOY
OBSESSION: GETTING ATTENTION
FAVORITE FOOD: 'SNAUSAGES' IN A BLANKET
KNOWN ACCOMPLICES: YOGI BEAR AND SHERPA
FAVORITE PASTIME: PLAYING WITH HIS BLUE DOG TOY
PET PEEVE: BIG DOGS THAT THINK THEY'RE THE BOSS
NAUGHTIEST DEED: ESCAPING TO GO ON AN ADVENTURE

PET PEEVE: *BIRDS FLYING OVERHEAD*
OBSESSION: *CONVERSATIONS WITH PEOPLE*
FAVORITE FOOD: *'SNAUSAGES' IN A BLANKET*
KNOWN ACCOMPLICES: *YOGI BEAR AND SHERPA*
FAVORITE PASTIME: *SITTING WITH BILL ON HIS CHAIR*
NAUGHTIEST DEED: *ESCAPING TO GO ON AN ADVENTURE*

CHARDONNAY

CIDER

PET PEEVE: BATHS
KNOWN ACCOMPLICE: BELL
OBSESSION: PLAYING NON-STOP
FAVORITE TOYS: FRISBEE AND STICKS
NAUGHTIEST DEED: STANDING ON TOP OF THE PATIO TABLE
FAVORITE PASTIMES: PLAYING FRISBEE AND FETCHING STICKS

WILLIAMSON VINEYARDS CALDWELL, ID | BORDER COLLIE X, 8 MONTHS | OWNER: BEVERLEY WILLIAMSON MAC

FAVORITE FOOD: BROCCOLI
PET PEEVE: THE CAT GETTING
TOO MUCH ATTENTION
KNOWN ACCOMPLICES: CHILDREN
OBSESSION: RETRIEVING ANYTHING
FAVORITE PASTIME: PLAYING SOCCER
NAUGHTIEST DEED: SNEAKING INTO
THE PANTRY AND EATING THE CAT'S FOOD

MILLA

KARMA

FAVORITE TOY: BALL
FAVORITE FOOD: DOG BISCUIT
OBSESSION: FETCHING A BALL
FAVORITE PASTIME: FETCHING A BALL
NAUGHTIEST DEED: CHEWING UP BEDS

FAVORITE TOY: KONG
FAVORITE FOOD: "COOKIE"
PET PEEVE: AIRPLANES
FAVORITE PASTIME: SLEEPING
NAUGHTIEST DEED: SNEAKING INTO
THE HOUSE TO SLEEP NEXT TO THE BED

SYRAH

BUTLER

FAVORITE TOY: KONG
KNOWN ACCOMPLICE: AVA
FAVORITE FOOD: CHICKEN GIBLETS
FAVORITE PASTIME: RUNNING IN THE VINEYARD
PET PEEVE: WHEN VISITORS WILL NOT PLAY STICK
NAUGHTIEST DEED: GETTING THE NEIGHBOR'S DOGS TO BARK

FAVORITE FOOD: "COOKIE"
KNOWN ACCOMPLICE: BUTLER
FAVORITE TOY: WATER BOTTLE
NAUGHTIEST DEED: PLAYING IN THE TOILET
FAVORITE PASTIME: RUNNING IN THE VINEYARD
PET PEEVE: NOT BEING ALLOWED IN THE TASTING ROOM

AVA

ROUSSANNE

FAVORITE FOOD: DOG COOKIES

KNOWN ACCOMPLICE: CABERNET

NAUGHTIEST DEED: TAKING A STEAK OFF
A PLATE BEFORE A WINEMAKER DINNER

FAVORITE PASTIMES: PLAYING BALL AND
LOOKING FOR DROPPED WINERY CRACKERS

FAVORITE TOYS: TENNIS BALLS AND GARY

PET PEEVE: WHEN GARY AND MARCY LEAVE

OBSESSION: CROSSING HER FRONT LEGS LIKE A REAL LADY

FAVORITE PASTIMES: PLAYING BALL
AND SWIMMING IN THE EBERLE POND
FAVORITE TOYS: TENNIS BALLS AND GARY
NAUGHTIEST DEED: WET CROTCH GREETINGS
FAVORITE FOOD: TASTING ROOM CRACKERS
OBSESSION: NUDGING PEOPLE TO PET HIM
KNOWN ACCOMPLICE: ROUSSANNE
PET PEEVE: BEING TEASED
BY THE TWO DOGS NEXT DOOR

CABERNE

HEIDI

OBSESSION: HUNTING
FAVORITE PASTIME: HUNTING
FAVORITE FOOD: DOG BISCUITS
FAVORITE TOY: TRAINING BUCK
NAUGHTIEST DEED: LEAVING THE
PROPERTY TO HUNT WITHOUT DICK
KNOWN ACCOMPLICES: PARIS AND LONDON

OBSESSION: CORKS
FAVORITE TOY: CORKS
FAVORITE FOOD: PIG EARS
PET PEEVE: BEING IGNORED
KNOWN ACCOMPLICE: MATILDA
NAUGHTIEST DEED: STEALING CORKS
FAVORITE PASTIME: RIDING ON THE TRACTOR

GIDGET

BART

FAVORITE TOY: KONG
FAVORITE FOOD: STEAK
OBSESSION: SWIMMING
FAVORITE PASTIME: HIKING
PET PEEVE: NOT GETTING ENOUGH ATTENTION
NAUGHTIEST DEED: CHEWING UP BACK SEAT OF CAR

GARY FARRELL HEALDSBURG, CA | GERMAN SHEPHERD, 7 | OWNER: SUSAN REED

OBSESSION: AFFECTION
FAVORITE FOOD: ANYTHING
THAT HITS THE FLOOR
PET PEEVE: DAD'S BAD SHOTS
NAUGHTIEST DEED: OPENING DOORS
AND LEAVING THEM OPEN
KNOWN ACCOMPLICE: ABI-NORMAL THE CAT
FAVORITE PASTIME: HUNTING UPLAND BIRDS

GRACIE

OWNER: GARY ARCHER | GOLDEN RETRIEVER, 7 | **GARY FARRELL** HEALDSBURG, CA

PET PEEVE: QUINCY THE ROTTY
OBSESSION: COUNTER SURFING
NAUGHTIEST DEED:
HAVING AN INTERNAL
ALARM CLOCK
FAVORITE FOODS: LOAF OF BREAD AND STICKS OF BUTTER
FAVORITE PASTIME: MORNING WALKS TO THE COFFEE SHOP

MILES

NAUGHTIEST DEED: CELLAR LEAKAGE
PET PEEVE: HAVING HER TAIL PULLED
FAVORITE FOOD: ON A STRICT LIFELONG DIET
FAVORITE PASTIME: SUPERVISING BARREL CREW SPILLAGE
KNOWN ACCOMPLICES: ASSOCIATES OF J. LOHR WINERY,
WILDHORSE WINERY AND THE VIA VEGA VINEYARD

LUCY

ROBBIE

PET PEEVE: DOGS
FAVORITE TOYS: CUSTOMERS
OBSESSION: HOSTING GUESTS
FAVORITE FOOD: WILD SALMON
FAVORITE PASTIME: GETTING TUMMY RUBS
KNOWN ACCOMPLICES: THE KENDALL-JACKSON STAFF

FAVORITE FOOD: CAT FOOD
FAVORITE TOY: SQUEAKY TOYS
FAVORITE PASTIME: TAKING MUD BATHS
KNOWN ACCOMPLICES: SIENA, GORDIE AND BUDDY
OBSESSION: ROLLING IN VARIOUS UNSAVORY SUBSTANCES
NAUGHTIEST DEED: SHREDDING HOMEWORK AND FURNITURE
PET PEEVE: BEING LEFT ALONE FOR LONGER THAN FIVE MINUTES

NOELLE

DUJAC AKA 'BIG HEAD'

FAVORITE TOY: TAYLOR'S SOCKS
FAVORITE PASTIME: GUARDING THE CAR
FAVORITE FOOD: CHEESE ON THE COUNTER
OBSESSIONS: VOLES, CATS AND SQUIRRELS
PET PEEVES: THE UPS MAN AND ANY MEN IN BROWN
KNOWN ACCOMPLICE: ANYONE WHO GIVES HIM LOVE
NAUGHTIEST DEED: SHOWING HIS BITS TO FEMALE VISITORS

THE WORLD'S SMARTEST WINE DOG?

A WELL-KNOWN NAPA VALLEY BUTCHER was recently seen shooing a hound from his shop. Then the butcher spots $20 and a note in the dog's mouth, reading: "Four Angus beef steaks, please." Amazed, he takes the money, puts a bag of steaks in the dog's mouth, and quickly locks up the shop.

He follows the dog and observes him wait for a green light, look both ways, and trot across the road to a bus stop. The dog checks the timetable and sits on the bench. When a bus arrives, he walks around to the front of the bus and looks at the number before boarding. The butcher follows, in disbelief. As the bus travels out of Napa down Highway 29 towards St. Helena, the dog takes in the scenery. After a while he stands on his back legs to push the stop button, and the butcher follows him off.

The dog runs up to a Calistoga winery and approaches the tasting room, dropping his bag on the step. He goes back down the path, takes a big run, and throws himself – whallop! – against the door. He does this repeatedly – yet there is no answer. So he jumps on a wall, walks around the garden, taps on the glass of a window, jumps off, and reappears at the door of the tasting room.

The wine-maker opens the door and starts cursing and yelling at the dog. The butcher runs up and screams at the guy: "What the hell are you doing? This dog's a genius!" The wine-maker responds, "Genius, my ass. It's the second time this week he's forgotten his key!"

CODY

PET PEEVE: OTHER DOGS

FAVORITE FOOD: AMERICAN CHEESE

FAVORITE PASTIMES: SNOOZING AND HANGING OUT IN THE REX HILL GARDENS IN THE SUMMER

FAVORITE TOY: TENNIS BALLS – SHE EATS THE FUZZ

OBSESSIONS: SEEING WHO'S IN THE TASTING ROOM AND LOOKING FOR FOOD IN THE KITCHEN

NAUGHTIEST DEED: EATING THE SHEETS OFF THE BED

PET PEEVE: *HER BOOTIES*
FAVORITE TOY: *STUFFED SQUIRREL*
OBSESSIONS: *SQUIRRELS AND HER BACKPACK*
FAVORITE PASTIMES: *CHASING LLAMAS AND LONG-DISTANCE HIKING*
NAUGHTIEST DEEDS: *ROLLING IN LIVESTOCK MANURE AND PEEING WHEN EXCITED*
FAVORITE FOODS: *MEDIUM-RARE BACON, DOUBLE CHEESEBURGER AND SQUIRRELS*

PACHA

RENOWNED CHEF MICHAEL CHIARELLO is very passionate about the Napa Valley – its lifestyle, culture, and glorious produce. He spends time tending the 95-year-old vines around his home to craft highly rated, estate-grown wines. It is a labor of love he shares with his family and Dash, his trusty golden retriever – truly a 'Napa-style' wine dog if ever there was one.

FAVORITE TOY: ANYTHING HIS
BABY BROTHER AIDAN LEAVES OUTSIDE
PET PEEVE: ANY PARTY HE'S NOT INVITED TO
FAVORITE FOOD: ORGANIC SHORT-RIB BONES
NAUGHTIEST DEED: YANKING A FOUR-WEEK
AGED FOUR-INCH PRIME RIBEYE OFF THE GRILL
FAVORITE PASTIME: DUCK HUNTING WITH MICHAEL

DASH

TERRA XINA WINES WILSONVILLE, OR | AUSTRALIAN SHEPHERD, 10 | OWNERS: CAROLE, KARL AND ROXANNE DINGE

FAVORITE FOOD: CHEESE
PET PEEVE: SOMEONE NOT PLAYING WITH
HER WHEN SHE LAYS A TOY IN THEIR LAP
OBSESSION: HAVING A TOY IN HER MOUTH
FAVORITE TOY: GREEN HURLEY OR ANY BALL
NAUGHTIEST DEED: BARKING AT NEIGHBORS
FAVORITE PASTIMES: SWIMMING AND PLAYING FETCH

DAKOTA

RUBY

OBSESSION: THE FLASHLIGHT
PET PEEVE: LACK OF OPEN DOORS
FAVORITE PASTIME: SITTING BY THE HEATER
FAVORITE TOYS: THE PENGUIN AND SQUEAKY RAT
FAVORITE FOOD: ANYTHING THAT CROSSES HER PATH
NAUGHTIEST DEED: RETRIEVING A BIRD BUT NOT COMING BACK WITH IT

OBSESSION: VISITORS
FAVORITE FOOD: KIBBLE AU JUS
PET PEEVE: COYOTES ON HER PROPERTY
FAVORITE TOY: ANYTHING THAT SQUEAKS
KNOWN ACCOMPLICES: VINEYARD WORKERS
FAVORITE PASTIME: RUNNING IN THE VINEYARDS
NAUGHTIEST DEED: EATING A WHOLE FAMILY DINNER

MOLLY

FAVORITE TOY: ROPE
OBSESSION: SLEEPING
FAVORITE FOOD: ANY MEAT
KNOWN ACCOMPLICE: BILL THE BOXER
PET PEEVE: NOT GETTING TO GO WITH DAD
NAUGHTIEST DEED: GETTING INTO THE TRASH
FAVORITE PASTIME: RIDING ON THE FOUR-WHEELER

JACK

SAWTOOTH WINERY NAMPA, ID | JACK RUSSELL TERRIER X 3 | OWNER: AARON MAI

ROVER, BORDEAUX COLLIE

by Lori Crantford

IF YOU'VE BEEN LUCKY ENOUGH to find yourself deep in the heart of California wine country, even if just for a day, then you've heard the legend. Of a dog. A dog of unparalleled intelligence, unrivaled good looks, and ball-licking skills the envy of every canine and pro wrestler west of the Mississippi.

Well, the legend's true. I'm Rover, Bordeaux Collie. And here's my story.

My people were originally East Coast folks. You know, Central Barkers. Sure there were lots of advantages to that life: gourmet doggie bags and pedigreed bitches as far as the eye could see. A city where anything is possible. Where else could a Golden Retriever learn to talk, walk upright, comb his hair over and call himself Donald Trump?

By the time I came around, my people had plenty of fine wine experience. (Oh come on. Yes, dogs drink wine. I Shih Tzu not. Ever get that sneaking feeling every time you left your wine glass unattended at a party, that when you returned it was less full than you remembered? That was us. My aunt Vi – or Viognier if you know what's good for you – holds the record for party tastings. For a Corgi, that girl can hold her liquor. Their secret? Low center of gravity. Oh, and drinking out of the toilet? Strictly palette cleansing.)

Party tastings weren't enough for me, however. I needed to be where the action was, where it all started. Wasn't I all about soil? Wasn't I all about tannins? You know, those little things that explode during the holidays? The one with the song: O Tannin Bombs. Wasn't I just like a great wine, excellent from nose to finish? Yes. I. Was.

With California as my destination, I set out on a cross-country trek that would make Lassie look like a pussy ... cat. I encountered every kind of terrain, every kind of weather, every kind of creature known and unknown to man. And that was just in Jersey.

In Kentucky I met a drop-dead gorgeous Cocker Spaniel named Red – I think she was a blend – who was sweet-tempered until she threw back a few distilled peaches. You know, some fruits are meant to be drunk, and others are just meant to be served over ice cream.

By the time I made Oklahoma, I was beginning to appreciate those wide-open spaces.

There was something appealing about those never-ending skies, that tumbleweed tundra. For a couple of days, I considered staying there, being at home, home on the range. "Range Rover." It had a nice ring to it.

But I pushed onward to my goal. In LA I met a flirty but flighty little Miniature Poodle with whom I whiled away a memorable evening. As they all do, she begged me to stay, but I don't roll over for beggars. In wine terminology, we'd call her a real corker, which is to say she had a screwcap loose.

With great determination, I miraculously made my way straight through San Francisco, across the great Golden Gate Bridge – which has been marked big time, my friend, so don't even think about it – and up into God's country, which we all know, if you listen to it backwards, is Dog's country.

Now I live where I was born to live, and my cross-country journey is the stuff of legends. I patrol the fields, keep watch over the grapes, and judging by the "Oh my!" and "I never!" and "If I could do that I wouldn't have gotten married!" phrases that are uttered by our winery customers, I know that my ball-licking skills are only adding to business. When you come visit, make sure to taste the Red Rover Reserve. It pairs well with nuts.

LORI CRANTFORD IS AN EMMY-AWARD WINNING WRITER LIVING IN INDIANAPOLIS, INDIANA. SHE HAS TWO CATS AND A PSYCHOTIC COCKATIEL; SHE BORROWED A NEIGHBOR'S DOG AND A FAIR AMOUNT OF THEIR WINE FOR THIS STORY'S INSPIRATION.

FAVORITE TOY: SOCKS
FAVORITE FOOD: MEATBALLS
OBSESSION: ROMEO THE CAT
FAVORITE PASTIME: BEING CHASED
NAUGHTIEST DEED: EATING CHECKS
KNOWN ACCOMPLICES: BEN, JAKE AND SOMETIMES ROMEO
PET PEEVE: NOT BEING CHASED WHEN SHE RUNS THROUGH THE WHEAT

KEIRA

HUNTER

NAUGHTIEST DEED: CHEWING UP TIN CANS
FAVORITE PASTIMES: HUNTING ANYTHING THAT
MOVES AND SLEEPING IN HIS FAVORITE CHAIR
OBSESSION: MAKING SURE HE'S COMFORTABLE AT ALL TIMES
PET PEEVE: PUTTING HIS NOSE IN HIS WATER WHEN HE DRINKS
KNOWN ACCOMPLICES: BUSTER, SILVERADO AND WINCHESTER

PET PEEVE: DISORDER
FAVORITE TOY: TENNIS BALLS
OBSESSION: PLAYING FETCH
NAUGHTIEST DEED: DIGGING
KNOWN ACCOMPLICE: MAGNUM
FAVORITE FOODS: CHICKEN AND RICE
FAVORITE PASTIMES: SWIMMING AND SLEEPING

OBSESSION: SUCKING HIS TOYS
NAUGHTIEST DEED: PULLING DOWN
AND CHEWING UP THE OUTSIDE BLINDS
FAVORITE TOYS: ALL HIS STUFFED ANIMALS
FAVORITE PASTIMES: EATING AND SLEEPING ON THE COUCH
KNOWN ACCOMPLICES: BUSTER, SILVERADO AND WINCHESTER

LUKE

MINI

PET PEEVE: SHOWERS
FAVORITE FOOD: HOTDOGS
KNOWN ACCOMPLICE: HER BROTHER LEO
FAVORITE TOY: WHICHEVER TOY LEO HAS
FAVORITE PASTIME: SITTING IN HERTA'S LAP
OBSESSION: BEING THE CENTER OF ATTENTION
NAUGHTIEST DEED: STEALING FOOD WHEN NO ONE'S LOOKING

FAVORITE TOY: PUPPET SHARK
FAVORITE FOOD: TURKEY DOGS
PET PEEVE: GETTING BLOW DRIED
OBSESSION: PULLING MINI'S EARS OR TAIL
FAVORITE PASTIME: PLAYING WITH HIS SISTER MINI
NAUGHTIEST DEED: GETTING HIS FEET MUDDY AND RUNNING ALL OVER THE WHITE CARPET

LEO

OBSESSION: FOOD
FAVORITE PASTIME: SLEEPING
FAVORITE FOOD: CHEW BONE
NAUGHTIEST DEED: BARKING AT BIRDS
KNOWN ACCOMPLICE: MEG FROM HARTWELL
PET PEEVES: THE RAIN AND THE NAIL CLIPPER

FAVORITE TOY: TENNIS BALL
OBSESSION: CHASING RABBITS
NAUGHTIEST DEED: BEING NEEDY
PET PEEVE: HAVING A SHOWER
FAVORITE PASTIME: SNIFFING
AROUND FOR FOOD OR A RABBIT

TANA

FAVORITE TOY: CHEW TOYS
PET PEEVE: PLAYING HIDE-N-SEEK WITH LINDA
KNOWN ACCOMPLICES: MISSY, TANA AND V'INDIA
FAVORITE PASTIME: BARKING AT DOGS ON THE TV
OBSESSION: HIDING UNDER THE BED WHILE CHEWING UP STOLEN CLOTHING
NAUGHTIEST DEED: CHEWING UP AN INK PEN AND RUINING THE CARPET

MEG

FAVORITE TOY: SHOES
FAVORITE FOOD: CHEESE
FAVORITE PASTIME: SLEEPING
OBSESSION: SLEEPING IN BED
NAUGHTIEST DEED: STEALING SHOES
PET PEEVES: RAIN AND SWIMMING POOLS
KNOWN ACCOMPLICES: THE FAMILY CAT AND PIG

TIG

KNOWN ACCOMPLICES: SCRAPPY AND ANDY
FAVORITE TOY: PLUSH SQUEAKY SQUIRREL TOY
FAVORITE FOOD: DOG TREATS FROM THE OFFICE
FAVORITE PASTIMES: SWIMMING AND CHASING SQUIRRELS
NAUGHTIEST DEED: STEALING STUFFED ANIMALS FROM ALICIA'S ROOM

BUCK

FAVORITE FOOD: SOUP BONES
KNOWN ACCOMPLICES: PARKER AND LINUS
FAVORITE TOY: SMALL STUFFED WHITE BEAR
OBSESSION: OTHER FEMALE DOGS ON HER PROPERTY
NAUGHTIEST DEED: CHASING THE NEIGHBOR'S LONG-HORNED STEERS
PET PEEVE: GUYS WITH BIG BLACK BOOTS SHOWING UP UNANNOUNCED
FAVORITE PASTIME: WATCHING FOR RABBITS, COYOTES, DEER AND TURKEYS

KARA

STAGLIN FAMILY VINEYARD RUTHERFORD, CA | ANATOLIAN SHEPHERD ♀ | OWNERS: SHARI AND GAREN STAGL

LIFE WITH OUR JACK RUSSELLS...
by Garen Staglin

LIFE WITH JACK RUSSELL TERRIERS is like a never-ending treadmill of activity. One is a handful, and two of them are a crazy combination of chaos and delight.

No dogs (in our opinion) are smarter, more ready to run, jump, chase, chew (anything... couch, furniture, wood, you name it), bark, and then crash, than this breed. When the doorbell rings you would think aliens are invading. When lizards are hatching in the summer and frogs in the springtime they are on a non-stop mission to sniff out and eradicate the "enemy" who has intruded on their territory. No matter if that involves going through poison ivy which they then bring into the house... no problem!

They are always ready for a scratch and a treat of any kind, dog variety or human food (preferred). How can an animal jump five times their height – straight up? Food on any counter, at any height, is not safe when they are around. And with all this, they always have a tail wag, a lick, and a nuzzle for their owners!

Until you've experienced life with a Jack Russell, you can only imagine it and we can only partially describe it. We are Jack Russell lovers through and through!

IN LOVING MEMORY OF DEUCE AND SAMI

THE STAGLIN FAMILY, RUTHERFORD, NAPA VALLEY, CALIFORNIA

POPPY

NAUGHTIEST DEED:
DRAGGING THE CAT BY THE TAIL
FAVORITE PASTIME: CHASING THE CAT
FAVORITE TOY: STUFFED SQUIRREL
KNOWN ACCOMPLICE: ANNIE
FAVORITE FOOD: STEAK
PET PEEVE: BEING TOLD
THAT I LOOK LIKE A LAMB
OBSESSION: STUFFED TOYS

HEITZ WINE CELLARS ST. HELENA, CA | BEDLINGTON TERRIER, 10 MONTHS | OWNERS: DAVID AND CH

OBSESSION: WATER FROM THE HOSE
FAVORITE TOY: FERMENTATION BUNG
FAVORITE PASTIME: SLEEPING UNDER TANKS
KNOWN ACCOMPLICES: HARRY AND IKIS
FAVORITE FOOD: CHICKEN NECKS
NAUGHTIEST DEED: PULLING
BUNGS FROM BARREL TOPS

SOPHIE

FAVORITE FOOD: HILL SCIENCE DIET
OBSESSION: UNTYING SHOELACES
PET PEEVE: AN EMPTY FOOD BOWL
FAVORITE PASTIMES: SNORING AND
PLAYING WITH JACK AND THOMAS
NAUGHTIEST DEED: LEAVING "PRESENTS"
KNOWN ACCOMPLICES: JACK, THOMAS AND UGA VI
FAVORITE TOY: KONG FILLED WITH CREAM CHEESE

VIVI

GARRETSON WINE COMPANY, PASO ROBLES, CA | ENGLISH BULLDOG, 3 MONTHS | OWNER, MAT GARRETSON

MIDNIGHT IN THE
WINERY OF GOOD AND EVIL

by Mat Garretson

ABOUT SIX MONTHS AGO we lost our beloved white bulldog, Fireball. We still don't know how it happened, but over the course of two weeks she lost all motor functions. It was a tough time for us, and we miss her dearly.

In early November, I was back in Athens, Georgia for the Homecoming game against Troy State (a game that was a LOT closer than anyone would have guessed pre-season). Before the game I caught up with Sonny Seiler, owner of UGA (pronounced, "ug-ga"), Georgia's beloved bulldog mascot. Sonny's a bit of a legend amongst Dawg fans. For over 50 years, the Seiler family has sired these dogs. For those of you counting, we're currently on UGA VI.

Sonny and UGA have also been immortalized in the book, Midnight in the Garden of Good and Evil *by John Berendt, as well as in the 1997 movie adaptation. In the movie, UGA played himself, while Sonny played a judge. Those of you who are real UGA fans probably know that actor Jack Thompson played Sonny.*

"Sorry to hear about the loss of your Dawg," Sonny said, "you let me know when your family is ready for another one." I told Mr. Seiler that I appreciated both the condolences and the offer, an offer I couldn't help but wonder if it was just polite conversation or the 'real deal'. I've known of more than a few folks who'd asked Sonny for a bulldog pup, only to be politely told no. Being offered a puppy who's daddy is THE UGA is high cotton where I come from. It's tantamount to being offered a winning lottery ticket: it doesn't happen often, and you'd be a damn fool to decline it.

In between flights on my way home, I called Amie and mentioned Sonny's offer. "Do you think he was serious?" was her response. "We shall see," I said. We didn't have to wait long. As a matter of fact, as my final plane landed in San Luis, I turned on my cellphone and noticed I had one voicemail message. It was from a "Miss Becky" in Moultrie, Georgia. "Mr. Garretson? Mr. Sonny asked me to give you a call. He's told me to put you at the top of the list for a puppy."

True to his word, Sonny wasted no time in extending his most generous offer. Six weeks ago, UGA VI sired a litter, only one of which was an all-white ... a little girl. As this is UGA's coloring, all-whites are especially prized. The fact that our Fireball was an all-white girl made the decision even easier ... we wanted – and got – dibs on this puppy.

It will be a few more weeks before the litter is old enough to leave their parents, and I'll be heading back to Georgia to pick her up. And, yes, we've already settled on her name: VIVI (pronounced, "viv-vee"). Amie's always wanted a dog with that name, and as her daddy's UGA VI, it just seems a natural!

IN THE LAST 28 YEARS, **MAT GARRETSON** HAS HELD VIRTUALLY EVERY POSITION POSSIBLE IN THE WINE INDUSTRY, FROM RETAILER TO IMPORTER TO WINERY OWNER, FROM SALES DIRECTOR TO GENERAL MANAGER TO WINEMAKER. HE IS GENERALLY CREDITED FOR BEING ONE OF THE DRIVING FORCES BEHIND THE RHONE WINE MOVEMENT IN THE U.S., HAVING FOUNDED HOSPICE DU RHONE (HOSPICEDURHONE.ORG), THE WORLD'S PREEMINENT ORGANIZATION FOR THE PROMOTION OF THESE WINES. IT WAS ONLY NATURAL THAT MAT'S LOVE FOR ALL THINGS RHONE WOULD LEAD TO THE STARTING OF HIS OWN RHONE-INSPIRED WINERY, GARRETSON WINE COMPANY. WHEN NOT CONVERTING THE WORLD TO RHONE WINES, MAT ENJOYS GOLF, FLYING, THE UNIVERSITY OF GEORGIA BULLDOGS AND SLEEP.

FAVORITE FOOD: STEAK
FAVORITE TOY: SQUEAKY BONE
OBSESSION: HANGING WITH JERRY
KNOWN ACCOMPLICES: ZIG AND TULLE
PET PEEVE: NOT GOING SWIMMING ENOUGH
FAVORITE PASTIMES: HUNTING AND SWIMMING
NAUGHTIEST DEED: SLEEPING UNDER THE COVERS IN PAT AND JERRY'S BED

RED

FAVORITE FOOD: PIZZA
PET PEEVE: HAVING HIS TEETH BRUSHED
OBSESSION: CARRYING A TOY IN HIS MOUTH
KNOWN ACCOMPLICES: TUCKER AND
DAKOTA WARD, AND BRITNEY SPEARS THE CAT
NAUGHTIEST DEED: CHEWING UP PAPER TOWELS
FAVORITE PASTIMES: PLAYING TUG AND BEING BRUSHED
FAVORITE TOYS: USC FOOTBALL TUG AND HEDGEHOG TOY

ZACK

MILO

FAVORITE TOY: MOM
FAVORITE PASTIME: EATING
FAVORITE FOOD: EVERYTHING
OBSESSION: BEGGIN' STRIPS
NAUGHTIEST DEED: POOPING ON THE RUG
PET PEEVE: GEORGE BUSH'S DOG BARNEY

FAVORITE FOOD: CHEESE
PET PEEVE: DICK CHENEY
FAVORITE TOY: CHARCOAL THE CAT
FAVORITE PASTIME: RIDING IN THE CAR
OBSESSION: STEALING MILO'S BONES
NAUGHTIEST DEED: GROWLING AT MILO
KNOWN ACCOMPLICES: MILO AND CHUCK NORRIS

PET PEEVE: THE VACUUM CLEANER
FAVORITE TOYS: BALLS AND FLOWERS
OBSESSIONS: BLANKETS AND STEALING
SOCKS FROM THE LAUNDRY BASKET
KNOWN ACCOMPLICES: PAOLO, ECHOES AND LAYLA
NAUGHTIEST DEED: EATING EVERYTHING IN THE GARDEN
FAVORITE PASTIME: BEING CHASED BY HIS BROTHER PAOLO

LOUIS

PAOLO

FAVORITE FOOD: HORS D'OEUVRES
FAVORITE PASTIME: RUNNING AT THE BEACH
NAUGHTIEST DEED: EATING CHOCOLATE-COVERED
STRAWBERRIES AT THE CHRISTMAS PARTY
PET PEEVES: CATS AND BEING LEFT ALONE
FAVORITE TOYS: STICKS, SQUEAKY TOYS AND STUFFED ANIMALS
OBSESSIONS: CHASING BIRDS AND HAVING PEOPLE CHASE HIM

FAVORITE FOOD: CARROTS
FAVORITE PASTIMES: SLEEPING AND WATCHING
THE NEIGHBORHOOD FROM THE FRONT STEP
FAVORITE TOY: LUCKY, THE STUFFED DALMATIAN
OBSESSIONS: SEARCHING FOR CRUMBS
AND ATTACKING THE WASHING MACHINE
NAUGHTIEST DEED: CHEWING UP DAD'S YEARBOOK
PET PEEVES: MARTHA STEWART, NEIGHBORHOOD CATS AND COFFEE TABLE LEGS

OLIVIA

MAX

OBSESSION: BIRDS
FAVORITE FOOD: RABBIT
KNOWN ACCOMPLICE: L.E.
FAVORITE TOY: BONDO'S GROW TUBE
FAVORITE PASTIME: HUNTING RABBITS

PET PEEVE: BONDO
KNOWN ACCOMPLICES:
THE TUMANS FROM NEXT DOOR
NAUGHTIEST DEED: BURYING BONDO'S BONES

FAVORITE FOOD: BUTTER
FAVORITE PASTIME: BIRD HUNTING
OBSESSION: BABYSITTING BABY ANIMALS
FAVORITE TOY: NONE – TOYS ARE FOR KIDS, HE'S A BIRD DOG

L.E.

BONDO

KNOWN ACCOMPLICE: MAX
FAVORITE FOOD: CHILIS
PET PEEVE: GUNSHOTS
OBSESSION: FOOD
FAVORITE PASTIMES: SLEEPING AND GREETING TASTING ROOM VISITORS
NAUGHTIEST DEED: POOPING ON PAUL'S SLIPPER AFTER HE SCOLDED HIM

OBSESSION: TOYS
FAVORITE PASTIMES: EATING
AND RUNNING IN THE VINEYARD
FAVORITE FOOD: INNOVA PUPPY FOOD
NAUGHTIEST DEED: ESCAPING TO PLAY
KNOWN ACCOMPLICES: COCO AND MOLLY
PET PEEVE: NOT GETTING TO GO EVERYWHERE

GEORGEANNE

NAUGHTIEST DEED: DIGGING
FAVORITE FOOD: DOG BISCUITS
OBSESSION: CHASING SHADOWS
FAVORITE PASTIME: BEING PETTED
FAVORITE TOY: SQUEAKY SOFT TOYS
PET PEEVE: WALKING ON THE STREET
BECAUSE SHE'S AFRAID OF CARS

ROXY

CALLIE

OBSESSION: SHOE COLLECTING
FAVORITE TOY: WENDY'S SHOES
KNOWN ACCOMPLICE: INDIGO
PET PEEVE: HAVING TO STAY AT HOME
FAVORITE FOOD: ANYTHING INDIGO LIKES
FAVORITE PASTIME: SLEEPING UNDER THE COVERS

KNOWN ACCOMPLICE: CALLIE
FAVORITE TOY: FLYING SQUIRREL
FAVORITE FOOD: ANYBODY ELSE'S
PET PEEVE: BEING TOLD WHAT TO DO
OBSESSION: GUARDING THE FRONT DOOR
NAUGHTIEST DEED: HERDING THE NEIGHBOR
FAVORITE PASTIME: EXERTING MIND-CONTROL OVER OTHER DOGS

INDIGO

SASSY

PET PEEVE: CATS
OBSESSION: BIRDS
FAVORITE TOY: SOCCER BALL
FAVORITE FOODS: COOKIES AND DOG BONES
KNOWN ACCOMPLICES: CHARLEY AND WILLY
NAUGHTIEST DEED: JUMPING IN OTHER PEOPLE'S CARS
FAVORITE PASTIMES: RUNNING, PLAYING AND SWIMMING

FAVORITE FOOD: CARROTS
OBSESSION: DESTROYING TOYS
FAVORITE PASTIME: PLAYING FETCH
PET PEEVE: BEING BOSSED AROUND
NAUGHTIEST DEED: GOING 'POTTY' IN THE HOUSE
KNOWN ACCOMPLICES: AMIKA, MR HIGGINS AND BOOMER
FAVORITE TOY: ANYTHING THAT CAN BE CHEWED ON FOR HOURS

OPIE

OBSESSION: SNAILS
PET PEEVE: RABBITS
FAVORITE TOY: BUCKET
FAVORITE FOOD: PEDIGREE
FAVORITE PASTIME: RUNNING
NAUGHTIEST DEED: BITING THE CAMERA

MANCHAS

OBSESSION: GOPHERS
FAVORITE TOY: GOPHERS
PET PEEVE: DELAY IN TAKING A WALK
FAVORITE FOOD: T-BONE STEAK BONE
KNOWN ACCOMPLICES: OTIS AND LUKE
NAUGHTIEST DEED: EATING WORKERS' BOOTS, GLOVES AND LUNCHES
FAVORITE PASTIMES: WALKS IN THE VINEYARD AND DIGGING FOR GOPHERS

JACK

W O L F

THE MAN STOOD AT THE WINDOW looking down on the vines in the moonlight. The room behind him was lit with a single shaded lamp; in the bed his wife sat with pillows at her back, feeding the baby. The man could see the vines silvered by the moon, and he could hear the soft sucking of the baby at the woman's breast. There was no other sound. He almost thought he could hear the vines growing, imagine the turning and loosening of the buds. He gripped the rail of the balcony and liked the feel of the cold metal in his hands.

Suddenly he saw a movement towards the end of a row, a swift dark shadow passing along the end posts. There it was again. He didn't move. It was impossible to pick out different shades at that distance, despite the brightness of the moon.

From the bed the woman said, 'Are you coming in? She's finished.' She carried on talking, murmuring to the baby.

He stepped back into the room. It seemed darker than outside. He said, 'There's something out there. In the vines. A dog, I think.' He climbed under the covers and raised a hand to cup the sleeping baby's warm powdery head.

'What was it doing?' the woman asked.

'I don't know. I don't even know it was a dog. It might have been a wolf.'

'A wolf,' she said. 'There aren't any wolves.'

'Up here? You'd be surprised. Further down, no. But at this height, in the forest.'

'Wolves,' she said. 'I'd like to see one.'

The next night, he stood on the balcony again. This time he strained to see movement, and turned his head at every imagined shape. Then he saw it, and was certain.

The dog moved with an easy, loping gait up the row of vines. It stopped about fifty yards from the house and stood, ears sharp on its head, tail sprung inwards. It stared at the house as if it hadn't expected to see it there, and for a moment the man stared back.

155

He felt he was on ground equally his and the dog's. He realized he was gripping the balcony rail and slowly relaxed his fingers. The dog turned and trotted back down the row.

In the morning, the man found a flattened circle of grass about a yard wide. There was hair among the stones and dust. He knelt and laid his hand on the ground, and said quietly, 'Where are you from?'

'He sleeps on the end of the row,' he told his wife in bed that evening. 'I saw where he'd been sleeping.'

'That's your wolf then,' she said.

That night he heard a shrieking in the woods, and saw the dog come purposefully along – closer to the house than he had ever seen it – with something heavy and limp swaying in its jaws. Not for the first time he wondered about the depth of the forest, and again thought of the land they seemed to borrow, not own.

The trees were densest just where they met the vines. Further in, where the slope gave way to rocky escarpment, they were thinner and hardier, curling exposed roots round massive boulders. But here, from the house, the black trunks looked impenetrable.

'Let's get out,' he'd said, when they knew she was pregnant. So in the space of three months he'd handed in his notice at the winery, sold the bungalow and bought the vineyard. It had 50-year-old zinfandel and cabernet sloping away from the two-storey cabin they spent the summer and half the winter making habitable.

'You know what? We can make this work,' they had said.

The next night, the moon shone so brightly you could pick out individual stones under the vines.

The man said, 'I'm just going out,' but saw his wife was asleep, curled around the baby on the bed beside her.

He pulled on trousers and boots and went downstairs. He stood on the porch and waited for a moment, feeling the chill night air. The rows ran down the hill and disappeared into the darkness and the woods beyond.

The dog saw him when it was ten yards away and stopped. It gave a low growl. The man waited, and slowly held out a hand. The dog approached, sniffed, and the growl quietened.

He breathed out and realized sweat was trickling down his sides. When he moved to touch the dog's flank he could feel rather than hear the quickening warning rumble.

It was a bitch, a cross-breed, German shepherd mixed with, what – husky? It had the elegant lines of the shepherd but with an extra heft to the chest.

'You're a beauty,' he said. The dog allowed him to run a hand along its side, feel its protruding ribs, sense the heart pumping, the alertness of it. He thought of winter days out working the vines, the dog alongside him.

At breakfast he said, 'It's a good one. There's all sorts in it. Husky for a start. It's thin though.'

His wife asked, 'Where do you think it's from?'

'Maybe it was dumped, or ran away.'

Over the next weeks, as spring caught hold and the days grew longer, the family took meals on the wooden porch that looked down over the budding vines. The dog became trusting, losing its nocturnal habits. It had once been tame, that was obvious. It ate the meat the man left out for it, and slept under the porch, on an old blanket on the hard earth. It would not come into the house.

He spent most of the day in the vineyard now, tending the vines, clearing weeds, repairing posts and wires, positioning shoots. The dog would sit and look over into the forest, and he would talk to it as he worked his way along a row.

'We should give her a name,' his wife said.

'Maybe. Have to get to know her first.'

A month later, with the vines now in flower, the man stood on the balcony in the night. He felt at peace as he looked down with satisfaction on his work; when he saw the low shape coming out of the woods he thought it was the dog.

But even at a distance he could see this was different. It trotted along the edge of the vineyard, its movements loose-limbed and savage. It gave him a jolt as he recognized what it was.

Below, the dog came slowly out from under the porch. She sniffed the air and stood, as if listening.

'Shit,' he said, and ran downstairs. In the kitchen he stood irresolute, then unlocked the metal gun cupboard.

His wife was coming out of the bathroom as he mounted the stairs. She looked at him.

'What's going on? What are you doing with that?'

'It's a wolf,' he said, holding the rifle. 'It'll attack the dog.'

'Let me see,' she said, 'put that gun down. Jesus. Are you mad?'

She went onto the balcony. 'God, look at it,' she whispered.

The dog and the wolf were circling each other, nose to tail. The dog looked fine-boned, civilized, beside the gaunt wild beast. Slowly they turned, and a low cold rumble could be heard, both animals beginning to bare teeth. Then, as if on a signal, the circling turned to snarling conflict. They rolled in a blur of limbs and snapping teeth.

The man and woman watched aghast. The fight lasted seconds – before any possibility of separating them, the dog was lying in the dust, a dark tangle of intestines hanging from a great wound in its belly.

The wolf skulked around the corpse, sniffing, then it moved off swiftly into the vineyard.

Later in the year, after a perfect summer, the ripened grapes hung in fat bunches. Deer and rabbits came and nibbled at the fruit, and weeds grew tall between the rows. The house was deserted now, and under the sagging porch, on the old blanket, the wolf made a bed for her cubs.

ADAM LECHMERE IS EDITOR AT LARGE OF *DECANTER* MAGAZINE. HE LIVES IN LONDON WITH HIS WIFE AND THREE DAUGHTERS, AND SPENDS A GOOD DEAL OF TIME IN WINE COUNTRY FROM BORDEAUX TO BAROSSA VIA CALIFORNIA AND BURGUNDY. HE HAS A TASTE FOR GREAT BORDEAUX AND GREAT PINOT, AND WILL GO MANY MILES FOR THE PERFECT BOTTLE OF GRUNER VELTLINER.

OBSESSION: FOOD
PET PEEVE: LUCIA
FAVORITE TOY: SQUEAKIES
FAVORITE FOOD: ANYTHING EDIBLE
FAVORITE PASTIME: LOOKING FOR THINGS TO EAT
KNOWN ACCOMPLICES: LUCIA, REUBEN AND MAURICE
NAUGHTIEST DEED: ROLLING IN SMELLY THINGS BY THE POND

LUCY

LUCIA

FAVORITE FOOD: PUP-PERONI TREATS
OBSESSION: MOVING JACQUE'S SHOES
FAVORITE TOY: SQUEAKY STUFFED ANIMALS
NAUGHTIEST DEEDS: TAKING THE BRIE OFF THE
TABLE AT AN EVENT AND EATING THE TV REMOTE
KNOWN ACCOMPLICES: DAKOTA, AMY AND PATTY
PET PEEVES: SUDDEN LOUD NOISES AND BEING LEFT ALONE
FAVORITE PASTIME: GREETING TASTING ROOM CUSTOMERS

REUBEN

MAURICE

OBSESSION: GUARDING BONES
FAVORITE FOOD: CHICKEN STRIPS
PET PEEVE: BEING SEPARATED FROM HIS MAMA
FAVORITE PASTIME: GOING FOR A RIDE TO THE WINERY

FAVORITE TOY: FUZZY SQUEAKY TOYS
PET PEEVE: PEOPLE NOT SAYING HELLO
KNOWN ACCOMPLICES: LUCY AND LUCIA
OBSESSION: CHASING GEESE INTO THE POND
NAUGHTIEST DEED: ROLLING IN SMELLY THINGS BY THE POND

OWNER: JACQUE HOGGE | POODLES, 11 | **COOPER VINEYARDS** LOUISA, VA

BELLA

OBSESSION: RED KONG BALLS
FAVORITE TOY: SADIE'S COLLAR
FAVORITE FOOD: APPLES
PET PEEVE: YAPPY LITTLE DOGS
KNOWN ACCOMPLICE: DUDE, THE WINERY CAT
FAVORITE PASTIMES: HELPING PRUNING IN THE VINEYARD
AND LAPPING UP SPILLED WINE DURING PUMP OVERS
NAUGHTIEST DEED: JUMPING ON THE COUCH AND THROWING PILLOWS OFF

BELLA LUNA WINERY TEMPLETON, CA | ENGLISH BULL TERRIER, 6 | OWNERS: SHERM AND LAURIE SMOOT

FAVORITE FOOD: DOG BISCUITS
FAVORITE TOY: ANYTHING SQUEAKY
PET PEEVE: BELLA GETTING MORE ATTENTION
OBSESSIONS: FETCHING BALL AND GOING FOR CAR RIDES
KNOWN ACCOMPLICES: BELLA AND DUDE THE WINERY CAT
NAUGHTIEST DEED: EATING ALL THE CHOCOLATE OFF THE KITCHEN COUNTER
FAVORITE PASTIMES: SLEEPING IN FRONT OF WINERY AND GREETING CUSTOMERS

SADIE

CHARLIE

FAVORITE FOOD: ICE CUBES
KNOWN ACCOMPLICES: BOGEY AND CASSIE
OBSESSIONS: SQUIRRELS AND WINE CORKS
FAVORITE PASTIME: PRETENDING HE'S HUMAN
NAUGHTIEST DEED: CHEWING A HOLE IN THE TV REMOTE
PET PEEVE: BEING PETTED WHEN HE'S TRYING TO CONCENTRATE
FAVORITE TOY: ANYTHING WITH A SQUEAKER THAT HE CAN TEAR OUT

OBSESSION: BONES
FAVORITE TOY: TENNIS BALLS
KNOWN ACCOMPLICE: CHARLIE
FAVORITE PASTIME: MAKING DOG SNOW-ANGELS
PET PEEVES: BEING AWOKEN FROM A NAP OR POUNCED ON BY CHARLIE
NAUGHTIEST DEED: EATING A FRIEND'S ENTIRE SALMON FILET FROM OFF THE COUNTER

BOGEY

FAVORITE TOY: BALL
FAVORITE FOODS: CHEESE AND TOFU
FAVORITE PASTIME: CHASING BIRDS
KNOWN ACCOMPLICES: DAISY, SMOKEY AND BIZU
PET PEEVE: NOT GETTING TO GO EVERYWHERE HIS MOM GOES
OBSESSION: HIS CAT, SMOKEY, BEING THE CENTER OF ATTENTION
NAUGHTIEST DEED: EATING A PLATTER OF CHEESE FOR A WINE EVENT

KOKOPELLI

OWNER: LISA PRETTY | STANDARD POODLE, 5 | **PRETTY-SMITH VINEYARDS AND WINERY** SAN MIGUEL, CA

BUDDY

FAVORITE FOOD: CHEESE
OBSESSION: CAR RIDES
PET PEEVE: FIREWORKS
FAVORITE TOY: TENNIS BALL
FAVORITE PASTIME: CHASING STICKS
NAUGHTIEST DEED: CHEWING SLIPPERS

NAUGHTIEST DEED: RUNNING
AWAY FROM THE DOG PARK
PET PEEVE: HOT AIR BALLOONS
FAVORITE FOOD: WHIPPED CREAM
FAVORITE PASTIME: CHASING ROCKS
FAVORITE TOY: RUBBER SQUEAKY PIG
OBSESSION: SWIMMING IN THE OCEAN

GIRARD WINERY YOUNTVILLE, CA | JACK RUSSELL TERRIERS, 5 AND 6 | OWNER: STEVE ROSS

B I T C H ...

by Zoe Williams

– I don't understand why you even care.

– I don't care.

He pulled his chin into his neck, brought his eyebrows together and looked at me
askance. From a distance, it could have been constipation or scepticism. 50-50. I knew
which.

– I don't care.

– You care.

This struggle breaks out on the scabby, scorching porch outside my house. My adversary,
also best friend, and I have thrashed out many things here but never, I don't think, have
we got on each other's nerves as much as we are doing today. The subject of this discord
looks up from a snooze. His body is still stretched out, legs criss-crossing, suggesting
motion even in stillness, like a statue of a running dog. Stan is a Rhodesian Ridgeback.
I have heard these dogs described, variously, as racist, as slave hunters, as lion tamers,
and even the last slightly offends me, as if you can possibly describe the great strength
and determination of this animal in terms of the petty-minded ambitions of men. My
canine ramblings contrast with my reticence otherwise. I would guess that there are
one or two people under 25 in this area who have known me all their lives and never
heard me speak.

– I don't care. I will admit to a very slight anxiety, but that is all.

*– What are you anxious about? Do you think the other dogs are going to take the piss?
I'll have a word with Bonny, but I'm sure she wouldn't.*

Richard takes jokes too far, only one notch, but a miss is as good as a mile in this
respect, and I look at him wearily. He did not appear to find me cutting, not in the
smallest amount.

I used to think Rose took me pretty seriously, took my displeasure seriously, but it's possible that nobody does, and when Rose looked affected, she was just being courteous. She'd read some book on courtesy within a marriage, maybe. Take an Interest. Pretend to Mind.

– I'm worried... I'm, look, it's no big deal.

– Tell me what you're worried about.

– Look, he's just a dog, it's no big deal. But he's an adult dog. Something changes with an adult dog, it's not puberty, is it? He's not gonna grow a new dick, his voice isn't going to break. Something changes with a dog, you think maybe that dog is ill.

– So take him to a vet.

– I'm not taking him to the vet.

– Why not?

– What do I say to the vet?

Picturing myself at the vet, I get an embarrassment so refined and precise that it's an actual physical pain. Stan seems to infer this, somehow, and he stands, relinquishing his shade in spite of the heat, and slopes over with his head bowed, hulking into my shadow as I sit, and nudging my thigh. I grab an ear of his.

– Don't worry, old man. We're not going to the vet.

– You are a hard man to help, did you know that?

I stay silent. Richard hates it when I do that, and I think that explains his next remark, because he's not a jerk.

– I imagine Rose will have told you that, one way or another.

– She wasn't trying... she wasn't living to help me. We helped each other.

I shake my head at myself, that wasn't what I was trying to say.

– We didn't help each other, we weren't crutches for each other. Why are you...

I let this hang. Now we're both annoyed, and Stan has his head on my leg, resting it there, he has all day, he has all the time in the world. Richard won't be happy until he thinks I'm opening up, and I can't decide whether or not I've got it in me to pretend to be opening up. Because here's the thing, I could pretend; and I could say the very words, the exact words, that I would say if I really meant it. I could say the things that are true, I'm not proud, but I still wouldn't mean them because I feel dead. So I can't be bothered.

– I feel dead.

He looks up. He waits for ages. It really feels like hours.

– Talk to me.

– Oh God, all that's happened is my wife's left me. I haven't got a whole new personality. If I could get a whole new personality, she probably wouldn't have left me.

– Just talk a little bit. Just carry on talking.

Now I wait for ages. Stan is stock still, leaning on me still, watching nothing. Closing his eyes slowly, opening them again. "I still have all the time in the world," he says, with his dog blinking. I keep on waiting. And then finally I tell him, still taking my time.

I miss the way she had begun to lean over, quite formally, bending from the waist, and kiss me like a mechanised woodpecker, even though I know now and I knew then that it meant she was going to leave me. I miss where her family were from, even though it was a family she'd never met and nor had I. They lived in the Ardèche, in France, what do you even call them, ancestors? Pâté shopping is hell for me. I miss her funny corrugated hair. The other day I pulled up in traffic alongside a butterscotch Volvo with a woman in it who seemed to be everything she might be, in twenty years' time, and it was like sitting there watching, while my future got trashed, got ripped away, in front of my eyes, and then I still had to hit go when the lights said go.

But Stan has started pissing like a bitch. He's 8 years old, and he doesn't cock his leg anymore, stopped overnight, the week after Rose left. And I wouldn't mind, who cares how a dog pees, I don't really think he's ill.

I think he's doing it to make me feel better. That bothers me more than all the rest of it put together.

ZOE WILLIAMS IS A COLUMNIST FOR *THE GUARDIAN*, ALONG WITH SUNDRY OTHER ENGLISH PUBLICATIONS AND THE ODD IN-FLIGHT MAGAZINE. SHE HAS A STAFFIE-RIDGEBACK CROSS CALLED SPOT; AS YET, NO VINEYARD.

OBSESSION: BISCUITS
FAVORITE TOY: VINE CANES
PET PEEVE: BEING TREATED LIKE A DOG
NAUGHTIEST DEED: SITTING IN DAD'S CHAIR
FAVORITE FOODS: CHICKEN, BISCUITS AND CABERNET
FAVORITE PASTIME: HUNTING GOPHERS, SQUIRRELS AND RABBITS

FAVORITE TOY: GOPHERS
PET PEEVE: OTHER DOGS
FAVORITE FOOD: GOPHERS
FAVORITE PASTIME: PICKING ON THE YOUNGER DOGS
KNOWN ACCOMPLICES: CIRA, EDANA, BUSTER AND DANIKA
NAUGHTIEST DEED: STEALING A WHOLE TRI-TIP OFF THE BARBEQUE
OBSESSIONS: PROVING SHE'S TOUGH AND HAVING HER BELLY RUBBED

LACY

LEIFE

PET PEEVE: CAR TRAVEL
FAVORITE FOOD: TURKEY
FAVORITE PASTIME: HUNTING
OBSESSION: RATTLESNAKES
FAVORITE TOY: STUFFED ANIMALS
NAUGHTIEST DEEDS: BRINGING HOME
DEAD ANIMALS AND BARKING AT THE CATTLE

FAVORITE FOOD: TURKEY
KNOWN ACCOMPLICE: LEIFE
FAVORITE TOY: STUFFED ANIMALS
FAVORITE PASTIME: WALKING IN THE
VINEYARD AND HILLS WITH HIS MASTER
PET PEEVE: BEING LEASHED UP AND BRUSHED

SCOOTER

FAVORITE TOY: STUFFED BLUE HERON
FAVORITE FOOD: STEAK OFF THE GRILL
OBSESSION: PLAYING FETCH WITH TOYS
FAVORITE PASTIME: BEING WITH PEOPLE
PET PEEVE: CATS SITTING ON FENCE TAUNTING HER
NAUGHTIEST DEED: TRYING TO LICK PEOPLE TO DEATH
KNOWN ACCOMPLICES: FLEA FLICKER, DAYTON, DALLIS AND SAGE

MARLI

MARTIN & WEYRICH WINERY PASO ROBLES, CA | BOXER, 4 | OWNER: MAURA OSBOURN

OBSESSION: BIRDS
FAVORITE FOOD: PIG EARS
FAVORITE TOY: BARREL BUNGS
PET PEEVE: WANTS TO GO, ALWAYS!
KNOWN ACCOMPLICES: KOBE AND BRUNO
FAVORITE PASTIME: CHASING RABBITS AND BIRDS
NAUGHTIEST DEED: CHEWING UP STUFFED ANIMALS

SAMMY

KOBE

PET PEEVE: BEING LEFT AT HOME
FAVORITE FOOD: ANY MEAT OFF THE BBQ
FAVORITE TOYS: FRISBEE AND ANY BALL
OBSESSION: CHASING ATVS THROUGH THE VINEYARD
FAVORITE PASTIME: RUNNING THROUGH THE VINEYARD
NAUGHTIEST DEED: DESTROYING THE CHRISTMAS TREE ANGEL

OBSESSION: THE BALL
FAVORITE FOOD: PUPPY CHOW
PET PEEVE: BEING OUTSIDE BY HIMSELF
FAVORITE PASTIMES: CHASING BALLS
AND NAPPING IN FRONT OF THE FIREPLACE
FAVORITE TOY: JUMBO-SIZE RAWHIDE CHEW
KNOWN ACCOMPLICES: KYLIE AND MARLI
NAUGHTIEST DEED: TEARING UP THE BACKYARD

FLEA FLICKER

OWNER: PETER PRICE | LABRADOR, 2 | **MARTIN & WEYRICH WINERY** PASO ROBLES, CA | 181

FAVORITE TOY: TENNIS BALL
FAVORITE FOOD: MILK BONES
OBSESSION: KITTY COP DUTY
KNOWN ACCOMPLICE: SYRAH THE CAT
NAUGHTIEST DEED: ROLLING IN THE DIRT
FAVORITE PASTIME: GREETING GUESTS AT THE WINERY
PET PEEVE: BEING OUTRUN BY RABBITS IN THE VINEYARD

BUD

FAVORITE TOY: STICKS
FAVORITE FOOD: PIG EARS
KNOWN ACCOMPLICE: GORDON
OBSESSION: SLEEPING IN THE SUN
FAVORITE PASTIME: TAKING LIFE EASY
NAUGHTIEST DEED: PASSING GAS IN THE TASTING ROOM
PET PEEVE: YOUNG FEISTY DOGS JUMPING AROUND HER

GOOSE

OWNER: JIM THOMAS | LABRADOR X, 15 | **COUNTRYSIDE VINEYARDS & WINERY** BLOUNTVILLE, TN | 183

GUS

FAVORITE FOOD: BISCUITS
FAVORITE TOY: HEDGEHOG
PET PEEVE: BEING IGNORED
OBSESSIONS: LOVE AND GOPHERS
KNOWN ACCOMPLICE: ZSI GMOND
NAUGHTIEST DEED: GETTING UNDER THE
COVERS AFTER YOU JUST MADE THE BED
FAVORITE PASTIME: SITTING ON YOUR LAP

FAVORITE TOY: HEDGEHOG
OBSESSION: RIDING IN THE TRUCK
PET PEEVE: NOT GETTING TO GO!
KNOWN ACCOMPLICE: SHERMAN
NAUGHTIEST DEED: STEALING THE
THANKSGIVING TURKEY OFF THE COUNTER
FAVORITE FOOD: ANYTHING YOU ARE EATING
FAVORITE PASTIME: SUNBATHING IN THE VINEYARD

ZSI ZSA

PET PEEVE: FLIES
FAVORITE TOY: HEDGEHOG
FAVORITE PASTIME: PLAYING AT THE BEACH
KNOWN ACCOMPLICE: LILY THE JACK RUSSELL
FAVORITE FOOD: THE HORSE'S CARROTS IN THE BARN
OBSESSIONS: HUNTING GOPHERS, LIZARDS AND BIRDS
NAUGHTIEST DEED: KNOCKING OVER THE PARAKEET CAGE

FAVORITE TOY: BALL
FAVORITE PASTIME: RUNNING
OBSESSION: GETTING THE MAIL
PET PEEVE: HAVING HIS PAWS HELD
FAVORITE FOOD: ANYTHING HE CAN STEAL
NAUGHTIEST DEED: STEALING A ROAST OFF THE KITCHEN COUNTER

AJAX

OWNERS: MIKE AND VICKIE LANCASTER | BORDER COLLIE, 3 | **TIN BARN VINEYARDS** SONOMA, CA

ASPEN

KNOWN ACCOMPLICES: SADIE AND CHEWY
FAVORITE PASTIME: CLIMBING THE FENCE
IN THE BACKYARD FOR MORE ADVENTURES
FAVORITE FOOD: ANYTHING MOMMY AND DADDY ARE EATING
NAUGHTIEST DEED: SHREDDING HER PEE-PEE PAD AFTER SHE HAD USED IT
PET PEEVE: STAYING WELL HYDRATED BY DRINKING AS MUCH AS POSSIBLE

OBSESSION: CECIL
FAVORITE FOOD: CHEESEBURGER
KNOWN ACCOMPLICE: JESUS, WHO
BRINGS HER FOOD EVERY NIGHT
FAVORITE TOY: STUFFED ANIMAL PUPPY
THAT SHE GIVES A BATH REGULARLY
NAUGHTIEST DEED: SNAPPING AT THE CATS
PET PEEVE: HARLEY-DAVIDSON MOTORCYCLES

DAISY

RUDY

PET PEEVE: GUN FIRE
FAVORITE FOOD: BACON
KNOWN ACCOMPLICE: PISTLE
FAVORITE TOY: DAY GLOW BALL
OBSESSION: FINDING OUT THE
COLOR OF HIS BEDDING STUFFING
FAVORITE PASTIME: LOOKING FOR THE CAT
NAUGHTIEST DEED: ESCAPING FROM THE DOG RUN

OBSESSION: PIZZA
FAVORITE TOY: GOLF BALLS
FAVORITE FOOD: ROASTED BONES
FAVORITE PASTIME: CHASING GOLF BALLS
PET PEEVE: CATS THAT FOLLOW HER EVERYWHERE
KNOWN ACCOMPLICES: HER CATS, LILLE AND STUBS
NAUGHTIEST DEED: ROLLING IN THE MUD AFTER A BATH

REBEL ROSE

SADIE

OBSESSION: CATS
FAVORITE TOY: CATS
KNOWN ACCOMPLICE: STUART
FAVORITE FOOD: SANDWICHES
NAUGHTIEST DEED: EATING FECAL MATTER
PET PEEVE: NOT GETTING TO RIDE IN THE PICKUP
FAVORITE PASTIMES: EATING AND CHASING CATS

OBSESSION: EGG
PET PEEVES: DAISYMAE
AND DUKE, THE BLOODHOUNDS
FAVORITE PASTIMES: HER MORNING HUNT
AND SNUGGLING AT NIGHT IN BED

PENNY

OWNER: JUDY ARON | WALKER HOUND, 8 | **ARONHILL VINEYARDS** TEMPLETON, CA | 193

ANNIE

OBSESSION: FOOD
FAVORITE FOOD: BREAD
PET PEEVE: NOT BEING PATTED FIRST
NAUGHTIEST DEED: COUNTER CRUISING
FAVORITE PASTIME: GOING TO THE BEACH
FAVORITE TOY: KONG FILLED WITH PEANUT BUTTER

ARONHILL VINEYARDS TEMPLETON, CA │ LABRADOR, 8 │ OWNER: JUDY ARON

OBSESSION: CATS
FAVORITE FOOD: EGG
FAVORITE TOY: CHEW STICK
NAUGHTIEST DEED: STEALING SHOES
FAVORITE PASTIME: CATCHING A SCENT
PET PEEVE: THE OTHER PACK MEMBERS

DUKE

SITKA

FAVORITE TOY: BONES
PET PEEVE: DRUNKS
FAVORITE FOOD: STEAK
KNOWN ACCOMPLICE: HEATHER
OBSESSION: ANYTHING THAT MOVES
FAVORITE PASTIMES: PLAYING AND CHASING
NAUGHTIEST DEED: CHEWING THE OAXACAN CARPET

FAVORITE TOY: 12-YEAR-OLD STUFFED DUCK
NAUGHTIEST DEED: STEALING OTHER HUNTERS' DUCKS
FAVORITE FOOD: A T-BONE WITH PLENTY OF SCRAPS ON THE BONE
OBSESSION: PROTECTING THE WINERY OWNER'S PICK-UP TRUCK
PET PEEVE: ENDURING JIM BUNDSCHU'S SAXOPHONE PRACTICE

ROSIE

KELSEY

FAVORITE FOOD: APPLES
PET PEEVE: CATS IN THE YARD
FAVORITE TOY: STUFFED SERPENT
OBSESSION: SUCKING ON HER BLANKY
FAVORITE PASTIME: GOING ON LONG WALKS
NAUGHTIEST DEED: SNEAKING ONTO THE
TABLE AND NIPPING MOMMY'S BREAKFAST
KNOWN ACCOMPLICE: HER BOYFRIEND, EVAN

FAVORITE TOY: LITTLE DUCKY
OBSESSION: STEALING SOCKS
KNOWN ACCOMPLICE: COUSIN ABIGAIL
FAVORITE PASTIME: CURLING UP ON ANY LAP
PET PEEVE: NOT BEING THE CENTER OF ATTENTION
NAUGHTIEST DEED: CHEWING UP MOM'S FAVORITE SHOES

FAVORITE TOY: OLD DEER BONES
FAVORITE FOOD: PILL POCKETS,
WHICH WRAP AROUND HIS VITAMINS
KNOWN ACCOMPLICE: HIS CAT MUFFIN
PET PEEVE: FOUR-YEAR-OLD BOYS WHO
RUN AT HIM WHILE HE'S ASLEEP IN THE SUN
FAVORITE PASTIME: GREETING WINERY GUESTS

TROOPER

FAVORITE FOOD: PEARS
FAVORITE TOY: HIS ROPE
PET PEEVE: BEING ALONE
OBSESSION: GUARDING HIS PACK
FAVORITE PASTIMES: PLAYING CHASE AND SLEEPING
NAUGHTIEST DEED: COMMANDEERING SIR DUKE'S
FAVORITE BOODA GIRAFFE WHILE HE IS PLAYING WITH IT
KNOWN ACCOMPLICES: SIR DUKE, CORTON, PETAL, CORKY AND GUINNESS

OLIVER

PET PEEVE: BEING LEFT ALONE
FAVORITE TOY: MANOLO BLAHNIK SHOE
OBSESSION: TRYING TO PROVE HE'S HUMAN
NAUGHTIEST DEED: BEING AN ESCAPE ARTIST
FAVORITE FOOD: THOMAS KELLER'S WAGYU BEEF
FAVORITE PASTIMES: NAPPING IN MEETINGS AT
THE WINERY AND ATTENDING WINERY DINNERS
KNOWN ACCOMPLICES: OLLIE, DUKE, JACKI, PETAL AND GO-GO

OBSESSION: ICE COLD WATER
FAVORITE TOY: BOODA GIRAFFE
PET PEEVE: BEING HOME ALONE
NAUGHTIEST DEED: DEVOURING AN ENTIRE
STICK OF BUTTER AND HALF A CHEESECAKE
FAVORITE PASTIME: MEDITATING ON HIS BACK
FAVORITE FOOD: ANYTHING HE FINDS IN THE VINEYARD
KNOWN ACCOMPLICES: CORTON, PETAL, OLLIE, TIM, ABIGAIL AND LITTLE DUKE

SIR DUKE

TEXAS

PET PEEVE: BEING TOLD TO "STAY"
OBSESSION: CHEWING ON EVERYTHING
KNOWN ACCOMPLICES: STING AND SPINCAT
NAUGHTIEST DEED: STEALING A PATRON'S PURSE
FAVORITE FOOD: ANYTHING OUT OF THE TRASH CAN
FAVORITE PASTIME: SWIMMING IN THE SPRING-FED POND
FAVORITE TOY: ROPE WITH A KNOT ON THE END TIED TO A 500LB BBQ PIT

FAVORITE FOOD: CARROTS
FAVORITE TOY: SILICONE BARREL BUNGS
KNOWN ACCOMPLICES: SCOUT, JAMES, LUCQUE AND TITUS
FAVORITE PASTIME: MOUNTAIN BIKING WITH MOM AND DAD
PET PEEVE: WHEN DAD GOES MOUNTAIN BIKING WITHOUT HIM
OBSESSION: WAKING PARENTS UP EVERY MORNING LIKE CLOCKWORK
NAUGHTIEST DEED: STEALING NEIGHBORING WINERIES' SILICONE BARREL BUNGS

BOWIE

PEARL

FAVORITE FOOD: ANYTHING
KNOWN ACCOMPLICE: MURPHY
NAUGHTIEST DEED: DIGGING IN THE TRASH
FAVORITE TOY: A PIECE OF ROPE WITH KNOTS
OBSESSION: CHASING THE JOHN DEERE GATOR
FAVORITE PASTIMES: DUCK HUNTING AND SWIMMING

A GRAND DAY OUT

by Heidi Barrett

THIS IS THE TALE of our previous two notorious winery dogs: Jenny, an energetic and highly-motivated-by-food black Lab and her sidekick, Lucky, a dog pound Dalmatian as cute as they come.

Jenny was famous for her "waffle swallow" which we found extremely entertaining on Sunday mornings. There were always the burnt ones and the extra ones, and feeding them to Jenny was fun. She never chewed or probably ever tasted one, just swallowed them whole with the characteristic jutting neck action similar to a pigeon walking along a ledge. One giant gulp per waffle. We were easily amused, but that's what happens living in the vineyards with no television all these years.

Lucky, the spotted one, had tons of the usual Dalmatian black dots, plus some odd large black patches that made him look like he was wearing pants. He was a gentle soul who wished he had been born a pampered poodle much of the time, instead of the winery and vineyard dog he actually was. The upside was he did love to chase jack rabbits and deer and occasionally even caught some. But his very favorite thing was rolling in whatever he could find that was the smelliest. And here's where this story begins...

On one particular occasion, Lucky found a really great (to him) fresh pile of horse manure. So fresh it was green. He coated himself thoroughly 'til he was shiny and green, then rolled through a patch of blooming mustard to festoon himself with some lovely yellow blossoms adding panache to his ensemble. (Reminds me of the 'Far Side' cartoon where the boy dog carrying flowers comes to the door to pick up his date. She comes to the door and he says "Oh Ginger, you look lovely, and whatever you rolled in sure does stink!") After completely decorating himself in this manner, he couldn't understand why we wouldn't let him in the house. All dressed up and nowhere to go. Or so we thought...

He and Jenny had other plans and set out on their big adventure unescorted to the winery at the ranch next door, Chateau Montelena. It's about a three-mile trip. But they went the long way visiting neighbors along the route, eating cat food and sniffing around, doing what dogs do. Jenny was not smelling pretty at this point either, practically mildewing from the winter before, but looking and smelling this good, they simple had to socialize.

They looked forward to the swim in the pond at the winery. Great pond scum could add another dimension. And yes, there'd be picnickers, easy marks ripe for begging cheese and salami. At first, the tourists always think, oh look, how cute, winery dogs! Let's pet them. And then the horror, the smell! The wet dogs shaking on our stuff and us. Too late. The realization that you just petted something you regret, that seemed cute but actually reeks! Duped again. Then, with huge grins on their faces, they are off ... this time to the tasting room. Oh no! These two made the rounds like no others I have seen. Picture two wet dogs trotting into the beautiful tasting room wagging their whole bodies practically exclaiming, "Look, they really like us!" They had such a blast and so many other similar adventures with their wonderful joie de vivre. I got the phone calls, "Lucky and Jenny are here". "OK, I'll be right over to pick them up". Replaced a lot of cat food too.

So next time you visit a winery and think you'll just be smelling and tasting the wine, if there is a winery dog, NO MATTER HOW CUTE, just give a little sniff before you pet.

HEIDI BARRETT IS A WELL-KNOWN PROFESSIONAL WINEMAKER IN THE NAPA VALLEY. SHE HAS A B.S. DEGREE IN FERMENTATION SCIENCE FROM UC DAVIS AND HAS WORKED IN THE WINE INDUSTRY FOR OVER THIRTY YEARS. SHE IS WINEMAKER/OWNER OF LA SIRENA AND AMUSE BOUCHE. HER OTHER CLIENTS ARE BARBOUR, PARADIGM, REVANA, LAMBORN, KENZO, AND FANTESCA. HEIDI WAS ALSO WINEMAKER FOR THE FAMOUS 'SCREAMING EAGLE' AS WELL AS 'GRACE FAMILY', 'DALLA VALLE', 'JONES', AND 'SHOWKET'.

KNOWN ACCOMPLICE: PEARL
OBSESSION: CHASING KITTIES
FAVORITE FOOD: MEAT OF ANY KIND
FAVORITE TOY: THINGS THAT SQUEAK
FAVORITE PASTIMES: CHASING JACK RABBITS
IN THE VINEYARD AND GETTING BELLY RUBS
NAUGHTIEST DEED: GETTING ON THE SOFA
PET PEEVES: HAVING HIS TAIL TOUCHED AND RETRIEVING ANYTHING

MURPHY

BEAR

FAVORITE PASTIME:
CHASING BUNGS

FAVORITE TOY: BUNG

FAVORITE FOOD: CAT FOOD

OBSESSION: BEING THE
KEEPER OF THE BUNG

NAUGHTIEST DEED:
TRASH CAN DIVING

DUHG AKA THE SCHEMING BEAGLE

PET PEEVE: CATS
FAVORITE FOOD: ROAST BEEF
OBSESSIONS: EATING AND SNOOZING
FAVORITE TOY: HUGE WOOLLY STUFFED BONE
KNOWN ACCOMPLICES: MILES AND TROOPER
FAVORITE PASTIMES: CHASING ARMADILLOS AT NIGHT,
PEACOCKS AND SQUIRRELS DURING THE DAY

CISCO

FAVORITE TOY: BASKETBALL
PET PEEVE: BEING IGNORED
OBSESSION: BIG BELLY RUBS
FAVORITE FOOD: THE OWNER'S RIB EYE STEAKS
NAUGHTIEST DEED: MOOCHING PICNIC SNACKS
KNOWN ACCOMPLICES: CALAMITY JANE AND MISS KITTY
FAVORITE PASTIME: GREETING CUSTOMERS IN THE TASTING ROOM

TOBIN JAMES CELLARS, PASO ROBLES, CA | AUSTRALIAN SHEPHERD, 44 | OWNER, TOBIN JAMES

OBSESSION: RABBITS
FAVORITE FOOD: BEEF
FAVORITE TOY: RABBITS
PET PEEVE: HER FOOD BEING TAKEN
KNOWN ACCOMPLICES: ROWDY AND THE FIVE WINERY CATS
FAVORITE PASTIMES: GREETING VISITORS AND BEING PETTED

MIKEY

WIMPY WINES

MURPHY

KNOWN ACCOMPLICE: FRANCI
FAVORITE TOY: RALLY MONKEY
FAVORITE FOOD: PULLED PORK
NAUGHTIEST DEED: BITING PETER
PET PEEVE: GETTING ON HIS SPOT
FAVORITE PASTIME: WALKING WITH FRANCI

OBSESSION: OTHER DOGS
PET PEEVE: BEING IGNORED
FAVORITE TOY: ROPE MONKEY
KNOWN ACCOMPLICE: HAVANA THE PUGGLE
FAVORITE FOOD: ANYTHING PEOPLE ARE EATING
NAUGHTIEST DEED: PULLING THE STUFFING OUT OF TOYS
FAVORITE PASTIMES: RUNNING AND CHASING WITH OTHER DOGS

CALI

BINDI

OBSESSION: CHASING LIZARDS
FAVORITE FOOD: COOKED CHICKEN
FAVORITE TOY: HER SQUEAKY SHEEP
FAVORITE PASTIME: HERDING SHEEP AND COWS
PET PEEVE: THE NEIGHBOR'S DOG GETTING TOO CLOSE TO THE FENCE
NAUGHTIEST DEED: TEARING OFF THE INSULATION WRAPPED AROUND THE PIPES

OBSESSION: CATS
FAVORITE FOOD: JERKY
FAVORITE TOY: HIS SQUEAKY BALL
FAVORITE PASTIME: CHASING SQUIRRELS
PET PEEVE: WHEN HIS PAL BINDI TAKES HIS TOYS
NAUGHTIEST DEED: USING THE CHRISTMAS TREE AS A PIT STOP

DALLAS

HABU

FAVORITE FOOD: MEAT
OBSESSION: DRINKING WATER
KNOWN ACCOMPLICE: MUDDY
PET PEEVE: HAVING HIS TOE NAILS CLIPPED
FAVORITE TOY: KONG FULL OF PEANUT BUTTER
FAVORITE PASTIME: HERDING ANYTHING THAT MOVES
NAUGHTIEST DEED: GETTING INTO A HUGE CAN OF DOG FOOD

PET PEEVE: HAVING A BATH
KNOWN ACCOMPLICE: HABU
FAVORITE TOY: BLACK KONG
OBSESSION: CHEWING BALLS
FAVORITE PASTIME: FETCHING STICKS
NAUGHTIEST DEED: DIGGING A HUGE HOLE IN THE LAWN

MUDDY

BLANCA

FAVORITE TOY: BALLS
FAVORITE FOOD: CHICKEN
FAVORITE PASTIME: SNUGGLING UP
PET PEEVE: SANGRIA STEALING HER FOOD
NAUGHTIEST DEED: SLEEPING IN THE FLOWER BED
KNOWN ACCOMPLICES: SANGRIA, EARL GREY AND WUGGINS

OBSESSION: MOTOR VEHICLES
PET PEEVES: THE UPS TRUCK AND THUNDER
FAVORITE PASTIME: BARKING AT VULTURES
NAUGHTIEST DEEDS: MAULING THE CAT AND BITING TIRES
KNOWN ACCOMPLICES: BLANCA, EARL GREY AND WUGGINS
FAVORITE FOODS: CHICKEN OR A RABBIT WHEN SHE CAN CATCH ONE

SANGRIA

ROSCOE

OBSESSION: HIS CHAIR
FAVORITE FOOD: FISH AND CHIPS
FAVORITE TOY: HIS BEST FRIEND'S TAIL
NAUGHTIEST DEED: CHEWING MOMMIE'S SHOES
PET PEEVE: BEING DISTURBED WHEN IN HIS CHAIR
KNOWN ACCOMPLICES: KAYA, MADDIE, SOPHIE AND CHARLIE
FAVORITE PASTIMES: GREETING CUSTOMERS AND SECURITY DETAIL

KNOWN ACCOMPLICE: BOW
FAVORITE TOY: WATER BOTTLES
NAUGHTIEST DEED: FOLLOWING A
WONDERFUL SCENT TOO FAR
FAVORITE PASTIMES: RUNNING AND
CHASING BIRDS IN THE VINEYARD
OBSESSIONS: FOUR-WHEELERS AND TRACTORS
PET PEEVE: THE CATS TRYING TO EAT HIS FOOD

HUDSON

OWNERS: THE BALLETTO FAMILY | LABRADOR, 2 | **BALLETTO VINEYARDS AND WINERY** SANTA ROSA, CA | 223

OBSESSION: SHOES
FAVORITE FOOD: TURKEY MEAT
FAVORITE TOY: TOY OPOSSUM
FAVORITE PASTIMES: LAYING IN
THE SUN AND PLAYING WITH POOKIE
NAUGHTIEST DEED: CHEWING ON PAPER
AND DRAGGING IT AROUND THE HOUSE
PET PEEVE: BEING PENNED UP WITHOUT
FREE RANGE OF THE HOUSE OR PROPERTY
KNOWN ACCOMPLICES: POOKIE AND PHAT KITTY

ZOË

NEVERIDLE VINEYARD TEMPLETON CA | YORKSHIRE TERRIER 7 MONTHS | OWNERS: THE CLARKE FAMILY

OBSESSION: CROWS
FAVORITE FOOD: CHICKEN
FAVORITE TOY: ANY STUFFED TOY
PET PEEVE: CROWS FLYING OVERHEAD
FAVORITE PASTIME: SLEEPING IN THE SUN
KNOWN ACCOMPLICE: MR JINGLES THE CAT
NAUGHTIEST DEED: STEALING PEOPLE'S FOOD

ROLEY

OWNERS: THE CLARKE FAMILY | AMERICAN ESKIMO, 14 | **NEVERIDLE VINEYARD** TEMPLETON, CA | 227

DJANGO

FAVORITE TOY: A FLOATING KONG
FAVORITE PASTIME: RETRIEVING ANYTHING
OBSESSION: HARASSING HIS OLDER BROTHER
KNOWN ACCOMPLICES: BOSWELL, PRUNE AND JACKSON
FAVORITE FOOD: ANYTHING – A COMPLETE OPPORTUNIVORE
NAUGHTIEST DEED: CHEWING HOLES IN TWO RUGS IN A THREE-DAY PERIOD
PET PEEVE: PEOPLE WHO DON'T WANT TO THROW THINGS FOR HIM TO RETRIEVE

DAVERO HEALDSBURG, CA | CHESAPEAKE RETRIEVER X, 8 MONTHS | OWNERS: RIDGELY EVERS AND COLLEEN McGLY...

FAVORITE PASTIME: PEOPLE
FAVORITE FOOD: BANANAS
FAVORITE TOY: A PULL ROPE
PET PEEVE: HIS YOUNGER BROTHER WHO TRIES
TO DROWN HIM WHILE PLAYING IN THE POOL
OBSESSIONS: AVOIDING HIS YOUNGER BROTHER
KNOWN ACCOMPLICES: DJANGO, JACKSON AND PRUNE

BOSWELL

TOOTSIE

PET PEEVE: OTHER DOGS
FAVORITE TOY: STUFFED ANIMALS
OBSESSION: BARKING AT TRUCKS
FAVORITE FOOD: AL PASTOR TACOS
KNOWN ACCOMPLICE: GOLDIE ROSIE
FAVORITE PASTIMES: ENTERTAINING TASTING
ROOM VISITORS, EATING TACOS AND SAVING LIVES

TOOTSIE TO THE RESCUE

by Shannon O'Neill

TOOTSIE ORIGINALLY BELONGED to the Medinas family in Fresno, California where she worked a 4000-acre broccoli farm as the resident ranch dog, eradicating unwanted animals like deer, coyotes and squirrels.

When Tootsie was only one year old, the Medinas traveled with her to the upper Sacramento River for a family picnic day. What started out as a fun family outing quickly turned into near-tragedy, as their five-year-old son got too close to the water's edge and accidentally fell in the rapidly flowing river. Within seconds, he was swept away and disappeared out of sight. As none of the Medina family knew how to swim, it was Toosie who jumped in to swim after the boy. They both disappeared with the strong current of the river, so the family called 911 for help. A helicopter rescue team searched for five long hours and, just before sunset, when all seemed hopeless, they spotted Tootsie with the boy in her mouth, clinging to a clump of trees miles down the river. Tootsie held the boy above the water for five hours in the freezing cold rapids until the rescue team arrived.

A rescue basket was lowered from the helicopter to retrieve the boy but Tootsie refused to let go of him. The boy was extremely hypothermic and in great peril, so the rescuers had to coax Tootsie to get her to release the boy. They finally were able to save them both, reuniting them with their family.

Tootsie was the big hero! She made the evening news and the local newspapers, with the EMT rescue team commenting that Tootsie was the smartest and bravest dog they had ever met. Toosie didn't know what all the fuss was about – all in a day's work, she thought to herself!

SHANNON AND MAUREEN O'NEILL ARE UC DAVIS GRADUATES WHO HAVE BEEN GROWING GRAPES IN PASO ROBLES SINCE 1982. SHANNON RECEIVED A DEGREE IN FERMENTATION SCIENCE AND HAS BEEN MAKING WINE SINCE 1984. MAUREEN WORKED IN THE SILICON VALLEY UNTIL 2002 WHEN THEY BOTH DECIDED TO MOVE TO PASO ROBLES AND BUILD A TASTING ROOM. COME VISIT THEM AND TRY SOME OF THEIR BIG, EXTRACTED, HAND-CRAFTED RED WINES.

WOLFIE

OBSESSION: SQUIRRELS
FAVORITE FOOD: RABBIT
FAVORITE TOY: HEDGEHOG
FAVORITE PASTIME: CHASING RABBITS
PET PEEVE: GETTING HIS NAILS CLIPPED
KNOWN ACCOMPLICES: SALUKI DOG SHOW FRIENDS
NAUGHTIEST DEED: EATING BUTTER OFF THE COUNTER

FAVORITE TOY: PILLOW
FAVORITE FOOD: CARROTS
PET PEEVE: TAKING SHOWERS
FAVORITE PASTIME: DIGGING HOLES
KNOWN ACCOMPLICES: REED AND JERZY
OBSESSION: HOWLING TO THE HARMONICA
NAUGHTIEST DEED: JUMPING OFF BALCONIES

TAZI

LUCKY

PET PEEVE: LEASHES
FAVORITE FOOD: RABBIT
FAVORITE TOY: TOY RABBIT
OBSESSION: WATCHING FOR RABBITS
FAVORITE PASTIME: HUNTING RABBITS
NAUGHTIEST DEED: HUNTING THE NEIGHBOR'S PET RABBITS
KNOWN ACCOMPLICES: CHOPPER, MEATBALL AND PEPPER

PET PEEVE: BATHS
FAVORITE FOOD: STEAK
FAVORITE TOY: A BONE
FAVORITE PASTIME: SLEEPING
NAUGHTIEST DEED: BARKING AT THE WIND
OBSESSION: LAYING IN THE TASTING ROOM
KNOWN ACCOMPLICES: LUCKY AND MEATBALL

CHOPPER

AERO

KNOWN ACCOMPLICE: IRIE
OBSESSION: STEALING (KLEPTOMANIAC)
PET PEEVE: NOT GETTING TO GO TO WORK
FAVORITE FOOD: BOLOGNA SANDWICH AT LUNCH TIME
FAVORITE TOY: ANYTHING HE CAN GET INTO HIS MOUTH
FAVORITE PASTIME: GOING WHEREVER JASON AND JENNIFER GO
NAUGHTIEST DEED: HIDING OUT IN THE CAR WHEN JASON AND JENNIFER ARE LEAVING

OBSESSION: STICKS
FAVORITE FOOD: POPCORN
FAVORITE TOY: A BALL WITH FEET
PET PEEVES: LASERS AND LIGHTS
NAUGHTIEST DEED: LICKING WALLS
KNOWN ACCOMPLICES: SAM, BOOMER AND CURLY
FAVORITE PASTIMES: CHEWING BONES AND DIGGING HOLES

TURBO

CJ JACKSON

FAVORITE TOY: TENNIS BALLS
FAVORITE FOODS: CHICKEN AND RABBITS
KNOWN ACCOMPLICES: LUCY, BEAR AND BOO
PET PEEVE: BEING EXCLUDED FROM WINE TASTING
OBSESSION: DRIVING IN THE MULE WITH GRANDPA
NAUGHTIEST DEED: BRINGING A DEAD BUNNY TO THE DOORSTEP
FAVORITE PASTIMES: SELLING JAX WINE AND FLIRTING WITH HIS GIRLFRIENDS

JAX VINEYARDS CALISTOGA, CA | GOLDEN RETRIEVER, 8 | OWNER: KIMBERLY JACKSON

FAVORITE FOOD: JERKY
PET PEEVE: BRIGHT LIGHT
FAVORITE TOY: HIS LEOPARD
FAVORITE PASTIME: SLEEPING
KNOWN ACCOMPLICE: HIS BROTHER HOJI
NAUGHTIEST DEED: DOING NO. 2 IN THE HOUSE
OBSESSION: TAKING THE STUFFING OUT OF HIS TOYS

PET PEEVE: FENCES
FAVORITE TOY: JACK
OBSESSION: RABBITS
KNOWN ACCOMPLICE: JACK
FAVORITE FOOD: GRAPE JUICE
FAVORITE PASTIMES: RUNNING AND EATING GRAPES
NAUGHTIEST DEED: RUNNING AWAY TO THE GOLF COURSE

HOJI

OWNER: ALASTAIR RIMMER | CATAHOULA LEOPARD DOGS, 2 AND 3 | DIABLO GRANDE, PATTERSON

JESSIE

OBSESSION: CATS
PET PEEVE: BEING LEFT HOME
FAVORITE FOOD: ANY PEOPLE FOOD
FAVORITE TOY: THE OLD GREEN STUFFED DUCK
KNOWN ACCOMPLICE: CARLOS THE RANCH HAND
FAVORITE PASTIME: PICNICS WITH THE STILL WATER GUESTS
NAUGHTIEST DEED: BRINGING A BABY SKUNK TO A TASTING ROOM GUEST

OF WINE AND DOGS
by John Potter

WINE IS ONE OF TWO SUBJECTS about which I can speak with a small amount of authority. The other is dogs.

In what now seems like another lifetime, I was co-owner/trainer of a dog training, boarding and day care facility. I spent two years – 365 days a year, 7 days a week and 12 or more hours a day – with dogs. And that doesn't count the pack of dogs I was living with at the time.

At first glance, there doesn't seem to be much similarity between these two subjects. The differences are pretty clear: one is a living, breathing animal and the other is a liquid (although Kermit Lynch would argue that good wine is also living). The more I consider it, however, the more I find in common between these two passions of mine.

The more you learn about wine, the more you realize you don't know. The same can be said about dogs. The sheer number of breeds and various mixes certainly rivals the number of grapes, blends and wines. People have spent lifetimes breeding and blending genetic traits in search of the perfect dog, just as winemakers pursue the perfect vintage or cuvée.

Although I know very little about winemaking, I think there are some similarities between making wine and teaching dogs. Both require lots of time, patience and experience. And for those who master either trade, the results of their work can be breathtaking. Anyone who has ever watched a service dog in action should understand.

Both wine and dogs never cease to amaze me. There is subtlety, beauty, grace, aggression, simplicity, complexity, strengths and defects to be found in each.

For an information junkie like me, there is an endless amount of knowledge waiting to be discovered on both subjects. And they both require hands-on learning; books can provide a foundation of knowledge, but can never replace the glass, or the leash, in your hand.

And just as each individual bottle of wine is different, so is each individual dog. No two Labrador Retrievers are carbon copies, any more than any two syrahs are exactly alike.

I imagine these two passions will stay with me until the end. I can't imagine a life without holding a nice glass of wine in one hand and stroking a dog's head with the other.

My dog is a Belgian Malinois Eastern North Carolina 1996. She's a little funky on the nose, but once you get past that, she's warm, delicate and soft, with undertones of neurosis and the suggestion of an impending bite.

I wouldn't trade her for two cases of Château Lafite-Rothschild 1961.

JOHN POTTER IS A WRITER AND SEMI-RETIRED DOG TRAINER. HE BLOGS ABOUT WINE, DOGS AND OTHER (SOMEWHAT) RELATED TOPICS AT BRIMTOTHEDREGS.COM.

FAVORITE FOOD: CRACKERS
OBSESSION: CHASING RABBITS
FAVORITE PASTIME: CHASING CARS
FAVORITE TOY: ANYTHING THAT SQUEAKS
PET PEEVE: BEING DISTURBED DURING NAP TIME
NAUGHTIEST DEED: CHEWING UP DAD'S JEEP SEAT
KNOWN ACCOMPLICES: THE NEIGHBORHOOD DOGS

JIMMIE

OWNERS: THE BITNER FAMILY | JACK RUSSELL TERRIER, 3 | **BITNER VINEYARDS** CALDWELL, ID | 247

BONNES MARES

PET PEEVE: BEING LEFT BEHIND
WHEN EVERYONE ELSE GOES FOR A RUN
FAVORITE FOOD: ANYTHING AND EVERYTHING
FAVORITE PASTIME: LOUNGING ON THE TILES
OBSESSION: OLD BOOKS WITH SWEET GLUE BINDINGS
FAVORITE TOY: A WARM HAND, READY TO RUB HIS JAW

FAVORITE FOOD: PORK TENDERLOIN
FAVORITE TOY: HER BUBBLE SQUEAKY BALL
NAUGHTIEST DEED: GOING WINE TASTING
(WITHOUT PERMISSION) TOO FAR AWAY FROM HOME
PET PEEVE: HAVING HER PAWS CHECKED FOR FOXTAILS
OBSESSION: GOING EVERYWHERE THAT JON AND JULIE GO
FAVORITE PASTIME: RIDING IN THE FRONT SEAT OF THE TRUCK

TEALLY

MUSIGNY AKA MOOSE

OBSESSIONS: GUINEA HENS
FAVORITE TOY: SMELLY SOCKS
PET PEEVE: BEING ON A LEASH
FAVORITE PASTIME: SNUGGLING WITH
JON WHILE WATCHING THE GIANTS
FAVORITE FOODS: CHICKEN AND BRIE
NAUGHTIEST DEED: FOLLOWING ZEAUX INTO THE WILD YONDER

OBSESSION: MAKING VISITORS SMILE

FAVORITE PASTIME: STEALING LOGS FROM THE
PIZZA OVENS AND USING THEM AS TOOTHPICKS

PET PEEVE: BEING STUCK IN THE BARREL ROOM

NAUGHTIEST DEED: STEALING TREATS FROM WINERY
GUESTS AS THEIR HANDS DANGLE AT MOUTH LEVEL

FAVORITE FOOD: CHEESE CRUMBS DROPPED BY WINERY VISITORS

KNOWN ACCOMPLICES: MILO, SOHO, CHELSEA, COOPER AND WILBUR

GUS

LAMBERT BRIDGE WINERY HEALDSBURG, CA | LABRADOR, 2 | OWNER: ANDY WILCOX

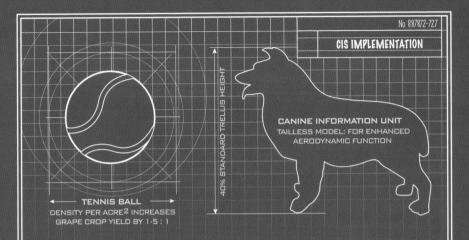

CIS IMPLEMENTATION

↑
40% STANDARD TRELLIS HEIGHT

CANINE INFORMATION UNIT
TAILLESS MODEL: FOR ENHANCED
AERODYNAMIC FUNCTION

← **TENNIS BALL** →
DENSITY PER ACRE^2 INCREASES
GRAPE CROP YIELD BY 1·5 : 1

WINERY AND VINEYARD MANAGEMENT

A Case Study in Canine Information Systems (CIS) Implementation

BY HANK THE ELVENGLADE WINE DOG

Canine Information Systems (CIS) play a critical role in precise management of vineyards and wineries. French vintners introduced the theory that *terroir* – meaning, the land – contributes significantly to the quality of the wine grape produced. Similarly, *grrr* – in any language, and in its many conjugations, declensions, shadings and nuances – is the very foundation of viticulture (*Ralston, Purina 1894*). Needless to say, the ability of CIS to integrate information from many sources is essential to any and all hope of success.

The integration of 'What's Going On?', 'Who's Doing What?', and 'What's That Smell?' evince benefits too obvious to belabor to the enlightened reader. Storage of this information in a CIS seamlessly streamlines the management of crops, facilities and wine production. Hours of tedious paperwork by the grower are thus eliminated.

A Case Study in CIS Implementation:
ELVENGLADE WINERY AND VINEYARDS

Planting commenced in 1986 in an abandoned orchard near Gaston, OR with approximately 10 acres of pinot gris. Nothing significant took place until the acquisition of CIS capabilities on Hank Williams' birthday in 2002. By that time, a total of 30 acres had been planted, a winery had been constructed, the Head Elf had quit his day job at Intel, and everything was going to hell in a handcart.

A CIS was selected as a means of storing this information in spatial databases for mapping and data analysis. A program to increase the density of tennis balls per acre (B_T/Ac) was initiated with commensurately dramatic increases in crop yields, wine production and profits.

The obvious advantages of CIS for human resources (HR) management result in dramatically increased productivity.

Note the clear eye; the steady gaze; the unflappable demeanor; the generous cranial vault for optimum processing capacity; the absence of a tail for enhanced aerodynamic efficiency (e.g., running *through* trellises versus going *all* the way around). The configuration of the CIS also anticipates future expansion of functionality (i.e., new tricks).

Bark to the Future

Entering the 21st century, Elvenglade Winery and Vineyards looks to leverage its CIS investment to further define operations and realize improved decision-making.

One interesting application of CIS technology is consumer education and public relations (e.g., Hank's Tennis Ball Discount).

HANK KELLEY IS AN AUSTRALIAN SHEPHERD AND VICE PRESIDENT OF CANINE INFORMATION SYSTEMS AT ELVENGLADE VINEYARDS. HE IS NAMED AFTER HANK WILLIAMS WITH WHOM HE SHARES A BIRTHDAY. HANK'S VERY FAVORITE BREAKFAST (OR LUNCH OR DINNER, FOR THAT MATTER) IF HE CAN'T HAVE HUMAN FOOD, IS A NICE DEAD GOPHER. HE CHASES (PROBABLY ATTEMPTING TO HERD) ANYTHING THAT MOVES, BUT PREFERS TENNIS BALLS OR FOUR-WHEELERS. WHEN THE CREW ARRIVES IN THE VINEYARD, HE MULTI-TASKS AS THEIR OFFICIAL FOOD TASTER. TO MAKE SURE THEY DON'T EAT ANYTHING THAT WOULD IMPINGE ON THEIR PRODUCTIVITY.

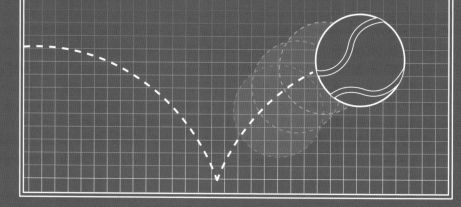

PET PEEVE: CATS
FAVORITE PASTIME: SLEEPING
FAVORITE FOOD: STEAK BONES
FAVORITE TOY: RUBBER BONE
OBSESSION: CHASING RABBITS
NAUGHTIEST DEED: OPENING PACKAGES
KNOWN ACCOMPLICES: JOHN AND CHRIS

SYRAH

RILEY

FAVORITE FOOD: CARROTS
FAVORITE TOY: TENNIS BALL
KNOWN ACCOMPLICES: MONTY AND EVIE
FAVORITE PASTIME: WRESTLING WITH EVIE
PET PEEVE: BEING TAUNTED ABOUT HIS WEIGHT
OBSESSION: STARING AT HIS REFLECTION IN THE POOL
NAUGHTIEST DEED: BATTING HIS EYELASHES FOR TREATS

FAVORITE FOOD: CHEETOS
FAVORITE TOY: QUACK QUACK DUCK
PET PEEVE: MOM MAKING HER WORK
OBSESSION: THE BIGGEST STICK SHE CAN FIND
KNOWN ACCOMPLICES: MAPLE VINEYARD DOGS
FAVORITE PASTIME: SWIMMING IN DUTCHER CREEK
NAUGHTIEST DEED: STEALING BUNGS OUT OF THE BARREL ROOM

DUTCHESS

ZUZU PETALS

NAUGHTIEST DEED:PLAYING KEEP AWAY
FAVORITE FOOD:TREATS, TREATS, TREATS
KNOWN ACCOMPLICES: LUCKY, RUDY THE CHIHUAHUA
AND BARNABAS THE HANDSOME NEWFOUNDLAND
OBSESSIONS: HER BLANKIE AND LAYING IN ICE OR SNOW
PET PEEVE: ANYONE SITTING IN HER FRONT SEAT IN THE CAR
FAVORITE PASTIMES: RETRIEVING AND NAPPING UNDER PEOPLE'S FEET

FAVORITE TOY: WUBBA-WUBBA
PET PEEVE: OTHER DOGS IN HER DOMAIN
FAVORITE PASTIME: HANGING OUT WITH DAD
ON THE DECK OVERLOOKING HER LAKE AND DOMAIN
KNOWN ACCOMPLICES: ZUZU PETALS AND MOMMY T
FAVORITE FOODS: GREEN BEANS AND SWEET POTATOES
OBSESSIONS: NOT A BIG FAN OF FOLKS WITH BOOTS AND/OR HATS
NAUGHTIEST DEED: OPENING CHRISTMAS PRESENTS TOO EARLY,
ESPECIALLY THOSE WITH CHOCOLATE AND COOKIES

JAZZ

ROOTY

FAVORITE TOY: TENNIS BALL
PET PEEVE: BEING LEFT AT HOME
KNOWN ACCOMPLICES: MITCHELL AND ZAKK
FAVORITE PASTIMES: CHASING TENNIS BALLS AND EATING
OBSESSIONS: PLAYING FETCH AND SWIMMING AT THE LAKE
NAUGHTIEST DEED: TAKING BUNGS OUT OF THE BARRELS

ZAKK AKA TINY

FAVORITE TOY: CAT TOYS
KNOWN ACCOMPLICE: ROOTY
PET PEEVE: BEING LEFT ALONE
FAVORITE PASTIME: TEASING CATS
OBSESSION: LICKING CUSTOMERS
NAUGHTIEST DEED: GOING 'POTTY' IN THE HOUSE

PACEY

FAVORITE FOODS: APPLES AND KIBBLES
PET PEEVE: LITTLE PUPPIES LICKING HIM
KNOWN ACCOMPLICES: SIENA AND DUKE
FAVORITE PASTIME: BEING THE VINEYARD DOORBELL
OBSESSION: GETTING TREATS FROM THE UPS DELIVERY MAN

OBSESSIONS: FOOD AND FETCH
FAVORITE FOOD: CARNITAS FROM
THE VINEYARD CREW'S LUNCH
PET PEEVE: NOT BEING TOP DOG
NAUGHTIEST DEED: GOING TO THE CREW
FOR HER SECOND HELPING OF LUNCH
FAVORITE PASTIME: SCOPING OUT LIZARDS
IN THE VINEYARD AND ON ROCK WALLS
KNOWN ACCOMPLICES: PACEY AND DUKE

SIENA

OWNERS:

DUKE

FAVORITE FOOD: KIBBLES
FAVORITE TOY: TUG-O-WAR ROPE
PET PEEVE: NOT GETTING ANY ATTENTION
KNOWN ACCOMPLICES: PACEY AND SIENA
FAVORITE PASTIMES: PLAYING WITH THE OLDER
DOGS AND CHEWING ANYTHING IN HIS WAY
NAUGHTIEST DEED: BEING A LITTLE ANKLE BITER
OBSESSION: LICKING THE OTHER DOGS TO GET THEM TO PLAY WITH HIM

YATES FAMILY VINEYARD NAPA, CA | LABRADOR, 10 WEEKS | OWNER: MARY YATES

KNOWN ACCOMPLICES: SYDNEY AND TILDA
FAVORITE PASTIME: HERDING THINGS THAT MOVE
OBSESSION: KEEPING DEER OUT OF THE VINEYARD
NAUGHTIEST DEED: NIPPING TILDA SO HARD IT REQUIRED STITCHES

RIA

PET PEEVE: GETTING A BATH
FAVORITE TOY: HER BEST FRIEND FANNY
FAVORITE FOOD: HOME-MADE DOGFOOD
FROM CHEF TOM AT VILLA CREEK RESTAURANT
KNOWN ACCOMPLICES: CLOVER AND FANNY
NAUGHTIEST DEED: CHEWING UP JOANN'S RABBIT SLIPPERS
FAVORITE PASTIMES: CHASING SQUIRRELS AND SUNBATHING
OBSESSION: HERDING THE CHICKENS AND GOAT ON THE PROPERTY

IZZY

PET PEEVE: HAVING HER FEET TICKLED
OBSESSION: WARM SLEEPING QUARTERS
FAVORITE PASTIME: RUNNING WITH JOANN
NAUGHTIEST DEED: JUMPING OUT OF THE TRUCK
KNOWN ACCOMPLICES: IZZY, JOLIE AND CLOVER
FAVORITE FOOD: HOME-MADE DOGFOOD
FROM CHEF TOM AT VILLA CREEK RESTAURANT
FAVORITE TOY: DEER PART FROM OUT OF THE WOODS

FANNY

GUY NOIR

FAVORITE FOOD: CAT FOOD
FAVORITE TOY: GAMAY ROUGE
NAUGHTIEST DEED: GETTING GAMAY PREGNANT
PET PEEVE: SHARING GAMAY'S ATTENTION WITH TREU BLEU
OBSESSION: CHASING BONNIE FROM NEXT DOOR ALONG THE DEER FENCE
KNOWN ACCOMPLICES: GAMAY ROUGE, TREU BLEU, BONNIE AND STELLA
FAVORITE PASTIME: GUARDING THE DOG FOOD LOCKER ON THE BACK PORCH

FAVORITE FOOD: CAT FOOD
FAVORITE TOY: DEAD GOPHERS
PET PEEVES: GOPHERS AND COYOTES
OBSESSION: DIGGING FOR GOPHERS
FAVORITE PASTIME: CHASING COYOTES
NAUGHTIEST DEED: GETTING PREGNANT BY GUY
KNOWN ACCOMPLICES: GUY NOIR, TREU BLEU, BONNIE AND STELLA

GAMAY ROUGE

OWNERS: DOUG FUNNELL AND MELISSA MILLS | IRISH SETTER, 13 | **BRICK HOUSE VINEYARDS** NEWBERG, OR

FAVORITE FOOD: CHICKEN
FAVORITE TOY: TENNIS BALL
PET PEEVE: BEING HOSED DOWN
OBSESSION: LOOKING IN RABBIT HOLES
KNOWN ACCOMPLICES: CAPTAIN AND LUCKY
FAVORITE PASTIME: FOLLOWING WORKERS IN THE VINEYARD
NAUGHTIEST DEED: PRESENTING DIANE AND MIKE WITH A DEAD RABBIT

LOLITA

NAGGIAR VINEYARDS GRASS VALLEY, CA | GOLDEN RETRIEVER X, 6 | OWNERS: DIANE AND MIKE NAGGIAR

FAVORITE TOY: FOOTBALL
FAVORITE FOOD: PUP-PERONI
PET PEEVE: BEING LEFT ALONE
KNOWN ACCOMPLICES: LOLITA AND LUCKY
OBSESSION: CHASING CRITTERS IN THE VINEYARD
NAUGHTIEST DEED: RUNNING AWAY TO CHASE RABBITS
FAVORITE PASTIME: CHASING RABBITS IN THE VINEYARDS

CAPTAIN

LUCKY

FAVORITE TOY: RUBBER BALL
PET PEEVE: BEING CONFINED
OBSESSIONS: SQUIRRELS AND RABBITS
NAUGHTIEST DEED: HOWLING AT NIGHT
FAVORITE PASTIME: FOLLOWING WORKERS
KNOWN ACCOMPLICES: LOLITA AND CAPTAIN

NAGGIAR VINEYARDS *GRASS VALLEY, CA* | *LABRADOR X, 9* | *OWNERS: DIANE AND MIKE NAGGIAR*

FAVORITE FOOD: SCIENCE DIET
FAVORITE TOY: TOY HAMBURGER
KNOWN ACCOMPLICE: SHRIMPO
NAUGHTIEST DEED: LICKING TOES
OBSESSION: SHAKING HER TEDDY BEAR
PET PEEVE: THE SOUND OF THE DOORBELL
FAVORITE PASTIME: PLAYING WITH HER SQUEAKY TOYS

TASHA

OWNERS: DIANE AND

SHAGGY

FAVORITE TOY: RUBBER BALL'
KNOWN ACCOMPLICES: KATY AND BEAU
FAVORITE FOOD: WHATEVER DROPS ON THE GROUND
PET PEEVE: OTHER ANIMALS COMING ONTO THE PROPERTY
FAVORITE PASTIMES: LOUNGING AROUND AND MOOCHING FOOD ON THE DECK
NAUGHTIEST DEED: SNEAKING ONTO THE LIVING ROOM COUCH WHEN NO ONE IS WATCHING

FAVORITE TOY: BALL
FAVORITE FOOD: CARROTS
PET PEEVE: THE DOOR BELL
KNOWN ACCOMPLICES: DAISY AND RANDY
OBSESSION: CHASING BUTTERFLY SHADOWS
NAUGHTIEST DEED: EATING PINOT NOIR GRAPES
FAVORITE PASTIMES: GREETING TASTING ROOM CUSTOMERS
AND CHASING RABBITS IN THE VINEYARD

BRIXIE

GODIVA

FAVORITE FOOD: PIZZA
OBSESSION: HER FOOD DISH
PET PEEVE: GOING TO THE GROOMER
FAVORITE PASTIME: CHASING CATS AND DEER
FAVORITE TOYS: LOVER BOY AND HER FOOD DISH
KNOWN ACCOMPLICES: LOVER BOY AND PRECIOUS
NAUGHTIEST DEEDS: STEALING THE DOG FOOD BOWL AND CHASING CATS

MARTERELLA WINERY WARRENTON, VA | BORDER COLLIE, 4 | OWNERS: JERRY AND KATE MARTERELLA

FAVORITE FOOD: PIZZA
OBSESSION: WATER FROM A HOSE
FAVORITE PASTIME: CHASING DEER
NAUGHTIEST DEED: TEARING UP HIS BED
KNOWN ACCOMPLICES: GODIVA AND CARLI
FAVORITE TOYS: DEER BONES AND GROUND HOGS
PET PEEVES: TAKING A BATH AND GODIVA PULLING HIS LEG

LOVER BOY

BOGART

FAVORITE TOY: HIS BED
PET PEEVE: GOING OUT IN THE RAIN
KNOWN ACCOMPLICES: PRECIOUS AND CARLI
OBSESSION: LICKING THE FLOOR AND CARPETS
FAVORITE FOODS: ROASTED CHICKEN AND STEAK
NAUGHTIEST DEED: PEEING IN THE LIVING ROOM
FAVORITE PASTIMES: SLEEPING AND CHASING GEESE

MARTERELLA WINERY WARRENTON, VA | SHIH TZU, 15 | OWNERS: JERRY AND KATE MARTERELLA

OBSESSION: COWS
FAVORITE TOY: PINK BED
FAVORITE FOOD: ROASTED CHICKEN
NAUGHTIEST DEED: PEEING IN THE HOUSE
PET PEEVE: LITTLE CHILDREN CORNERING HER
FAVORITE PASTIME: CHASING GEESE AND DEER
KNOWN ACCOMPLICES: PRECIOUS AND LOVER BOY

CARLI

PET PEEVE: THE HARMONICA
FAVORITE FOOD: HAMBURGER
FAVORITE PASTIME: SWIMMING
FAVORITE TOY: RUBBER SKELETON
NAUGHTIEST DEED: PLAYING WITH A BITING RATTLESNAKE
KNOWN ACCOMPLICES: FILSON, GUSTO, ZOE AND MOLEHILL KITTIES

OTIS

FAVORITE FOOD: YOURS
FAVORITE TO : CHILDREN
FAVORITE PASTIME: SLEEPING
PET PEEVE: WAKING UP EARLY
OBSESSION: RAWHIDE BONES
NAUGHTIEST DEED: SLEEPING IN A KING-SIZED
BED THAT DIDN'T BELONG TO HIM
KNOWN ACCOMPLICES: ZOE, GUSTO, OTIS AND MOLEHILL KITTIES

FILSON

GUSTO

OBSESSION: *THE DARK*
PET PEEVE: *DOORWAYS*
FAVORITE PASTIME: *DIGGING*
FAVORITE FOOD: *HAMBURGER*
NAUGHTIEST DEED: *PLANT KILLING*
FAVORITE TOY: *GIANT STUFFED BONES*

PET PEEVE: LEASHES
OBSESSION: PETTING
FAVORITE TOY: GUSTO
FAVORITE FOOD: ALMONDS
FAVORITE PASTIME: GOING FOR WALKS
NAUGHTIEST DEED: STRIPPING THE SIDING OFF THE HOUSE

ZOE

OWNERS: ROBIN, JON AND ERIN LAIL | BERNESE MOUNTAIN DOGS, 1 AND 9 | **LAIL VINEYARDS** ANGWIN, CA | 281

BIRDIE

FAVORITE TOY: TENNIS BALL
FAVORITE FOOD: PEANUT BUTTER
FAVORITE PASTIME: ACROBATIC DIVES
INTO BODIES OF WATER

HERMOSA VINEYARDS OAKVILLE, CA │ LABRADOR, 3 │ OWNERS: TODD AND KATIE TRAINA

PET PEEVE: LACK OF FETCH
KNOWN ACCOMPLICES: TIPPY, VICTOR AND LULU
NAUGHTIEST DEED: STEALING FOOD

BIRDIE

CASSIE

OBSESSION: TENNIS BALLS
FAVORITE TOY: KONG WITH TREATS
PET PEEVE: SQUIRRELS IN HER YARD
FAVORITE PASTIME: FETCHING TENNIS BALLS
KNOWN ACCOMPLICE: MAGGIE, HER DAUGHTER
NAUGHTIEST DEED: BURYING THE NEWSPAPER AFTER FETCHING IT

PET PEEVE: BIRDS
FAVORITE TOY: CATS
FAVORITE FOOD: SCRAPS
OBSESSION: CHASING CATS
NAUGHTIEST DEED: GETTING INTO THE GARBAGE
FAVORITE PASTIME: WANDERING THE PROPERTY CONSTRUCTION SITE

DUKE

OWNERS: KIM BELLINGER, JON AND ROSE MARSHALL | ROTTWEILER X, 12 | ADELSHEIM VINEYARD, NEWBERG

JOEY

OBSESSION: WATERMELON
FAVORITE TOY: SQUEAKY TOYS
FAVORITE FOOD: DRIED PIG EARS
KNOWN ACCOMPLICE: KITTY THE CAT
NAUGHTIEST DEED: CHEWING UP A COLLEGE
TEXT BOOK – THE BIG EXPENSIVE KIND
FAVORITE PASTIME: WATCHING PEOPLE FROM THE WINDOW
PET PEEVE: LOUD HIGH-PITCHED NOISES LIKE SMOKE ALARMS

FAVORITE TOY: BALL
OBSESSION: BALL CHASING
PET PEEVE: BEING LEFT BEHIND
FAVORITE FOOD: DRIED PIG EARS
KNOWN ACCOMPLICE: KITTY THE CAT
NAUGHTIEST DEED: DISAPPEARING FOR A WEEK
FAVORITE PASTIMES: CHASING BALLS AND SWIMMING

GERTIE

BELLA

FAVORITE TOY: BALLS
FAVORITE FOOD: STEAK
FAVORITE PASTIME: PLAYING
KNOWN ACCOMPLICE: MIDNIGHT
OBSESSION: BEING WITH FAMILY
NAUGHTIEST DEED: NIPPING AT HEELS

P U P I N O T

by Brian Doyle

JULY. WHEREAS WE GOT A PUPPY a while ago and the puppy is one wild adventure. I spend a lot of time with the puppy, and one roaring hot afternoon I come home from work and find no one home but the pup, my subtle research assistant being off somewhere doing something and the children off somewhere committing mischief and misdemeanor, and whereas it's been a really long day and it's stunning hot, the pup and I sprawl and loll in the grass with a bowl of water for her and a glass of clean crisp pinot blanc from Lange for me, the new wine just released a month ago, a lovely clear penetrating wine that carries cool peace right down my throat into my old moaning bones.

This is damn fine wine, I say to the pup, who yawns.

Don't yawn at me, dog, I say. This is excellent wine, and I'll tell you why, and you will be edified and educated, which is what you need, seems to me, because all of life is not bounding around chasing food and biting people and dreaming about sex. Some of life is contemplating and conversing and cogitating and admiring creativity in the human animal, which is a fascinating animal, not so much because of its capacity for language or philosophy or abstract thought, as some say, but because of its endless possibility for grace and generosity and epiphany. Seems to me that animals of my species are more capable of creativity than animals of your species, which is maybe why I am sitting here with wine and you are sitting there with water.

The pup knows the word water *and her ears and eyebrows do that startling-awake thing they do when she hears words like* food *and* walk *and* treat *and* ball *and* bad girl! *and* no! *and* get down from there! *and* my god don't eat that! *and* why don't you do me a huge favor and pee outside like the boys do? *which I have said to her many times even though my sons tell me it's too much of a rhetorical question for the pup to handle easily. I get her another bowl and water and get myself a second sip of the wine and make a mental note to tell Jesse that the new pinot blanc is an excellent wine to have while talking about moral evolution with your dog.*

BRIAN DOYLE IS THE EDITOR OF *PORTLAND MAGAZINE* AT THE UNIVERSITY OF PORTLAND IN OREGON. HE IS THE AUTHOR OF NINE BOOKS OF ESSAYS AND POEMS, MOST RECENTLY *THIRSTY FOR THE JOY: AUSTRALIAN & AMERICAN VOICES* (ONE DAY HILL, MELBOURNE, ONEDAYHILL.COM.AU).

LOLA

FAVORITE FOOD: TAPAS
FAVORITE TOY: STUFFED MOUSE
KNOWN ACCOMPLICES: IGGY AND MIA
OBSESSIONS: CORKS, FOOD AND SLEEPING
FAVORITE PASTIME: CHASING HER PET KITTEN
PET PEEVE: NOT BEING THE CENTER OF ATTENTION

FAVORITE FOOD: PIG EARS
PET PEEVE: VACUUM CLEANER
FAVORITE TOY: TENNIS BALL BONE
NAUGHTIEST DEED: SHREDDING AN ENVELOPE OFF
THE COUNTER CONTAINING PHOTOS FOR A WEDDING
FAVORITE PASTIMES: EATING ICE AND PLAYING IN HER WATER BOWL
KNOWN ACCOMPLICE: DOMENICA TOTTY, THE ASSOCIATE WINEMAKER

BRISTOW

TUCKER

FAVORITE FOOD: CHICKEN JERKY
OBSESSION: SLEEPING UNDER COVERS
NAUGHTIEST DEED: CHEWING ON RUGS
FAVORITE TOYS: CHEW TOYS AND PIG EARS
PET PEEVE: OTHER DOGS STEALING HIS TOYS
FAVORITE PASTIMES: LOUNGING ON THE COUCH AND LYING IN THE SUN.

FAVORITE FOOD: STEAK
FAVORITE TOY: SQUEAKY FROG
PET PEEVE: BEING LEFT AT HOME
FAVORITE PASTIME: CHEWING CORKS
NAUGHTIEST DEED: DESTROYING IMPORTANT PAPERS
KNOWN ACCOMPLICES: MGD AND PBR, THE TASTING ROOM CATS

CORKY

ELWAY

PET PEEVE: BAD MUSIC
FAVORITE FOOD: CHEESE
FAVORITE PASTIME: RUNNING
OBSESSION: THE DENVER BRONCOS
KNOWN ACCOMPLICES: BAILEY AND BEAR
NAUGHTIEST DEED: CHEWING EVERYTHING IN SIGHT

FAVORITE TOYS: BALLS AND BONES
PET PEEVE: NOT GETTING ATTENTION
NAUGHTIEST DEED: EATING EVERYTHING
KNOWN ACCOMPLICES: OPUS AND MIMIE
FAVORITE PASTIME: PLAYING WITH MIMIE AND OPUS

CASPER

ALL REVVED UP AND READY TO GO...

YOU TRAVEL UP THE WINDING ROAD, RISING ABOVE THE NAPA VALLEY, THROUGH SHADY TREES, TWISTS AND TURNS, EMERGING INTO A PANORAMA OF VINEYARDS, SUNLIGHT AND ROLLING HILLS. NESTLED INTO THE MOUNTAINS, SURROUNDED BY BREATHTAKING VIEWS, AND JUST UP THE HILL FROM THE WINERY, IS THE CHATEAU POTELLE TASTING ROOM — HOME TO FIVE WINE DOGS: MIMIE, CASPER, CHAVA, OPUS AND MURPHY. THEY ARE ALL READY FOR A HARD DAY'S WORK IN THE VINEYARD BUT NONE OF THEM CAN DRIVE...

MIMI

FAVORITE TOY: RABBITS
FAVORITE FOOD: DRIED MEAT CUBES
NAUGHTIEST DEED: DIGGING HOLES
KNOWN ACCOMPLICES: OPUS AND CASPER
FAVORITE PASTIMES: RUNNING AND CHASING RABBITS
PET PEEVES: GOING OUT IN THE RAIN AND BEING IGNORED

FAVORITE TOY: BED
NAUGHTIEST DEED: BEGGING
FAVORITE FOOD: PICNIC FOOD
KNOWN ACCOMPLICES: MIMIE AND CASPER
PET PEEVE: VISITORS BRINGING THEIR PETS
FAVORITE PASTIMES: GREETING GUESTS AND SLEEPING BY THE FIRE

OPUS

KYSHA

OBSESSIONS: JIM AND TENNIS BALLS
FAVORITE PASTIME: BEING JIM'S SHADOW
FAVORITE FOOD: CHICKEN JERKY STRIPS
NAUGHTIEST DEEDS: DIGGING IN ELIZA'S
GARDEN AND GETTING INTO THE GARBAGE
PET PEEVE: LOSING ONE OF HER TENNIS BALLS
KNOWN ACCOMPLICES: SHANDA, FURBALL, JON AND ASHLEY
FAVORITE TOY: HER BINKY, (TENNIS-BALL TYPE OF CHEW TOY)

FAVORITE TOY: MR. SEAL
PET PEEVE: BEING STONE-DEAF
FAVORITE FOOD: ANYTHING BUT MUSHROOMS
OBSESSIONS: PLAYING BALL AND CHASING STICKS
FAVORITE PASTIME: RIDING ON THE BACK OF THE ATV
NAUGHTIEST DEED: DIGGING IN ELIZA'S FLOWER GARDEN
KNOWN ACCOMPLICES: FURBALL, KYSHA , JENNA AND MISCHA

SHANDA

HOLLY HONEY

PET PEEVE: PATCH FINNEGAN

OBSESSIONS: THE CAT'S LITTERBOX

NAUGHTIEST DEED: EATING THE RIPE AND
READY-TO-EAT TOMATOES OFF THE VINES

KNOWN ACCOMPLICES: MURL AND NEEKO

FAVORITE TOY: THE SQUEAKY FLYING MONKEY

FAVORITE PASTIME: LICKING THE COUCH AND CHAIR
CUSHIONS FOR HOURS ON END FOR NO REASON

FAVORITE FOODS: WATERMELON RINDS AND WHOLE ORANGES

J. RICKARDS WINERY, COVERDALE, CA | GERMAN SHORT-HAIRED POINTER, 11 | OWNERS: THE HOLMAN FAMILY

FAVORITE FOOD: FOOD
FAVORITE PASTIME: EATING
FAVORITE TOY: ANYTHING EDIBLE
PET PEEVE: NOT GETTING FED ON TIME
OBSESSIONS: BREAKFAST, LUNCH AND DINNER
KNOWN ACCOMPLICES: BUTCHERS, GROCERY CLERKS, PIZZA DELIVERY
BOYS AND THE STARBUCKS DRIVE-THROUGH WINDOW ATTENDANT
NAUGHTIEST DEED: RAIDING THE APPETIZER TABLE AT THE HOLIDAY PARTY

PATCH FINNEGAN

OWNERS: ALEX AND ANNIE HOLMAN

ROSIE

FAVORITE TOY: BONES
OBSESSION: CRITTERS
FAVORITE FOOD: DRY FOOD
KNOWN ACCOMPLICE: MISSIE
FAVORITE PASTIME: CHASING LIFE
NAUGHTIEST DEED: EATING PLUGGED-IN EXTENSION CORDS

OBSESSION: ALL FOOD
KNOWN ACCOMPLICE: ROSIE
PET PEEVE: BEING LEFT AT HOME
NAUGHTIEST DEED: RUNNING OFF
FAVORITE FOOD: ANYTHING IN A DISH
FAVORITE TOYS: BALL, ROCK, STICK AND BALLOONS

MISSIE

OWNERS: WAYNE AND DEEDY PARKER | LABRADOR X, 6 | **MELROSE VINEYARDS** ROSEBURG, OR

305

BAILEY

FAVORITE PASTIME: SLEEPING
FAVORITE TOY: THE FIREWOOD
OBSESSION: GREETING VISITORS
KNOWN ACCOMPLICES: FESTUS,
TIGO, SUNSHINE, BOBBIE AND BETTY
FAVORITE FOOD: PLAIN DRY DOG FOOD
NAUGHTIEST DEED: EATING STINKY DEAD GOPHERS

306 | **PIPESTONE VINEYARDS** PASO ROBLES, CA | LABRADOR X, 14 | OWNER: JEFF PIPES

FAVORITE TOY: GWEN
OBSESSION: CHEWING
FAVORITE FOOD: FRIED RICE
FAVORITE PASTIME: PORCH PATROL
KNOWN ACCOMPLICES: GRACE AND GWEN
NAUGHTIEST DEED: CHEWING UP $300 WORTH
OF IRRIGATION EQUIPMENT IN ONE

ESTUS

FAVORITE PASTIME: HANGING
AROUND THE GOLF COURSE
FAVORITE TOY: VINE CUTTINGS
OBSESSION: GREETING VISITORS

FAVORITE FOOD: DOG FOOD
FAVORITE TOY: SQUEAKY BALL
PET PEEVE: DISHONEST PEOPLE
NAUGHTIEST DEED: CHEWING BARREL BUNGS
KNOWN ACCOMPLICE: SADIE AT BELLA LUNA WINERY
FAVORITE PASTIME: HANGING OUT IN THE TASTING ROOM

CLOVER

GUNNER

OBSESSION: CROWS
FAVORITE TOY: STICKS
KNOWN ACCOMPLICE: BRUNO
NAUGHTIEST DEED: SNEAKING
INTO THE HOUSE AFTER SWIMMING
FAVORITE FOOD: PROSCIUTTO PIZZA
PET PEEVES: SNEEZING AND GUNSHOTS
FAVORITE PASTIME: BEATING UP BREAKER

FAVORITE FOOD: FROGS
KNOWN ACCOMPLICE: SISSY
PET PEEVE: BEING LAUGHED AT
NAUGHTIEST DEED: STEALING BRAS
FAVORITE PASTIME: CHASING HER TAIL
FAVORITE TOY: HER BROTHER BREAKER

ROLAND

PET PEEVE: VETS
OBSESSION: COOKIES
FAVORITE PASTIME: SWIMMING
FAVORITE TOY: SOCCER BALLS
FAVORITE FOOD: BRUNO'S PASTA
NAUGHTIEST DEED: BITING TUCO THE HORSE'S NOSE

FAVORITE FOOD: HAM
FAVORITE TOY: BADGE
FAVORITE PASTIME: WALKS
KNOWN ACCOMPLICE: KRIS
PET PEEVE: EATING BREAKFAST
OBSESSION: CHILDREN (HE LOVES THEM)
NAUGHTIEST DEED: BREAKING HIS SISTER BADGE'S EAR

BREAKER

They are by our sides, or at least in our hearts, 100% of the time and only occasionally do they show any sign of distaste toward us: usually only when they are left at home. Fortunately, this distaste is only very fleeting, as they greet us at the door when we get home, with a smile on their face, a wagging tail and a "story" to tell us about their day without the winery, and without us.

We owe Wine Dogs our greatest respect, for they ultimately control the Yin and the Yang in the winery; the fine line between order and chaos. Only a few pats on the head, a kind word and some snippets from lunch will help maintain the balance of the winery, tasting room, vineyard and people.

Who needs Biodynamics? What really maintains the Chi of a winery, and in the hearts and souls of the people who love them, is a Wine Dog!!!

KRIS CURRAN GREW UP IN SANTA YNEZ VALLEY IN SANTA BARBARA COUNTY, CALIFORNIA. AFTER COMPLETING A DEGREE IN ANIMAL SCIENCE AT CAL PONY, SHE PURSUED A WINEMAKING DEGREE AT FRESNO STATE UNIVERSITY. KRIS HAS MADE AWARD-WINNING WINES AT CAMBRIA WINERY, KOEHLER WINERY, SEA SMOKE CELLARS AND FOLEY ESTATE. KRIS' OWN LABEL WAS STARTED IN 1997.

OBSESSION: *PLAYING BALL*
FAVORITE TOY: *ANYTHING THAT BOUNCES*
PET PEEVE: *HAVING THE KITTIES SIT NEXT TO HIM*
KNOWN ACCOMPLICES: *MO, SNOW BALL AND TIGER*
NAUGHTIEST DEED: *MAKING THE VINEYARD WORKERS*
THROW THE BALL TO HIM INSTEAD OF WORKING
FAVORITE PASTIME: *PICKING UP STICKS IN THE VINEYARD*
FAVORITE FOODS: *KITTY FOOD (ONLY IF HE CAN STEAL IT) OR STEAK*

SCOUT

ANYA

FAVORITE FOOD: YOURS
PET PEEVE: BEING IGNORED
KNOWN ACCOMPLICE: BRUTUS
OBSESSION: BOSSING EVERYONE AROUND
NAUGHTIEST DEED: STEALING STEAK OFF THE BBQ
FAVORITE PASTIME: BOSSING ANYONE WHO WILL LISTEN

PET PEEVE: *BEING LEFT BEHIND*
OBSESSION: *INVESTIGATING NOISES*
FAVORITE TOY: *ANYTHING THAT MOVES*
KNOWN ACCOMPLICES: *RINGO AND ZIGGY*
FAVORITE PASTIME: *SLEEPING ON TERRI'S LAP*
FAVORITE FOOD: *ANYTHING FROM THE MASTER'S TABLE*
NAUGHTIEST DEED: *STEALING THE OTHER DOGS' 'CATCHES'*
(MICE, RODENTS, EVEN AN OCCASIONAL SKUNK)

ZOE

TALLULAH

OBSESSIONS: KISSING AND SPLICING FILMS
TOGETHER WITH SHAWN AT THE CAMEO CINEMA
FAVOURITE TOY: SHAWN'S FACE AT 4:00AM
NAUGHTIEST DEED: THE FINE ART OF PUPPY SEDUCTION
FAVOURITE PASTIME: WATCHING RE-RUNS OF PEPE LEPEW
KNOWN ACCOMPLICES: MAX AND A PUGNACIOUS SOUTHERN BELLE PUG NAMED SOPHIE
PET PEEVE: PEOPLE WHO DON'T ACKNOWLEDGE HER CONSTANT REQUESTS FOR ATTENTION

MAXIMILLIAN

FAVORITE TOY: THE WORLD IS HIS TOY
FAVORITE PASTIME: TRICKING HIS OWNER INTO
THINKING HE MUST HAVE TREATS EVERY TEN MINUTES
NAUGHTIEST DEED: CONVINCING UNSUSPECTING HUMANS
TO SURRENDER THEIR BACON AND EGG BREAKFASTS
OBSESSIONS: MOM, FOOD, MOM, FOOD, MOM, MOM, MOM
KNOWN ACCOMPLICES: TALLULAH AND SOPHIA REGAN BUCK
FAVORITE FOOD: EVERYTHING – AN EQUAL OPPORTUNITY EATING MACHINE

LUCY

OBSESSION: MOM
PET PEEVE: SUITCASES
FAVORITE TOY: STUFFED PLATYPUS
FAVORITE PASTIME: ANNOYING MAGNUM
FAVORITE FOOD: ORGANIC VANILLA YOGHURT
NAUGHTIEST DEED: NOT COMING WHEN CALLED
KNOWN ACCOMPLICES: MAGNUM, WINECLUB MEMBERS AND BASIL

PET PEEVE: *DADDY'S SALES TRIPS*
OBSESSIONS: *RED SQUEAKY BALL AND CRUNCHIES*
FAVORITE TOYS: *RED SQUEAKY BALL AND TWO-INCH CORKS*
FAVORITE PASTIME: *WATCHING MOVIES ON 600-THREAD-COUNT SHEETS*
KNOWN ACCOMPLICES: *LUCY, CLYDE, BASIL AND THE PRODUCTION CREW*

MAGNUM

OWNER: *JESSE LANGE* | *GOLDEN RETRIEVER, 2* | **LANGE ESTATE WINERY** *DUNDEE, OR* 321

PHILEAS

FAVORITE TOY: TENNIS BALL
KNOWN ACCOMPLICE: BRUISER
PET PEEVE: GETTING PHOTOGRAPHED
FAVORITE PASTIME: CHASING RABBITS
OBSESSION: BEING BRUSHED AND GROOMED
FAVORITE FOOD: ANYTHING THE BABY DOESN'T FINISH
NAUGHTIEST DEED: NOT COMING HOME FOR TWO DAYS

FLORA SPRINGS WINERY ST. HELENA, CA | GOLDEN RETRIEVER, 10 | OWNERS: NAT AND ANNE KOMES

FAVORITE FOOD: ITALIAN
PET PEEVE: THE MAILMAN
FAVORITE TOY: MIMI DOLL
FAVORITE PASTIME: SLEEPING
OBSESSIONS: CHEESE AND HIGH HEELS
KNOWN ACCOMPLICES: MUGSY AND FRANK
NAUGHTIEST DEED: ATTACKING THE SWEET MAILMAN

MOOSE

BRUISER

PET PEEVE: BATHS
FAVORITE PASTIME: CHEWING
FAVORITE TOY: RAWHIDE BONE
NAUGHTIEST DEED: BARKING AT CARS
FAVORITE FOODS: HAMBURGER OR STEAK

FAVORITE FOOD: STEAK
PET PEEVE: LOUD NOISES
NAUGHTIEST DEED: USING ELEVATORS
OBSESSION: PERSONALLY GREETING EACH VISITOR
KNOWN ACCOMPLICES: ANGEL AND MOSES THE CATS
FAVORITE PASTIMES: VISITING NEIGHBORS AND RIDING IN CARS

TUCKER

OWNER: RICHARD MATHER | GERMAN SHEPHERD X, 8 | **DAVID FULTON** ST. HELENA, CA

HARLEY D.

KNOWN ACCOMPLICES: KOJAK, STAR AND CASH
PET PEEVE: AIRPLANES FLYING OVER WINERY
FAVORITE PASTIMES: RUNNING AFTER
ANYTHING AND WATCHING TELEVISION
NAUGHTIEST DEED: BEING HOUDINI
OBSESSION: EVERYTHING
FAVORITE TOY: SQUEAKER
FAVORITE FOOD: TREATS

TOLOSA WINERY, SAN LUIS OBISPO, CA | TERRIER X, 5 MONTHS | OWNERS: JIM AND JEANETTE FERA

FAVORITE TOY: CROAKING FROG
OBSESSION: CHASING SQUIRRELS
KNOWN ACCOMPLICE: SHELLEY SUZANNE
FAVORITE PASTIME: RUNNING AROUND THE VINEYARD
NAUGHTIEST DEED: BRINGING GOPHERS INTO THE HOUSE

HAILEY

TAFFY

FAVORITE TOY: BLUE BALL
KNOWN ACCOMPLICES: LUCKY AND BRANDY
FAVORITE PASTIME: THROWING THE BALL BACK
FAVORITE FOOD: ANYTHING THE FAMILY IS EATING
PET PEEVE: SOMEONE ELSE GETTING MORE ATTENTION
NAUGHTIEST DEED: DIGGING HOLES IN THE GARDEN BIG ENOUGH TO LIE IN
OBSESSIONS: BLUE RUBBER HANDBALL AND NEW FUZZY YELLOW TENNIS BALLS

FAVORITE FOOD: CHEESE
OBSESSION: SQUIRRELS
PET PEEVE: BEING LEFT BEHIND
FAVORITE TOY: SQUEAKY MALLARD DUCK
FAVORITE PASTIMES: PROWLING THE PERIMETER
OF THE PROPERTY AND CHASING SQUIRRELS
NAUGHTIEST DEED: CATCHING A CAT (BUT NOT HURTING IT)

LUCKY

ANDRE

OBSESSION: ELVIS
PET PEEVE: BEING FED AFTER 8AM
FAVORITE FOOD: KIBBLES WITH EXTRA BITS
NAUGHTIEST DEED: STEALING A PAIR OF SUNGLASSES
KNOWN ACCOMPLICES: THE UPS MAN AND ANYONE ELSE WHO WILL THROW A BALL
FAVORITE PASTIME: EATING PINOT NOIR GRAPES THAT FALL OFF THE SORTING TABLE

SOKOL BLOSSER WINERY DAYTON, OR | LABRADOR, 9 | OWNER: ALEX SOKOL BLOSSER

A DOG NAMED ANDRE

by Susan Sokol Blosser

ANDRE, MY SON ALEX'S YELLOW LAB, is almost 10 years old now. Adorable as a puppy, destructive as an adolescent, Andre has matured into a sweet, if quirky, adult. His eyes shine and he smiles when you pet him; he still barks a lot; he excels at frisbee; and every day he runs up the hill to the winery alongside Alex on his bike. Andre is the dean of our three winery dogs.

No other dogs we've had around have shown the slightest interest in grapes, but Andre adores them. He clearly considers himself part of the harvest team, stationed at the crush pad as grapes come in. Any berries hitting the ground, and there are a lot, fall prey to his long pink tongue. Andre helped with harvest for years before someone told us grapes were harmful to dogs. He seemed all the better for it, so continued as before. We never see him eat grapes off the vine, but he sure keeps the crush area clean.

Wine grapes aren't Andre's only culinary delight. His appetite and ability to sneak food is legendary. Given the chance, he will pilfer the vineyard crew's lunches from the equipment shed, sneak baked treats brought for the harvest team to share during break, and appear suddenly whenever a sandwich or snack is opened. We all remember the time he stole two sticks of butter off the table carefully set for a winery dinner in the tasting room courtyard. Someone turned his back and within seconds a half pound of butter was gone. His nose is fine-tuned and we have learned to watch him carefully.

Andre is only happy when he is at Alex's side. At work, Alex sits at his desk and Andre lies underneath on a large fleece cushion. When Alex gets up to leave the room, Andre is right behind him. If he is left outside, Andre has learned that if he jumps vertically, he can look in the window to see if Alex is there. Many times, I've come upon Andre jumping straight up, not touching the door, trying to get a good look. If he can't see Alex, he runs around to another door and starts jumping to see in that window. If you're inside, all you see is a dog's head bobbing up and down as if on a pogo stick, scanning the room for his master.

When Alex leaves Andre at home, Andre sits on the front porch and waits for his return. He recognizes the car and starts barking when Alex turns in the drive, almost a quarter mile away. No sneaking home for Alex!

Next to being with Alex, Andre wants to play fetch and is always carrying something around, hoping to find someone to throw it for him. Tennis balls, blocks of wood, grape cuttings, and the occasional dog toy. He will fetch almost anything you can throw and bring it back for you to throw again. And again. And again. If you tire before he does and want to stop, he will beg you to continue by picking the item up, all wet and slimy by now, dropping it repeatedly at your feet, and then looking at you longingly. Frisbees are a favorite and he carried a nylon one around with him until it got so tattered it had no loft. Whenever we have our staff frisbee golf tournaments, Alex has to lock his dog up in his office or Andre will leap in front of everyone to snatch the frisbee out of the air.

It's a dog's life. But being a winery dog makes it a good one.

OREGON WINE INDUSTRY PIONEER, CO-FOUNDER OF SOKOL BLOSSER WINERY, AND AUTHOR, **SUSAN SOKOL BLOSSER** HAS RETIRED TO DEVOTE MORE TIME TO HER PUPPY, HER GRANDCHILDREN, AND HER GARDEN.

PET PEEVE: WEEKENDS
OBSESSION: OPENING DOORS
FAVORITE TOYS: ROPE TOYS AND GRAPE VINES
NAUGHTIEST DEED: STEALING A RAW PORK
TENDERLOIN OFF THE COUNTER AND TRYING TO EAT IT
FAVORITE PASTIME: ACCESSORIZING FOR HALLOWEEN
FAVORITE FOOD: WHATEVER FALLS ON THE FLOOR DURING DINNER TIME

TWIX

OBSESSION: BEING BRADLEY'S SHADOW
FAVORITE FOOD: MOM'S GOURMET COOKING
FAVORITE TOY: ANYTHING FUZZY OR CHEWY
NAUGHTIEST DEED: EATING HALEY'S SLIPPERS
KNOWN ACCOMPLICES: BRAD, LILY AND GANDOLF
FAVORITE PASTIMES: TRIPS IN THE MOTORHOME
AND HIDE-N-SEEK WITH BRADLEY
PET PEEVE: IF LILY GETS TO GO SOMEWHERE WITHOUT HER

DIVA

FAVORITE TOY: HOT PINK PURSE
OBSESSION: TO BE IN ANYBODY'S LAP
KNOWN ACCOMPLICES: DIVA AND FREAK
PET PEEVE: IF DIVA GETS TO GO OUT WITHOUT HER
NAUGHTIEST DEED: CHEWING DONALD PLINER SHOES
FAVORITE FOODS: COOKIES AND MOM'S GOURMET COOKING
FAVORITE PASTIME: RUNNING AROUND THE VINEYARD WITH SUSAN

LILY

DARBY

FAVORITE TOY: BUNGS
OBSESSION: MUSTARDS GRILL
PET PEEVE: NOT GETTING ENOUGH LOVE
FAVORITE PASTIME: GOING TO MUSTARDS GRILL
FAVORITE FOOD: ANYTHING FROM MUSTARDS GRILL
NAUGHTIEST DEED: DODGING CARS ON HIGHWAY 29
KNOWN ACCOMPLICES: PUTTER, JAKE AND MARIO, THE CELLAR MASTER

FAVORITE TOY: GOLF BALLS
OBSESSION: BEING CHASED
KNOWN ACCOMPLICE: ANYONE WITH FOOD
PET PEEVE: OTHER DOGS BARKING TOO LOUD
FAVORITE FOODS: TOMATOES AND ENGLISH PEAS
FAVORITE PASTIME: WATCHING 'ANIMAL PLANET' ON TV
NAUGHTIEST DEED: GOING TO THE BATHROOM ON THE PUTTING GREEN

PUTTER

OWNER: MITCH COSENTINO | PEMBROKE WELSH CORGI, 5 | **COSENTINO WINERY** YOUNTVILLE, CA | 337

HENDRY NAPA, CA | LABRADOR, 2 | OWNERS: MIKE HENDRY AND MOLLY BLAIR

JAKE

FAVORITE FOOD: STEAK
OBSESSION: THE ORANGE BALL
FAVORITE TOY: THE ORANGE BALL
FAVORITE PASTIME: CHASING THE ORANGE BALL
NAUGHTIEST DEED: STEALING BUNGS FROM BARRELS
KNOWN ACCOMPLICES: WHEEZER AND GUS

OBSESSION: SALAMI
FAVORITE TOY: CHEETAH
FAVORITE FOODS: CELERY AND SALAMI
PET PEEVE: STAYING HOME AND MISSING ADVENTURES
KNOWN ACCOMPLICE: SCARLET FROM SADDLEBACK CELLARS
FAVORITE PASTIMES: LEARNING NEW TRICKS AND TRAVELING

MOXIE

TURBO JAGUAR

PET PEEVE: BATHS
FAVORITE TOYS: BALL AND DUCK DUMMY
OBSESSIONS: SOCCER AND TENNIS BALLS
KNOWN ACCOMPLICE: STEVE ROBERTSON
FAVORITE PASTIMES: EATING AND HUNTING
FAVORITE FOODS: WALNUTS, CHEESE AND CRUMBS
NAUGHTIEST DEED: EATING BIRD SEED OUT OF THE BAG

FAVORITE TOY: A ROPE TOY
FAVORITE FOOD: CHICKEN TIDBITS
FAVORITE PASTIME: GNAWING ON BONES
OBSESSION: NIPPING AT PEOPLE'S HEELS
KNOWN ACCOMPLICE: BETTY THE SIAMESE CAT
NAUGHTIEST DEED: ESCAPING HIS YARD AND
SNEAKING DOWN TO THE WINERY TO VISIT GUESTS
PET PEEVE: BEING PUT OUT IN THE RAIN TO DO HIS BUSINESS

SPIKE

FAVORITE FOOD: LIVER
FAVORITE TOY: TENNIS BALL
KNOWN ACCOMPLICE: SYDNEY
OBSESSION: LICKING HIS PAW
PET PEEVE: GETTING WOKEN UP
NAUGHTIEST DEED: EATING KEVIN'S
SIGNED COLLECTION OF GENESIS CDS
FAVORITE PASTIMES: WALKING AND SNIFFING

ROO

MIDLIFE CRISIS WINERY, PASO ROBLES, CA | AUSTRALIAN SHEPHERD, 11 | OWNERS: KEVIN AND JILL MITTAN

FAVORITE TOY: TUG TOY
FAVORITE FOOD: CHEESE
OBSESSION: TUG TOY FIGHTS
NAUGHTIEST DEED: DIGGING
HOLES AROUND THE ROSES
FAVORITE PASTIME: TORTURING ROO
PET PEEVE: NOT BEING LOVED ENOUGH

SYDNEY

REAGAN

KNOWN ACCOMPLICE: COCO
FAVORITE PASTIME: EATING
FAVORITE TOY: KATHRYN'S PILLOW
PET PEEVE: BEING LEFT BEHIND
OBSESSIONS: HER NEXT MEAL AND BEING TOP DOG
NAUGHTIEST DEED: CHASING COYOTES IN THE VINEYARD

KNOWN ACCOMPLICE: REAGAN
FAVORITE TOY: SQUEAKY SQUEEZE BALL
OBSESSION: BEING THE CENTER OF ATTENTION
NAUGHTIEST DEED: CHEWING KATHRYN'S SHOES
FAVORITE PASTIME: PLAYING FETCH INCESSANTLY
PET PEEVE: HOUSE GUESTS WHO WON'T PLAY FETCH
FAVORITE FOOD: ANYTHING IN REAGAN'S FOOD DISH

COCO

BELLA

FAVORITE FOOD: RAVIOLI
FAVORITE TOY: NICK'S FEET
PET PEEVE: THE NEIGHBORS
KNOWN ACCOMPLICE: NICK
NAUGHTIEST DEEDS: BEING CHASED
BY A BEAR AND PLAYING WITH COYOTES
FAVORITE PASTIMES: BARKING AND RUNNING
FROM GATE OF VINEYARD TO WINERY BUILDINGS

FAVORITE FOOD: STEAK BONES
PET PEEVE: BEING LEFT ALONE
FAVORITE TOY: GINGERBREAD MAN
FAVORITE PASTIME: CHASING SQUIRRELS
OBSESSION: EATING THE CAT'S FOOD
NAUGHTIEST DEED: CHASING THE NEIGHBOR'S BULL
KNOWN ACCOMPLICES: ALEXANDER, DINGO AND BLAZER THE CAT

MAX

OWNERS: JOHN AND BETTY PATACCOLI | SOFT-COATED WHEATEN TERRIER, 6 | **REDHAWK WINERY** SALEM, OR | 347

BRODIE

FAVORITE TOY: SOFTBALL
NAUGHTIEST DEED: CHEWING SLIPPERS
KNOWN ACCOMPLICES: REAGAN, OLLIE AND LIV
FAVORITE PASTIMES: DIGGING AND BELLY SCRATCHES
OBSESSIONS: DIGGING AND CHASING THE NEIGHBOR'S CAT
PET PEEVE: THE NEIGHBOR'S CATS SLEEPING IN THE KENNEL

SEVERINO CELLARS ZILLAH, WA | WEST HIGHLAND TERRIER, 7 MONTHS | OWNERS: LINDA AND JAY SPURLOC

KNOWN ACCOMPLICES: GOLDIE
THE CAT, BRIAN AND BRADEN
PET PEEVE: HAVING TO COME IN THE HOUSE
FAVORITE PASTIME: PLAYING WITH THE CAT
NAUGHTIEST DEED: POOPING ON THE LAWN
OBSESSION: BEING SHY AROUND STRANGERS
FAVORITE FOODS: CHICKEN AND RICE DOG FOOD

VINO TOO

LITTLE MISSY

FAVORITE TOY: TENNIS BALLS

PET PEEVES: FOXTAILS, BURRS OR LOUD ADULTS

FAVORITE PASTIMES: GREETING VISITORS AND TENDING BAR

FAVORITE FOODS: TRUFFLED PATÉ AND ST. ANDRE CHEESE

OBSESSION: POSSIBLE ALIEN INVASION – FREQUENTLY WEARS AN ALUMINUM FOIL HAT TO PREVENT MIND CONTROL

KNOWN ACCOMPLICE: CAPTAIN COURAGE, A BOSTON TERRIER MIX – TOGETHER THEY ROAM THE VINEYARD, SIGHTING CRIME AND PROTECTING THE INNOCENT

PET PEEVE: WAITING FOR BREAKFAST
FAVORITE PASTIME: WATCHING SAGANO
THE CAT GREETING VISITORS AT THE WINERY
NAUGHTIEST DEED: NOT LISTENING WHEN
HE WANTS TO TAKE OFF ON A RUN
OBSESSION: HIS FRIEND SAGANO THE CAT
FAVORITE FOODS: BEEF JERKY AND ICE CREAM
KNOWN ACCOMPLICES: KAREN, SUE AND DONN

BODHI

BELLE

OBSESSION: YELLOW JACKETS
PET PEEVE: MIKE THE UPS GUY
FAVORITE FOOD: DOGGY TREATS
FAVORITE TOYS: STICKS AND LIMBS
KNOWN ACCOMPLICES: BUNGEE AND GUNNER
FAVORITE PASTIMES: LOUNGING AND CHILLING OUT
NAUGHTIEST DEED: BARKING AT WINERY GUESTS BEFORE BEFRIENDING THEM

FAVORITE PASTIME: FETCH
FAVORITE TOY: TENNIS BALL
FAVORITE FOOD: LAMB CHOPS
OBSESSION: RIDING SHOTGUN IN THE CAR
NAUGHTIEST DEED: EATING THE ENTIRE LOT OF
CHRISTMAS CHOCOLATES SHE UNCOVERED IN THE GARAGE
PET PEEVE: PLAYING SECOND FIDDLE TO MELVIS THE CAT
KNOWN ACCOMPLICES: MELVIS, LEFTFOOT AND BIGFOOT

ANNABELLE

GRACIE

FAVORITE FOOD: *CARNE ASADA*
OBSESSION: *BEING PETTED*
FAVORITE TOY: *JERRY*
KNOWN ACCOMPLICES: *WILLIE NELSON, LUCY, BELLA AND BAD BAD LEROY BROWN*
NAUGHTIEST DEED: *CHEWING SEATBELTS*
PET PEEVE: *SEEING HER OWNERS PET OTHER DOGS*
FAVORITE PASTIME: *GREETING VISITORS WHILE WORKING THE VINEYARD CIRCUIT: PATTON VALLEY VINEYARDS, TUALATIN ESTATE VINEYARD AND WILLAMETTE VALLEY VINEYARDS*

PATTON VALLEY VINEYARD

PATTON VALLEY VINEYARD *GASTON, OR* | *BEAGLE X* | *OWNERS: TERRY D. MURRAY AND MEG HURSH*

OBSESSION: PEOPLE
PET PEEVE: OTHER DOGS
FAVORITE TOY: A STUFFED LIZARD DOLL
FAVORITE PASTIME: LAYING ON THE COUCH
NAUGHTIEST DEED: TORMENTING HIS BROTHER

FAVORITE TOY: TENNIS BALL
OBSESSION: CHASING A TENNIS BALL
NAUGHTIEST DEED: STEALING FOOD OFF THE COUNTER
PET PEEVE: PEOPLE NOT THROWING THE TENNIS BALL

SNEAD

ROXY

FAVORITE TOY: SQUEAKING MONKEY ROPE TOW
FAVORITE FOOD: TREATS THAT VISITING FOLKS GIVE HER
PET PEEVE: FOXES WHO OUTRUN HER (WHICH IS ALL OF THEM)
NAUGHTIEST DEED: BARKING AT CUSTOMERS WHO DON'T BUY WINE
OBSESSIONS: TALLY, DOG TREATS AND HER PARENTS' ALMA MATER – VIRGINIA TECH

PET PEEVE: SQUIRRELS
FAVORITE FOOD: PIG EARS
OBSESSIONS: ROXY AND DUCKS
FAVORITE TOYS: BALLS AND PULL ROPE
NAUGHTIEST DEED: CHEWING ON SHOES
KNOWN ACCOMPLICES: ROXY, BULLET AND SHANNON
FAVORITE PASTIME: SHARING A DENTASTIX WITH BULLET AND SHANNON

LOOKSHA

FAVORITE FOOD: CHEESE RINDS
OBSESSION: ANYTHING THAT SQUEAKS
KNOWN ACCOMPLICE: LOUIS THE SHAR-PIT
FAVORITE PASTIMES: CHASING DUCKS, HUNTING
CHIPMUNKS AND WALLOWING IN MUD PUDDLES
FAVORITE TOY: SQUEAKY DOUGHNUT WITH SPRINKLES
PET PEEVE: ANYTHING THE NEXT DOOR NEIGHBOR DOES
NAUGHTIEST DEED: SNEAKING A WHOLE ROUND OF TALEGGIO CHEESE

OBSESSION: HAVING HER TUMMY RUBBED
FAVORITE TOYS: STUFFED SHEEP AND LOBSTER
PET PEEVE: GETTING A HAIRCUT EVERY OTHER MONTH
FAVORITE PASTIME: RIDING IN THE PINZGAUER VEHICLE
FAVORITE FOODS: GOPHERS AND CABERNET SAUVIGNON
KNOWN ACCOMPLICES: COUSIN SMUGGLER AND LOLITA THE CAT
NAUGHTIEST DEED: EATING A WHOLE CARTON OF EGGS LEFT ON THE COUNTER

FLOOZY

PET PEEVE: BEING TOLD TO STAY
FAVORITE PASTIME: QUAIL HUNTING
FAVORITE FOOD: RARE PRIME RIBS
NAUGHTIEST DEED: ROLLING IN FILTH
AND THEN JUMPING INTO SCOTT'S TRUCK

GUINEA

OWNERS: SCOTT AND KATHLEEN McLEOD | LABRADOR, 8 | **RUBICON ESTATE** RUTHERFORD, CA 361

OBSESSION: CRAIG
PET PEEVE: BEING CHAINED UP
FAVORITE PASTIME: LAYING IN THE SUN
KNOWN ACCOMPLICES: TUCKER AND MONTANA
FAVORITE FOOD: ANYTHING ON THE DINNER TABLE
NAUGHTIEST DEED: PEEING ON THE DINING ROOM RUG
FAVORITE TOYS: PLASTIC SQUEAKY BONE AND HAMBURGER

TIPSY

WOOD WINERY ARROYO GRANDE, CA | BEAGLE, 4 | OWNERS: CRAIG AND SHERI WOOD

PET PEEVE: CATS
OBSESSION: CATS
FAVORITE TOY: ANY BALL
NAUGHTIEST DEED: CHEWING ON THE DRIP SYSTEM
FAVORITE FOOD: ANYTHING OTHER THAN WHAT IS IN HIS DISH
FAVORITE PASTIME: SLEEPING ON THE GRASS IN FRONT OF TASTING ROOM
KNOWN ACCOMPLICES: JACK, FRANK, LILLY AND THE LOVE OF HIS LIFE, SYRAH

CHIEF

ROY

OBSESSION: AGED RED WINE
FAVORITE TOY: A SQUEAKING BUNNY
FAVORITE PASTIME: NAPS IN THE SUN
FAVORITE FOOD: CHEESE OF ANY KIND
PET PEEVE: PEOPLE TOUCHING HIS TAIL
KNOWN ACCOMPLICES: CHARLIE AT RIVERBENCH,
OSWALD FROM OSSEUS AND MAMBO AT CONSILIENCE
NAUGHTIEST DEED: STEALING LUNCHES OFF THE PICNIC TABLES

FAVORITE FOODS: HAM AND BACON
FAVORITE TOYS: VINEYARD ROCKS AND CANES
NAUGHTIEST DEED: CHASING NEIGHBORHOOD CATS
OBSESSION: AFTERNOON NAPS ON THE TRUCK'S TOOLBOX
FAVORITE PASTIME: CHASING VINEYARD SQUIRRELS AND BIRDS
PET PEEVES: COLD MORNINGS AND BEING SPRAYED WITH WATER

CHARLIE

OWNER: JIM STOLLBERG | LABRADOR X, 8 | **RIVERBENCH VINEYARD** SANTA MARIA, CA

PET PEEVE: VET VISITS
FAVORITE FOOD: BACON
FAVORITE TOY: CANE'S SANITY
OBSESSION: THE CRACKERS AT THE TASTING ROOM
NAUGHTIEST DEED: PLAYING IN THE NEIGHBOR'S FOUNTAIN
FAVORITE PASTIME: PLAYING WITH ALL THINGS WATER-RELATED

MIRA

FAVORITE TOY: LOUIS THE CAT
PET PEEVE: GANGS OF TODDLERS
FAVORITE FOOD: WINERY GUESTS' PICNIC ITEMS
NAUGHTIEST DEED: PRETENDING HE DOES NOT WANT
TO GET ON YOUR LAP AS HE GETS ON YOUR LAP
FAVORITE PASTIME: CHASING ANYTHING THAT RUNS EXCEPT THE WILD TURKEYS
OBSESSION: NAPPING IN THE SUN, ESPECIALLY WHEN HE BLOCKS THE FRONT DOOR

VINO

LUCY

PET PEEVE: STAYING HOME
FAVORITE TOY: RUBBER BONE
FAVORITE FOOD: PEOPLE FOOD
OBSESSIONS: PEOPLE FOOD AND CATS
NAUGHTIEST DEED: EATING UNDERWEAR
KNOWN ACCOMPLICES: COPPER AND TARBY
FAVORITE PASTIME: PATROLING THE PROPERTY

PEBBLES

OBSESSION: PEOPLE
FAVORITE TOY: SQUEAKY BALL
FAVORITE FOOD: OATMEAL DOG COOKIES
FAVORITE PASTIME: CHASING BIRDS AND LIZARDS
KNOWN ACCOMPLICES: ASHLEE, SUNSHINE AND DAISY
NAUGHTIEST DEED: RUNNING AWAY TO VISIT THE TASTING ROOM NEXT DOOR
PET PEEVE: NOT BEING ALLOWED TO VISIT THE TASTING ROOM NEXT DOOR

OWNERS: RAY AND PAM DERBY | BOXER, 4 | **DERBY WINE ESTATES** PASO ROBLES, CA

SOPHIE

FAVORITE FOOD: POPCORN
FAVORITE TOY: STUFFED ANIMALS
NAUGHTIEST DEED: POND DIVING
FAVORITE PASTIME: ROMPING WITH GUS
KNOWN ACCOMPLICES: OTIS, GUS AND YOGI
PET PEEVE: WHEN PEOPLE STOP PETTING HER

MILLER WINE WORKS NAPA, CA | GOLDEN RETRIEVER, 5 | OWNERS: GARY AND KIM MILLER

FAVORITE TOY: THE TINIEST BALL
FAVORITE FOOD: ANYTHING BUT DOG FOOD
PET PEEVE: NOT GETTING HER TREATS ON TIME
FAVORITE PASTIME: RIDING IN JOSE'S TRUCK WITH PINTO
KNOWN ACCOMPLICES: AGNES, PINTO, VENUS AND BRUNO

SODA

BUSTER DOUGLAS BROWN

FAVORITE TOY: COW EARS
FAVORITE PASTIME: WORKING COWS
PET PEEVES: WHISTLES AND FIREWORKS
KNOWN ACCOMPLICES: THE MAGGOT PACK
FAVORITE FOOD: BEN AND JERRY'S VANILLA ICE CREAM
NAUGHTIEST DEED: EATING A BOX OF OREOS ON TOP OF THE FRIDGE

PET PEEVE: SIRENS
FAVORITE PASTIME: SWIMMING
OBSESSION: HUNTING ANYTHING THAT MOVES
FAVORITE TOY: GEORGE THE GIANT STUFFED MONKEY
KNOWN ACCOMPLICE: TANK, A NEIGHBOR'S 8-YEAR-OLD BOXER
NAUGHTIEST DEED: DIGGING THROUGH THE CARPET TO GET TO A MOUSE
FAVORITE FOOD: ANY PEOPLE FOOD HE CAN "BORROW" FROM PICNICKERS

HANK

NADIE

OBSESSION: SQUEAKY TOYS
FAVORITE FOOD: ANYTHING SHE CAN GET
FAVORITE PASTIME: PLAYING FETCH AND TUG-OF-WAR
FAVORITE TOY: ANYTHING THAT MAKES A SQUEAKY NOISE
NAUGHTIEST DEED: SNEAKING OFF WITH UNSUSPECTING LUNCHES LEFT UNATTENDED

FAVORITE TOY: ROPE
OBSESSION: SQUIRRELS
PET PEEVE: BEING LEFT ALONE
FAVORITE PASTIME: RUNNING
FAVORITE FOOD: CAESAR SALAD
KNOWN ACCOMPLICES: RICKY AND LUCY
NAUGHTIEST DEED: EATING ANY ACCESSIBLE PAPERWORK IN THE CAR

ALLIE

NUS

HANNAH "BEAR"

KNOWN ACCOMPLICE: LUCY
PET PEEVE: BEING IGNORED
FAVORITE TOY: HER GREEN WEASEL
FAVORITE PASTIME: PERSIMMON HUNTING
NAUGHTIEST DEED: EATING TOO MANY GRAPES
OBSESSION: GETTING ATTENTION FROM CUSTOMERS
FAVORITE FOOD: ANYTHING AS LONG AS IT HAS SAUCE ON IT

OWNER: ASHLEE WILLIAMSON | GOLDEN RETRIEVER, 11 | SILENUS VINTNERS NAPA, CA   377

FAVORITE TOY: CORKS
OBSESSION: DIGGING
FAVORITE FOOD: COTTAGE CHEESE
PET PEEVE: PEOPLE WEARING HATS
KNOWN ACCOMPLICES: IGGY, MOXIE AND LOLA
NAUGHTIEST DEED: POOPING IN THE WINERY CONFERENCE ROOM
FAVORITE PASTIMES: PLAYING WITH CORKS AND CHASING SQUIRRELS

MIA

LODI VINTNERS WOODBRIDGE, CA | DACHSHUND X, 3 | OWNER: TYSON RIPPEY

FAVORITE TOY: FRISBEE
OBSESSION: CHASING SQUIRRELS
KNOWN ACCOMPLICES: MIA AND LOLA
FAVORITE FOODS: STEAK AND CHICKEN
FAVORITE PASTIMES: RUNNING AND EATING
NAUGHTIEST DEED: CRAPPING ON THE STATE CAPITAL LAWN

LILY

OBSESSION: BARREL BUNGS
FAVORITE TOY: GREEN SQUEAKY ALIEN
FAVORITE FOOD: PORT-SOAKED CHEESE
FAVORITE PASTIME: BEING A SNEAK THIEF
PET PEEVE: PEOPLE WHO DON'T LIKE TO PLAY
KNOWN ACCOMPLICES: KRISTEN, MATT AND TRAVIS
NAUGHTIEST DEED: EATING THE VINEYARD WORKERS' LUNCH

FAVORITE FOOD: *PEOPLE FOOD*
OBSESSION: *CATCHING ANYTHING*
NAUGHTIEST DEED: *GETTING DIRTY*
KNOWN ACCOMPLICES: *MARK AND FRAN*
FAVORITE TOY: *STUFFED TALKING ELMO*
PET PEEVE: *HAVING NO ONE TO THROW THE BALL*
FAVORITE PASTIMES: *SWIMMING AND FRISBEE PLAYING*

SPENCER

CINNAMON

OBSESSION: THE CATS
FAVORITE TOY: CHEW TOY
KNOWN ACCOMPLICE: ZIGGY
PET PEEVE: HAVING HIS EARS TICKLED
NAUGHTIEST DEED: JUMPING ON THE BED
FAVORITE PASTIME: WALKING IN THE VINEYARD
FAVORITE FOODS: COTTAGE CHEESE AND PEANUT BUTTER

ARGER-MARTUCCI ST. HELENA, CA │ BOXER X, 4 │ OWNERS: KATIE AND VINCE MARTUCCI

The Woof Street Times

"ALL THE NEWS THAT'S FIT TO PAW" | **6th JANUARY, 2008** | *FORECAST: (you guessed it..) RAINING CATS & DOGS*

BAN BITES BONA FIDE BITCH

BY ZAR AND ELENA BROOKS

For the small crowd of curious onlookers the sight of high-flying canine executive Ms. Madison D. Dog, Bone Co. founding hound and CEO, whimpering in a communal cage with common mutts at the city pound, came with full bowl of schadenfreude.

Unceremoniously led by a short leash into the lock-up, choker chain tightened by the pound's Pawlice, Ms. Madison D. Dog's signature designer kit (dark Pawda Sunglasses,

Ms. Madison D. Dog, founding hound and CEO of Bone Co. at the city pound.

WAG Heuer watch, Chewy Vuitton Handbag and Bark Jacobs pumps) was replaced with pound-issue collar, city-issued dog tags and khaki kennel jumpsuit. Even Madison's trademark bounding gait was not on offer; the only remnant of her previously high-flying life as Wine Dog and Bone Co CEO was a faint whiff of Coco Chewnel #19.

Instead, assembled puppyrazzi and disgruntled investors sniffed and stared at Ms. Madison D. Dog whose tail was most certainly between her legs. In what was to be the talk amongst the parks across America, the question remained, how did one of the most powerful bitches get rolled over so easily?

It quickly came to light that it had been the lure of a large dog park complete with a "No Leash" policy and a spritely young South African by the name of Ridge Back who had caught her attention at a Napa Valley restaurant, that was to prove her undoing.

Celebrating her 'Dog of the Year' award by the influential *Bone Aficionado* magazine and ordering the obligatory Kobe and Wagu beef tartar entree for her entourage, she barked viciously at the wait staff after they cited health and safety and liquor licensing concerns over her party's pre-disposition to mark their respective tables, and soon detained by a short haired pointer.

Young Ridge came to Ms. D. Dog's rescue, offering the restaurant owner three large lamb leg bones in exchange for her release – a fair deal in any dog's language; he didn't need the attention of a few wet noses pressed against the door…

MUTUAL SNIFFING SOCIETY

Ms. Madison D. Dog showed her appreciation with a low rise extended stretch and after a few minutes of mutual sniffing and circling, a friendship was born. Little did Ridge know the bitch he had encountered or what he would find under the oak tree the following month.

Public accusations of provocative sniffing had chased Ms. Madison D. Dog over the last few months. A long-time champion of the Boneatarian movement, Ms. Madison D. Dog's personal commitment to everything 'orgo-bio-dio' had come into question of late, wagging in the face of her company's sustainable claims.

Famously her collared line 'that humans had not been tested (much) in the development of products' was itself under a number of state and federal examinations, resulting in the now infamous worldwide ban on Bone Co. products.

At press conference held behind a butcher's yard in the Napa Valley, company spokesperson, Tammi Scratch, announced that there was great news ahead for Bone Co. "We at Bone Co. recognize the challenges we face in managing the ongoing plateau of our signature blends, combined with the enforced stop on sales for the signature 'Terroir-based product'.

However, this reduced activity is also reducing the company's carbon footprint and fuel costs – all of which reflect our corporate sustainability positioning."

NO BONES ABOUT IT...

The ban on the D. Dog's signature product had unsettled investors over the ensuing two months. However, the biggest bite for Bone Co. came at the AGM when it was revealed, despite extra funding, there was a huge discrepancy in the 'stock on hand' figures.

Recent assertions at Bone Co's AGM beggared belief. Bone Co's business was based on investors funding the maturation of bones of terroir, the bones processed and then buried in some of the finest vineyards in the United States.

However, it seems there had been more digging and fetching than returning, with a potential gap in burials to retrievals at a ratio of two-to-one. It would have gone unnoticed, had Ms. Madison D. Dog not fallen to the sniffing advances of aforementioned Ridge Back who retrieved a tennis ball destined for the doggy-bag of the head of the New Bark Stick Exchange in return for his growling silence over the whole affair.

Upon digging up this incriminating information, Ms D. Dog immediately denounced young Master Back as a "stick chasing immigrant with a bad coat job, seeking only to gnaw on her fame and fortune."

SENT TO THE DOG HOUSE

Howling and growling with disdain, young Ridge headed to the local dumpster to drown his sorrows in the bones and remnants of a restaurant alleyway.

It was here he met Lab Rador – a puppy editor sniffing for stories and a penchant for pack leaders himself. Conversation ensued as Ridge recounted his story, and a pact was formed to bring down the neutered bitch – something sure to make young Lab lead pound editor at the *Tree Street Journal* by year's end.

As the headlines went to print and she gazed at her bruised paws from the pawlice handcuffs, Madison D. Dog lay on the cold kennel floor, replete with common mutts who were in for far lesser crimes – chasing parked cars, biting mailmen and the like.

Sitting upright on the steps of Wine and Bone Co, company spokesperson Ms. Scratch clamoured to put the obligatory spin on the topic, "only once full details are disclosed, will it be proven a young pup of questionable provenance was in this for his own mating pleasure; sanity will prevail and Wine Dog and Bone Co will again grace the floor of the New Bark Stick Exchange."

Madison D. Dog has been arraigned to face trail with a date to be set.

ZAR BROOKS OF PAPER EAGLE WINES ENTIRELY CREDITS HIS WINEMAKER AND WIFE, **ELENA**, AND THEIR UNWITTING PUBLICIST, **MS REBECCA HOPKINS**, FOR EVERYTHING AND, OF COURSE, EVERYONE'S MENTOR OBERON KANT AO BSE.

FAVORITE TOY: THE PINK PIG
PET PEEVE: STRANGE NOISES
FAVORITE FOOD: FAT FIELD MICE
KNOWN ACCOMPLICE: THE PINK PIG
OBSESSION: CATCHING "FAST EDDY" THE BIG GRAY SQUIRREL
FAVORITE PASTIME: RIDING SHOT-GUN IN THE WINERY TRUCK

COOPER

OWNERS: TOM AND KERRY EDDY | CHOW CHOW X, 9 | **TOM EDDY WINERY** CALISTOGA, CA | 385

HIGGENBOTHAM

FAVORITE FOOD: RIBS
OBSESSION: RABBITS
PET PEEVE: JUMPING
FAVORITE TOY: TENNIS BALL
FAVORITE PASTIME: CHASING DEER
KNOWN ACCOMPLICES: LADY AND KO KO
NAUGHTIEST DEED: PEEING ON AN EMPTY WINE BARREL

PET PEEVE: PEOPLE WHO IGNORE HIM
KNOWN ACCOMPLICES: OSO AND SUGAR
FAVORITE TOY: ANYTHING THAT SQUEAKS
OBSESSIONS: WATER AND CHASING RABBITS
FAVORITE PASTIME: PLAYING AT THE DOG PARK
NAUGHTIEST DEED: EATING KLEENEX OUT OF THE GARBAGE

DUNDEE

OBSESSION: SQUIRRELS
FAVORITE FOOD: STEAK BONES
FAVORITE TOY: STUFFED SQUIRREL
FAVORITE PASTIME: SQUIRREL SIGHTING
NAUGHTIEST DEED: CATCHING SQUIRRELS
PET PEEVE: DELIVERYMEN NOT PETTING HER
KNOWN ACCOMPLICES: TESS, DAISY AND STELLA

LILY

FAVORITE TOY: STELLA'S EARS
FAVORITE FOOD: STEAK BONES
KNOWN ACCOMPLICES: LILY, STELLA AND TESS
OBSESSION: GETTING THE UPPER HAND ON STELLA
FAVORITE PASTIME: PLAYING WITH STELLA THE GOLDENDOODLE
PET PEEVE: BEING STUCK IN THE BACK SEAT WHEN DAD'S DRIVING
NAUGHTIEST DEED: HANGING FROM STELLA'S EARS AND MOUSTACHE

DAISY

OBSESSION: FOOD
KNOWN ACCOMPLICE: CARMEL
FAVORITE TOY: PEANUT BUTTER RUBBER BALL
FAVORITE PASTIMES: SLEEPING, RUNNING, WRESTLING AND EATING
NAUGHTIEST DEED: STANDING ON THE TABLE AND DRINKING COFFEE

BARON VON TEEGARDEN

LADY

PET PEEVE: *BEING ALONE*
FAVORITE TOY: *TEDDY BEAR*
FAVORITE PASTIME: *FETCHING BALLS*
FAVORITE FOOD: *PASTA AND MEATBALLS*
OBSESSION: *CHASING RABBITS IN VINEYARDS*
KNOWN ACCOMPLICE: *SOLO THE HIMALAYAN SIAMESE CAT*
NAUGHTIEST DEED: *GREETING PEOPLE BY JUMPING ON THEM*

FAVORITE FOOD: PIZZA
PET PEEVE: MEAN ROTTWEILERS
FAVORITE TOY: SQUEAKY HEART TOY
FAVORITE PASTIME: HANGING WITH THE GUESTS
OBSESSIONS: CHASING THE 4-WHEELER AND MAKING WINE
KNOWN ACCOMPLICE: DITCH FROM STONY MOUNTAIN WINERY
NAUGHTIEST DEED: EATING A BOX OF CHOCOLATE TRUFFLES THEN THROWING UP ON RANDY

CHUCK

GUINNESS

FAVORITE TOY: DIRTY SOCKS
OBSESSION: CHASING COYOTES
FAVORITE FOOD: DOG BISCUITS
KNOWN ACCOMPLICE: NEIGHBOR'S DOGS
FAVORITE PASTIME: PLAYING WITH STICKS
PET PEEVE: THE BIRDS EATING HIS DOG FOOD
NAUGHTIEST DEEDS: KNOCKING OVER
CINDY'S HOUSEPLANTS AND EATING HIS BED

FAVORITE FOOD: LIVER TREATS
FAVORITE TOY: STUFFED HEDGEHOG
OBSESSION: LEANING AGAINST HIS OWNER'S LEGS
NAUGHTIEST DEED: COLLECTING CAT POOP AND
ARRANGING IT IN A NEAT PILE ON THE LIVING ROOM RUG
FAVORITE PASTIME: GETTING INTO MUD AT THE DOG PARK
KNOWN ACCOMPLICES: CATIE THE CAT, CHARLEY AND ELIZABETH

ELVIS

OWNERS: ERIC AND ERICA SKLAR | SHEPHERD X, 11 MONTHS | **ALPHA OMEGA** RUTHERFORD, CA 393

SPIKE

FAVORITE PASTIME: SLEEPING
KNOWN ACCOMPLICE: ANGUS
OBSESSION: BEING WITH PEOPLE
PET PEEVE: BEING LEFT HOME ALONE
NAUGHTIEST DEED: PICKING HIS OWN
VEGETABLES FROM THE GARDEN
FAVORITE TOY: HIS BABY (AKA TEDDY BEAR)

FAVORITE FOOD: CHEESE
FAVORITE TOY: HEDGEHOG
OBSESSION: HUMAN COMPANIONSHIP
FAVORITE PASTIME: GREETING PEOPLE AT CHIMNEY ROCK
KNOWN ACCOMPLICES: PHOEBE AND TASTING ROOM GUESTS

BUSTER

FAVORITE TOY: BODHI
PET PEEVE: THE MAILMAN
OBSESSION: WHOEVER IS WALKING
OUTSIDE THE HOUSE AT 3AM
FAVORITE PASTIME: RAISING HELL
KNOWN ACCOMPLICES: ZOOEY AND EMERSON
NAUGHTIEST DEED: TOO NUMEROUS TO COUNT
FAVORITE FOOD: WHATEVER FITS IN HER MOUTH

PANTHER CREEK CELLARS McMINNVILLE, OR | ROTTWEILER X, 3 | OWNER: ANDREA FEERO

OBSESSION: MICHAEL'S WHEREABOUTS
FAVORITE PASTIME: BEING WITH MICHAEL
KNOWN ACCOMPLICES: STELLA AND FRANKIE
FAVORITE FOOD: WHATEVER FITS IN HER MOUTH
NAUGHTIEST DEED: EATING STEAK OFF THE TABLE
WHILE MICHAEL WAS WATCHING COLLEGE FOOTBALL
PET PEEVE: BEING PETTED WHILE SHE IS TRYING TO SLEEP

ZOOEY

OWNER: MICHAEL STEVENSON | PIT BULL TERRIER X, 5 | **PANTHER CREEK CELLARS** McMINNVILLE, OR | 397

LULU

PET PEEVE: BATHS
FAVORITE TOY: TEDDY BEAR
FAVORITE FOOD: PEOPLE FOOD
OBSESSION: VINEYARD RABBITS
FAVORITE PASTIME: PLAYING WITH OTHER DOGS
KNOWN ACCOMPLICES: SCOUT, MAX AND TALULAH
NAUGHTIEST DEED: STEALING CHEESE DIP OFF THE TABLE

FAVORITE PASTIME:
HANGING OUT IN THE OFFICE
PET PEEVE: NOT GOING TO
WORK WITH STEVE EVERY DAY
FAVORITE TOY: SILICON BUNGS
OBSESSION: RETRIEVING BIRDS
NAUGHTIEST DEED: RUNNING IN FRONT OF AN
ELECTRIC VEHICLE AND NEARLY BREAKING HIS LEGS

KENO

FAVORITE TOY: CATS
FAVORITE FOOD: PRIME RIB
OBSESSION: CHASING CATS
NAUGHTIEST DEED: LEAVING A HALF
EATEN OPOSSUM IN THE DRIVEWAY
PET PEEVE: MEETING NEW PEOPLE
FAVORITE PASTIMES: SMILING AND BEING HUGGED

LOLA

OBSESSION: DIGGING
PET PEEVE: TAKING A BATH
FAVORITE FOOD: BACON STRIPS
KNOWN ACCOMPLICE: FINA THE BOXER
NAUGHTIEST DEED: PEEING IN THE HOUSE
FAVORITE TOY: "DOG PERSON" CHEW SQUEAK TOY
FAVORITE PASTIME: LAYING ON HER BLANKET BY THE FIRE

ZOE

OBSESSION: FOOD
KNOWN ACCOMPLICE: MOCHA
FAVORITE TOY: ANYTHING THAT SQUEAKS
PET PEEVES: SHOWERS, WATER AND BEING IGNORED
FAVORITE PASTIMES: INTERRUPTING MEETINGS AND STEALING FOOD
NAUGHTIEST DEED: CLEARING OUT THE CONFERENCE ROOM WITH HER GAS

AMBER

CLOS LACHANCE WINERY SAN MARTIN, CA | RHODESIAN RIDGEBACK, 11 | OWNERS: BRENDA AND BILL MURPH

OBSESSION: CHEWING BONES
FAVORITE TOY: CHILDREN'S TOYS
PET PEEVE: WHEN AMBER STEALS HER BONES
FAVORITE PASTIME: RUNNING IN THE VINEYARD
KNOWN ACCOMPLICES: AJ DURZY, AMBER AND LILA
FAVORITE FOOD: ANYTHING DROPPED FROM THE HIGH CHAIR
NAUGHTIEST DEED: STEALING SOCKS AND LEAVING THEM ALL OVER THE HOUSE

MOCHA

OWNER: CHERYL MURPHY DURZY | LABRADOR, 8 | **CLOS LACHANCE WINERY** SAN MARTIN, CA | 403

LOLA

PET PEEVE: BEING TIED UP
NAUGHTIEST DEED: STEALING SOCKS
FAVORITE FOOD: ANYTHING CHEWABLE
KNOWN ACCOMPLICES: AMBER AND MOCHA
FAVORITE TOY: "LEANNA LINX" STUFFED ANIMAL
FAVORITE PASTIMES: SLEEPING, CHEWING AND EATING
OBSESSIONS: TAKING AND SLEEPING ON TOM'S SHOES AND CLOTHES

OBSESSION: RABBITS
FAVORITE TOY: WALNUTS
PET PEEVE: PEOPLE WHO KILL FLIES
KNOWN ACCOMPLICES: JJ AT VINCENT ARROYO WINERY
FAVORITE PASTIME: HANGING OUT, BEING A "WATCHDOG!"
NAUGHTIEST DEED: EATING GRAPES OUT OF THE PICKING BINS

LIBBY

REMINGTON

FAVORITE TOY: BEAR
KNOWN ACCOMPLICE: MAGGIE
OBSESSION: SHOWING PEOPLE HIS BEAR TOY
FAVORITE PASTIME: PLAYING WITH HIS BEAR TOY
NAUGHTIEST DEED: EATING THE THANKSGIVING
TURKEY WHILE IT WAS COOLING ON THE PORCH

FAVORITE PASTIMES: SCROUNGING FOR
SNACKS AND PLAYING CATCH WITH THE BALL
NAUGHTIEST DEED: TAKING DIRTY PLATES
OFF THE TABLE AND LICKING THEM CLEAN
KNOWN ACCOMPLICE: HER UNCLE BELZ
PET PEEVE: BEING LEFT ALONE FOR ONE SECOND
FAVORITE FOOD: ANYTHING RYLEE AND HAYLEE ARE EATING

NESTA SZEP

FAVORITE TOY: BALLS
FAVORITE FOOD: STEAK
OBSESSION: FINDING GOLF BALLS
FAVORITE PASTIME: CHEWING ANYTHING
NAUGHTIEST DEED: CHEWING THE AIR-CONDITIONING UNIT
PET PEEVE: ANOTHER PET GETTING TOO MUCH ATTENTION

ROCK

AMBULLNEO VINEYARDS S

FAVORITE FOOD: CAT FOOD
PET PEEVE: MEAN BULLY DOGS
FAVORITE TOY: SQUEAKY SQUIRREL
OBSESSION: LOOKING FOR TREATS IN THE TRASH
FAVORITE PASTIME: SNIFFING AROUND LOS OLIVOS
NAUGHTIEST DEED: CHEWING THE WAX SEALS
OFF THE TOP OF THE MOST EXPENSIVE PINOT NOIR
KNOWN ACCOMPLICES: HENRY THE PUG AND DIANA

BUDDY

GABBY

PET PEEVE: CATS
OBSESSION: FOOD
FAVORITE PASTIME:
BEGGING FOR FOOD
FAVORITE TOY: THREE-YEAR-OLD
AIR-DRIED OREGON OAK STICKS

OBSESSION: TOYS
PET PEEVE: WHEN PEOPLE WON'T PLAY WITH HIM
FAVORITE TOYS: ANYTHING FROM BALLS TO PRUNED GRAPEVINES
FAVORITE PASTIMES: PLAYING AND RUNNING AROUND THE VINEYARD
NAUGHTIEST DEED: JUMPING UP ON COUNTERS TO GET LEFTOVER FOOD

JACK

FAVORITE FOOD: TORTILLA CHIPS
FAVORITE TOY: STUFFED SQUAWKING QUAIL
OBSESSIONS: SQUEAKY TOYS AND PAW-LICKING
NAUGHTIEST DEED: ESCAPING A SKIJORING HARNESS
FAVORITE PASTIME: MEDITATING TO YO-YO MA'S CELLO CONCERTOS
PET PEEVE: SQUIRRELS AND CHIPMUNKS WHO THINK THEY BELONG ON HIS BACK PORCH

RAPTOR RIDGE WINERY CARLTON, OR | LABRADOR, 6 | OWNERS: ANNIE AND SCOTTY SHULL

PET PEEVE: BABY TALK
OBSESSION: STALKING HOUSEFLIES
FAVORITE TOY: HIS BED ON THE FRONT PORCH
FAVORITE FOOD: ANYTHING DROPPED ON THE FLOOR
KNOWN ACCOMPLICE: THE OTHER WINERY DOG BIRDIE
FAVORITE PASTIME: CHASING DEER, COYOTES AND VOLES
NAUGHTIEST DEED: LIFTING HIS LEG ON HIS OWNER DURING OBEDIENCE CLASS

EMMIT

DAKOTA

FAVORITE FOOD: PESTO
FAVORITE TOY: TENNIS BALLS
NAUGHTIEST DEED: CATCHING A DEER
KNOWN ACCOMPLICES: SIERRA AND ELLA
PET PEEVE: PEOPLE BLOWING IN HIS FACE
OBSESSIONS: SLEEPING AND CHASING TENNIS BALLS
FAVORITE PASTIME: SLEEPING IN BED WITH HIS OWNER

PET PEEVE: BATHS
OBSESSIONS: CHASING DEER OUT OF
THE VINEYARD AND BEFRIENDING COYOTES
FAVORITE PASTIME: PLAYING WITH DANIELLE
AND LAURENT'S DAUGHTER SOLÉNA
NAUGHTIEST DEED: BEING DOG-NAPPED, RESULTING
IN A RELOCATION TO ANOTHER VINEYARD FOR 8 MONTHS
UNTIL HE WAS FOUND AND BROUGHT HOME

TACTE

WALDO THE WONDER DOG

FAVORITE FOOD: DOG COOKIES
PET PEEVE: BEING IGNORED
FAVORITE TOY: ANYONE WHO WILL PET HIM
NAUGHTIEST DEED: EATING SANDI'S SON'S
BABY DUCK AND THEN ACTING INNOCENT
FAVORITE PASTIMES: CHASING THE GREEN MACHINE
AND LAYING IN THE SHADE OF THE GRAPE VINES
OBSESSION: ANYTHING LOUD AND MECHANICAL

PET PEEVE: BATHS
OBSESSION: SQUIRRELS
FAVORITE FOOD: GREEN TRIPE
FAVORITE TOY: SQUEAKY TOY QUAIL
KNOWN ACCOMPLICES: NAT AND KURT
FAVORITE PASTIME: RUNNING IN THE VINEYARD
NAUGHTIEST DEED: RENOVATING THE LAUNDRY ROOM

JACKSON

TARA

PET PEEVE: MICE
FAVORITE FOOD: YOGHURT
KNOWN ACCOMPLICE: RITA
FAVORITE TOY: TOY SQUIRREL
FAVORITE PASTIME: HUNTING MICE
OBSESSION: JUMPING INTO A LAP

TRES HERMANAS WINERY SANTA MARIA, CA | RAT TERRIER, 4 | OWNER: PAULETTE TEIXEIRA

FAVORITE TOY: BALL
FAVORITE FOOD: NUTS
PET PEEVE: COLD WEATHER
KNOWN ACCOMPLICE: TARA
OBSESSION: RIDING IN THE CAR
NAUGHTIEST DEED: NOT COMING WHEN CALLED
FAVORITE PASTIMES: SLEEPING AND SUNBATHING

RITA

TOMMY

PET PEEVE: LEASHES
FAVORITE FOOD: CORN CHIPS
FAVORITE TOY: "FROSTY" SQUEAKY TOY
OBSESSION: BOX OF 100 SQUEAKY TOYS
FAVORITE PASTIME: WRESTLING
WITH HIS PET CAT, MISTER GRAY
NAUGHTIEST DEED: WALKING IN
THE MIDDLE OF FOXEN CANYON ROAD
KNOWN ACCOMPLICES: QUEENIE,
YAHI, MISTER GRAY AND LILY THE PRINCESS BITCH

PET PEEVE: BEES
FAVORITE TOY: SAWYER
KNOWN ACCOMPLICES: THE KITTENS
FAVORITE PASTIMES: SETTING OFF THE OTHER
DOGS' BARKING AND BEING A TROUBLE-MAKER
OBSESSION: BONES THAT ARE TWICE HER SIZE
NAUGHTIEST DEED: JUMPING ON THE TABLE AFTER DINNER

STAR

OWNER: PARKER RUSACK | DACHSHUND X, 5 | **RUSACK** SOLVANG, CA | 421

MANDY

OBSESSION: BALLS
FAVORITE TOY: BALLS
FAVORITE FOOD: IN-N-OUT BURGERS
FAVORITE PASTIME: LYING ON HER BACK
WITH ALL FOUR PAWS IN THE AIR
KNOWN ACCOMPLICES: SAWYER AND STAR
PET PEEVE: WHEN DAD GOES OUT OF TOWN
NAUGHTIEST DEED: STEALING SOCKS AND SHOES

FAVORITE FOOD: STEAK
PET PEEVE: LOUD NOISES
FAVORITE PASTIMES: SLEEPING, CHASING
RABBITS AND BARKING POINTLESSLY
KNOWN ACCOMPLICES: MANDY AND STAR
FAVORITE TOYS: STUFFED ROOSTER AND ORANGES
NAUGHTIEST DEED: GETTING SKUNKED REGULARLY
OBSESSION: CARRYING WATER BOTTLES AND TOWELS IN HIS MOUTH

SAWYER

OWNER: HUNTER RUSACK | GOLDEN RETRIEVER, 8 | **RUSACK** SOLVANG, CA

BUBBA

FAVORITE TOY: BASKETBALLS
FAVORITE FOODS: STEAK AND RIB BONES
KNOWN ACCOMPLICES: SUNNY AND PETE
FAVORITE PASTIME: RETRIEVING STICKS FROM THE CREEK
OBSESSION: CHASING RABBITS AND SQUIRRELS THROUGH THE VINEYARD
NAUGHTIEST DEED: EATING THE STAFF'S LUNCH WHEN THEY AREN'T LOOKING
PET PEEVE: NOT RECEIVING A TREAT WHEN EVERYONE GOES HOME FOR THE NIGHT

FAVORITE TOY: FOOTBALLS
FAVORITE FOOD: MEXICAN FOOD
KNOWN ACCOMPLICES: BUBBA AND SUNNY
OBSESSION: CHASING RABBITS AND SQUIRRELS
PET PEEVE: WHEN PEOPLE DON'T SCRATCH HIS BELLY
FAVORITE PASTIMES: LAYING IN THE SUN, SLEEPING AND EATING
NAUGHTIEST DEED: RIPPING THROUGH THE NEIGHBOR'S TRASH CANS

PETE

BEAUREGARD

PET PEEVE: IRIS' SON-IN-LAW
OBSESSION: LAYING AT PEOPLE'S FEET
FAVORITE FOODS: CHICKEN AND STEAKS
FAVORITE PASTIME: WALKING IN THE PARK
NAUGHTIEST DEED: WALKING HOME ALONE
KNOWN ACCOMPLICES: BLANCA AND CLEO
FAVORITE TOY: A NEW SQUEAKY TOY HE TAKES FROM THE BAG

RIDEAU VINEYARD SOLVANG, CA | LHASA APSO, 9 | OWNER: IRIS RIDEAU

PET PEEVE: BIRDS
FAVORITE TOY: GRAHAM
FAVORITE FOOD: SNAUSAGES
KNOWN ACCOMPLICE: GRAHAM
FAVORITE PASTIMES: CHASING BIRDS AND PLAYING WITH GRAHAM
OBSESSION: THE AUDACITY OF BIRDS WHO FLY ONTO HIS PROPERTY

BERTIE WOOSTER

OSCAR MEYER

OBSESSION: PLAYING BALL
PET PEEVE: BEING LEFT ALONE
FAVORITE FOOD: IN-N-OUT BURGER
FAVORITE TOY: SQUEAKY ROPE BALL
NAUGHTIEST DEED: PEEING ON THE RUG
KNOWN ACCOMPLICE: ANY HUMAN HOLDING A BALL
FAVORITE PASTIMES: EATING OFF YOUR PLATE AND LICKING WINE FROM YOUR LIPS

SALTY

FAVORITE TOYS: PEOPLE
FAVORITE FOOD: NOODLES
OBSESSION: SINGING WITH J STREET SLIM
PET PEEVE: FOOD TREATS HE DOESN'T LIKE
NAUGHTIEST DEED: GETTING PERFORMANCE ANXIETY
FAVORITE PASTIMES: SINGING AND WORKING AT THE WINERY
KNOWN ACCOMPLICES: DIANE, LYNDIE, PHAROAH AND CHRISTY

ROGER

OBSESSION: BALLS
FAVORITE TOY: STICKS
FAVORITE FOOD: DOG FOOD
KNOWN ACCOMPLICE: CODY
FAVORITE PASTIME: HUNTING PHEASANT
PET PEEVE: HAVING NO ONE TO PLAY WITH

PET PEEVE: BEING ALONE
OBSESSION: RETRIEVING
KNOWN ACCOMPLICE: CODY
FAVORITE FOOD: DOG FOOD
FAVORITE TOY: TENNIS BALLS
FAVORITE PASTIME: CHASING A BALL

WESSON

OWNER: CHRISTINA SMITH | LABRADORS, 2 AND 7 | **SMITH VINEYARD** GRASS VALLEY, CA

THREE PALMS VINEYARD CALISTOGA, CA | LABRADOR, 4 | OWNER: CAROLINE UPTON

CYRUS

OBSESSION: THE OCEAN
FAVORITE TOY: RED RUBBER KONG BALL
FAVORITE PASTIMES: SWIMMING AND
LOOKING FOR VINE MEALY BUGS IN VINEYARDS
NAUGHTIEST DEED: PULLING CAROLINE DOWN
IN THE SAND AND DRAGGING HER INTO THE OCEAN
PET PEEVES: WAITING TO GO TO WORK AND BEING STUCK IN THE CAR
KNOWN ACCOMPLICES: WILLOW, SCOUT, TUCKER AND RIXI

FAVORITE FOOD: CREAM CHEESE
FAVORITE TOY: STUFFED MANATEE
PET PEEVE: NOT GETTING TO MEET GUESTS
KNOWN ACCOMPLICES: CYRUS AND MILO
NAUGHTIEST DEED: SWIMMING IN THE WATER DISH
OBSESSION: TAKING THE BED TO THE FRONT DOOR TO MEET VISITORS
FAVORITE PASTIME: BEING WITH SLOAN AND PRISCILLA AT THE VINEYARD

WILLOW

OWNERS: SLOAN AND PRISCILLA UPTON | LABRADOR, 9 | **THREE PALMS VINEYARD** CALISTOGA, CA | 433

BANDIT

OBSESSION: GETTING OUT TO HUNT
FAVORITE FOODS: MEAT AND GRAPES
FAVORITE PASTIME: HUNTING PHEASANT
PET PEEVE: STAYING IN THE YARD BY HIMSELF

PET PEEVE: *OBEYING*
FAVORITE TOY: *TENNIS BALL*
OBSESSION: *GETTING ONTO THE BED*
FAVORITE PASTIME: *DIGGING IN THE YARD*

ZIZOU

PET PEEVE: BEING CLOSE
FAVORITE FOOD: BISCUITS
FAVORITE TOY: RUBBER CHEWY PUFFER FISH
KNOWN ACCOMPLICES: ANNIE, BUZZ AND SOPHIA
OBSESSION: CARRYING SOMETHING IN HER MOUTH
FAVORITE PASTIMES: CHASING RABBITS AND PLAYING WITH ANNIE

HONIG VINEYARD AND WINERY RUTHERFORD, CA | LABRADOR, 2 | OWNERS: MICHAEL AND STEPHANIE HONIG

FAVORITE TOY: TENNIS BALL
NAUGHTIEST DEED: EATING POOP
PET PEEVE: WALKING ON THE LEFT SIDE
OBSESSION: GOING ANYWHERE PATTI IS
FAVORITE FOOD: DOG BISCUITS AT BEDTIME
KNOWN ACCOMPLICES: RAISIN, BUZZ AND DOUG
FAVORITE PASTIMES: CHASING TENNIS BALLS AND
WALKING IN VINEYARDS WITH PATTI AND RAISIN

ANNIE

BELLA

KNOWN ACCOMPLICE: GEORGI
FAVORITE FOOD: TREATS OF ANY KIND
OBSESSION: RABBITS IN THE VINEYARD
FAVORITE PASTIME: RIDING IN THE BACK OF THE PICKUP
NAUGHTIEST DEED: REMOVING ALL THE PLANTS
AND THE DRIP HOSE IN A FRESHLY PLANTED GARDEN

MUNSELLE VINEYARDS GEYSERVILLE, CA | LABRADOR X, 3 | OWNERS: BRET AND KRISTEN MUNSELLE

FAVORITE FOOD: ANYTHING
FAVORITE PASTIME: SLEEPING
OBSESSION: STAYING ON THE GOLF CART

MAX

FRANKIE

OBSESSION: KONG BALL
FAVORITE FOOD: GREENIES
FAVORITE TOY: KONG BALL
NAUGHTIEST DEED: EXPLORING TRASH
FAVORITE PASTIMES: BEGGING FROM
PICNICKERS AND PLAYING WITH ALL DOGS
PET PEEVE: BEING KEPT AWAY FROM ANY PARTY

FAVORITE TOY: BALLS
FAVORITE PASTIME:
STAYING DOWN AT THE SHOP
PET PEEVES: BATHS, CATS
AND THUNDERSTORMS
OBSESSION: GETTING
INTO THE GARBAGE

SADIE

OWNERS: LEO AND EVELYN TRENTADUE | GERMAN SHEPHERD, 5 | **TRENTADUE WINERY** GEYSERVILLE, CA | 429

MARLEY

FAVORITE TOY: TOY DUCK
OBSESSION: PLAYING BALL
FAVORITE FOOD: LIVER TREATS
PET PEEVE: PEOPLE WHO DON'T PET HIM
FAVORITE PASTIMES: GREETING CUSTOMERS
AT THE WINERY AND PLAYING WITH MAZZY
KNOWN ACCOMPLICES: MAZZY, DENALI, CLEO AND PATRAH
NAUGHTIEST DEED: STEALING DISHES OUT OF THE KITCHEN SINK

FAVORITE TOY: TOY CAT
PET PEEVE: SQUIRRELS
FAVORITE FOOD: JERKY TREATS
NAUGHTIEST DEED: CHEWING UP UNDERWEAR
FAVORITE PASTIME: WRESTLING WITH MARLEY
KNOWN ACCOMPLICES: LUCI, MARLEY, PONCHO AND NINA
OBSESSION: FLINGING THE TOY CAT IN THE AIR EVERY MORNING

MAZZY

OWNER: SCOTT TAYLOR | JACK RUSSELL TERRIER, 3 | **SIERRA KNOLLS VINEYARD** GRASS VALLEY, CA | 443

PET PEEVE: BEING HARASSED BY LOLA
OBSESSIONS: ENSURING THE SAFETY OF THE
CHILDREN, LIKE AN OVERBEARING MOTHER
FAVORITE PASTIME: WATCHING LOLA GO CRAZY
FAVORITE TOYS: THE CHILDREN'S STUFFED ANIMALS
KNOWN ACCOMPLICES: LOLA, SOPHIA AND SAMANTHA
FAVORITE FOOD: LOLA'S FOOD, MADE SPECIFICALLY FOR PUGS
NAUGHTIEST DEED: MARKING HIS TERRITORY ...ON LOLA'S HEAD

ODDO

OBSESSIONS: ODDO
FAVORITE TOY: ODDO
FAVORITE PASTIME: PESTERING ODDO
FAVORITE FOOD: ODDO'S FOOD, MADE
SPECIFICALLY FOR GERMAN SHEPHERDS
PET PEEVE: BEING AWOKEN FROM HER NAPS
NAUGHTIEST DEED: BREAKING INTO FULL CHRISTMAS
STOCKINGS IN THE MIDDLE OF THE NIGHT

LOLA

GINGER

PET PEEVE: CATS
OBSESSION: OTHER DOGS' FOOD
FAVORITE PASTIME: STAR-GAZING
KNOWN ACCOMPLICES: GALAXY, VIOGNIER,
LILAC LILLY ROSE AND SAMMY SUGAR BALL

JAFFE ESTATE ST. HELENA, CA | CAVALIER KING CHARLES SPANIEL, 4 | OWNER: VIDA JAFFE

PET PEEVE: CATS
OBSESSION: SHOES
NAUGHTIEST DEED: EATING
A DINNER GUEST'S SHOE
FAVORITE PASTIME: ROUGH-HOUSING
WITH THE BLACK LABRADOR PUPPY

PEACHES

GHILLIE DUBH

PET PEEVE: RATTLESNAKES
OBSESSION: EATING KLEENEX
FAVORITE TOYS: KONG BALL AND BONE
FAVORITE PASTIMES: FOLLOWING MOM AND CHASING LIZARDS
NAUGHTIEST DEED: STEALING A CREAM SCONE RIGHT OUT OF KENT'S HAND
KNOWN ACCOMPLICES: WEBSTER AND CALVALEIGH THE PARAKEETS, KENT AND CELIA

FAVORITE TOY: KONG
PET PEEVE: SMALL DOGS
OBSESSION: EATING MERLOT GRAPES
FAVORITE FOOD: WHATEVER IS IN THE BOWL
FAVORITE PASTIME: SWIMMING IN THE NAPA RIVER
KNOWN ACCOMPLICES: GUS, KITTY JUNE, JAKE, OTTO AND RIVA
NAUGHTIEST DEED: STEALING THE CHEESE BOARD OUT OF THE TASTING ROOM

STOCKARD

OWNERS: JOAN AND STAN BOYD | LABRADOR, 10 | **BOYD FAMILY VINEYARD** NAPA, CA | 449

MIKE

FAVORITE FOOD: PÂTÉ
FAVORITE PASTIME: SLEEPING
OBSESSION: BARKING AT THE UPS MAN
NAUGHTIEST DEED: STEALING GUS' TREATS
KNOWN ACCOMPLICES: GUS AND STOCKARD
PET PEEVE: GUS OR STOCKARD STEALING HIS TREAT

FAVORITE TOY: EARL THE CHICKEN
KNOWN ACCOMPLICES: JAKE AT MONTICELLO
AND SWEET PEA AT MILLER WINE WORKS
PET PEEVE: DELIVERY TRUCKS WITHOUT TREATS
NAUGHTIEST DEED: STEALING VISITORS' BOTTLES OF WATER
FAVORITE PASTIME: LEADING TRIPS TO THE RIVER FOR A SWIM

GUS

OWNERS: JOAN AND STAN BOYD | BURGUNDIAN TRUFFLE HOUND 3 | **BOYD FAMILY VINEYARD** NAPA CA | 451

CHEWY

PET PEEVE: BEING LEFT HOME
FAVORITE TOYS: BALLS AND BONES
FAVORITE PASTIME: ATTENDING EVENTS SO
HE CAN LOVE AND LICK ALL THE ATTENDEES
OBSESSION: LEANING AGAINST PEOPLES' LEGS
NAUGHTIEST DEED: GETTING CAUGHT IN A
FOOT TRAP AND COMING HOME MINUS ONE TOE

SIERRA STARR GRASS VALLEY, CA | ROTTWEILER X, 4 | OWNERS: PHIL AND ANNE STARR

OBSESSION: SLEEPING
FAVORITE TOY: TENNIS BALL
FAVORITE FOOD: APPLE CORES
NAUGHTIEST DEED: RUNNING OFF
KNOWN ACCOMPLICE: CHEWY STARR
FAVORITE PASTIME: STICK! STICK! STICK!
PET PEEVE: HAVING HIS STICK TAKEN AWAY

BRUNO

BUCK

OBSESSION: BIG STICKS
FAVORITE FOOD: RIPE CABERNET GRAPES
FAVORITE TOY: THE BIGGEST STICK HE CAN FIND
PET PEEVE: ANYONE WHO WON'T PLAY WITH HIM
KNOWN ACCOMPLICES: LULU AND FRANKI AT JJ COLIN ESTATE
NAUGHTIEST DEED: CHEWING THE PHONE WIRES TO CELIA'S OFFICE
FAVORITE PASTIMES: CHASING WILD TURKEYS AND SWIMMING IN RESERVOIRS

CANINES, PARKER & ME

by Elin McCoy

WHEN I STARTED WRITING my biography of Robert M. Parker, Jr, The Emperor of Wine, little did I know how often dogs would nose their way into my several years of research and wind up in the narrative.

I don't know why I was so surprised. In three decades of visiting vineyards and wineries to cover the wine world, I've encountered hundreds of canines wagging their tails outside cellar doors, patrolling the vines, trailing winemakers as we toured and tasted, or just lounging in the sun as trucks rumbled in with harvested grapes. As a dog lover (schnauzers and bichons), I long ago started taking photos of each winery's dogs to add to my file of wine notes. (Ironically, I can think of only one that had a winery cat – Alta Vista in Argentina.) But these photos are just for my own amusement; the dogs don't make it into my columns and articles.

With my first visit to Robert Parker's home in Parkton, Maryland, it was clear dogs were going to feature big in my book. For one thing, as many know, Parker is almost as dog-obsessed as he is wine-obsessed and even rates one of his canines on his 100-point wine-rating system for the winedogs.com website.

As soon as I entered Parker's grey ranch house at the end of a narrow dead-end road, I met his brown-eyed, droopy-eared, short-legged basset hound Hoover (then age 3) and drooly bulldog George (then 9, now dead), whose eyes were like black patches in his squished-up face. Both sniffed deeply to check me out and demanded pats. Evidently I passed the bouquet test. While Parker and I settled in chairs in his messy office, with the fax humming in the background and my tape recorder running, they padded around, then settled down next to clusters of bottles. Joan Passman, then Parker's office manager, revealed that she shooed them out whenever they passed wind. Parker claimed that didn't interfere with his ability to assess wine.

Later, Hoover and George sprawled in the living room as we ate lunch in a light-filled dining area off the kitchen alongside Riedel glasses on shelves and dozens of plants. Neither showed any interest in wine.

Dogs in general seemed to be a Parker life leitmotif: his father, for example, kept blue tick hounds and once claimed he could tell the breed of a dog by its scent. Parker told *me that at the time he thought his father was joking, and only later realized his father had an unusually acute sense of smell, which Parker had apparently inherited.*

He abandoned the cocker spaniels of his childhood for basset hounds (Watson came first) when he married his highschool sweetheart, Pat. I thought the choice, which coincided with his increasingly serious interest in wine, seemed like some kind of omen, as I learned a basset hound's sense of smell is second only to that of a bloodhound. Surely it was an especially appropriate breed for a wine critic whose ability to smell is insured for one million bucks.

But Parker hasn't used the several basset hounds he's owned in any professional capacity. No secret help for his blind wine tastings. Not like Michelle Edwards, the winemaker at Napa Valley winery Cliff Lede, who recently trained her bloodhound to detect contaminated corks.

Dogs and dog comparisons kept popping up as I sniffed out reactions to Parker in various wine regions. In Bordeaux, where Parker made his name by championing the 1982 vintage, noted négociant Bill Blatch told me, "When it comes to wine, Parker has a nose like a dog." Did he mean a bloodhound? Or a basset hound? Many château owners made the same comparison, including those who were unhappy with his wine judgments and influence.

Ironically, anger with a low score for a wine was behind the most famous Parker dog story, which I heard several times in Bordeaux, as well as from Parker. The accounts don't completely match, of course. The owner of the great Château Cheval Blanc in St. Emilion, furious that Parker had called his 1981 wine "mediocre" and "disappointing," demanded Parker retaste it. When he pulled up the following evening at the small château surrounded by vines, a ferocious little schnauzer made straight for his leg, bit down hard, and wouldn't let go. Hébrard watched impassively as Parker finally shook the dog off and limped into the office. Parker claimed blood was running down his leg and Hébrard didn't offer him a bandage; Hébrard says there was no blood. But when the dog died, he let Parker know.

I chased down many apochryphal Parker-dog rumors in the region. Like the tale that Anthony Barton of Château Léoville-Barton had sent Parker a photograph of one of his dogs lapping up spilled wine on a table with a caption: A 100 point wine! Barton denied it. Too bad.

In perusing Parker's newsletter The Wine Advocate and his books, I discovered that Parker seemed to delight in his experiences with dogs at wineries. It took him three years to get the reclusive late owner/winemaker Jacques Reynaud of Château Rayas in the Rhône Valley's Châteauneuf du Pape region to see him. When he finally did, Parker reported, the visits were always chaotic, as "undisciplined dogs" roamed about the cellar. But none of them bit him.

One of the most entertaining dog tales I happened upon, which I didn't include in my book, involved Behrens & Hitchcock, a winery on the Napa Valley's Spring Mountain that came out of nowhere and rose to sell-out fame on high Parker scores. The dog is Lucy, a "wild and crazy" white Jack Russell terrier, who has reportedly "survived collisions with fork-lift trucks" as well as encounters with rattlesnakes. The dog inspired the winery's Le Chien Lunatique syrah, which Parker usually scores at 91 and up. But despite diligent analysis I found no evidence that he gives higher scores to wines with dog-type names.

Naturally, on the day I spent touring and tasting with Parker in the Napa Valley, we encountered several dogs. But the most amusing were at our first stop, Staglin Vineyards, at the end of Bella Oaks Lane in Rutherford. Parker pushed the buzzer at the iron gate across the winery drive, and we made our way slowly up through the vineyards to the built-into-the-mountain winery and cellar. The Staglins' two Jack Russell terriers, Sami and Deuce, yipped wildly at Parker as we joined the family at the just-completed cellar entrance. The canine hosts of a doggie dinner party that had raised $28,000 at a Napa Valley Wine Auction, they followed us into Staglin's new 24,000 square foot cave. Our tasting was punctuated by barks from the two dogs, but Parker was unfazed. Alas, Sami and Deuce are no more and the Staglins have an Anatolian shepherd named Kara whose pictures are on their website.

By the time I was making the last changes to the book, Parker's beloved bulldog George had died. His replacement Buddy didn't make it into my book.

As for me, I am temporarily without a dog, but won't be for long.

ELIN McCOY IS WINE COLUMNIST FOR BLOOMBERG NEWS AND THE AUTHOR OF *THE EMPEROR OF WINE: THE RISE OF ROBERT M. PARKER, JR., AND THE REIGN OF AMERICAN TASTE.* WHEN NOT TRACKING CANINES ON THE VINE IN WINE COUNTRY, SHE RESIDES IN CONNECTICUT.

BELLA

OBSESSION: MAKING SURE EVERYONE
KNOWS SHE IS THE CENTER OF ATTENTION
FAVORITE TOY: HER LITTLE SISTER BLOSSOM
PET PEEVE: NOT BEING ABLE TO DRIVE THE CAR
FAVORITE PASTIME: WATCHING THE SKY FOR HOT AIR BALLOONS
NAUGHTIEST DEED: NOT GETTING OUT OF THE DRIVER'S SEAT IN THE CAR

NAUGHTIEST DEEDS: CHEWING SHOES
AND JUMPING ON THE COUCH AND BED
FAVORITE FOOD: HER SISTER'S ADULT LITE
FAVORITE TOYS: WILT, SQUEAKY DUCKS AND GEESE
OBSESSIONS: EXPENSIVE SHOES AND WILT THE CAT
KNOWN ACCOMPLICES: WILT THE CAT, BELLA AND LUCY
FAVORITE PASTIME: PLAYING WITH HER SISTER BELLA

BLOSSOM

KNOWN ACCOMPLICE: YOWAH
FAVORITE TOY: PAPA'S SHOES
PET PEEVE: CATS SHE DOESN'T KNOW WELL
FAVORITE PASTIME: PRETENDING SHE'S A LAPDOG
FAVORITE FOODS: ROASTED CHICKEN AND CORN CHIPS
OBSESSION: LARGE BIRDS FLYING OVER THE VINEYARDS
NAUGHTIEST DEED: EXPLORING WAY PAST THE FENCELINE

MOOKA

LEMELSON VINEYARDS CARLTON, OR | GREAT PYRENEES, 5 | OWNER: ERIC LEMELSON

PET PEEVE: OTHER DOGS
FAVORITE FOOD: DOG BISCUITS
FAVORITE TOY: SQUEAK CHEW TOY
FAVORITE PASTIME: FOLLOWING HENRY
NAUGHTIEST DEED: PULLING THE PILLOW OUT
OF THE CAT'S PLAY HOUSE AND HIDING IT

SIERRA

MOON

FAVORITE TOY: TENNIS BALL
FAVORITE FOOD: SOW'S EARS
OBSESSION: FETCHING A THROWN BALL
KNOWN ACCOMPLICES: CHLOE AND KIRA
NAUGHTIEST DEED: DIGGING VERY LARGE
HOLES IN THE LAWN IN SEARCH OF GOPHERS
PET PEEVE: WATCHING WHILE THE CAT GETS FED
FAVORITE PASTIMES: CHASING BALLS, BIRDS AND CATS

FAVORITE FOOD: GRAPES
FAVORITE TOY: RUBBER KONG
KNOWN ACCOMPLICE: RUBBER KONG
PET PEEVE: SPENDING THE NIGHT IN HIS KENNEL
NAUGHTIEST DEED: GETTING IN CUSTOMERS' CARS
FAVORITE PASTIMES: DESTROYING HIS TOYS AND CHASING BIRDS

JACK

HEIDI

FAVORITE TOY: ANY BALL
PET PEEVE: BEING LEFT ALONE
OBSESSION: BEING WITH THE FAMILY
FAVORITE FOOD: HUMAN FOOD OF ANY TYPE
KNOWN ACCOMPLICE: RUFOUS, THE BLACK LAB THAT SHE RAISED FROM A PUPPY
FAVORITE PASTIMES: GREETING CUSTOMERS AND ANNOUNCING THEIR PRESENCE

OBSESSION: CHASING BIRDS
FAVORITE TOY: ANY GOLF BALL
KNOWN ACCOMPLICE: HEIDI, HIS MINI DACHSUND FRIEND
NAUGHTIEST DEED: LOCKING JOHN'S FRIEND OUT OF HER HOUSE
FAVORITE PASTIME: SHOWING CUSTOMERS TO THE TASTING ROOM

RUFOUS

STACY

FAVORITE TOY: GREEN FROG
FAVORITE PASTIME: FOLLOWING THE FAMILY
NAUGHTIEST DEED: GETTING INTO THE FROG POND
KNOWN ACCOMPLICE: BRUTUS, HER NEW BROTHER
OBSESSION: CARRYING ANYTHING SHE CAN FIND IN HER MOUTH
FAVORITE FOOD: ANYTHING SHE CAN FIND LEFT BEHIND BY EMRYS OR NELSON

FAVORITE TOY: BALLS OF ANY SIZE
NAUGHTIEST DEED: STEALING CHOCOLATE
FAVORITE PASTIME: SLEEPING INDOORS ON HIS DOG BED
KNOWN ACCOMPLICES: STACY AND BOOTS THE ORANGE CAT
OBSESSIONS: WATER BOTTLES THROWN BY ANYONE WHO HAS PATIENCE
FAVORITE FOOD: ANY TABLE SCRAPS THAT FALL FROM THE TODDLER'S PLATES

BRUTUS

WILBUR

FAVORITE FOOD: TREATS
FAVORITE PASTIME: SINGING
OBSESSION: GETTING PETTED
KNOWN ACCOMPLICE: SHEEBA
PET PEEVE: NOT GETTING ATTENTION
NAUGHTIEST DEED: HOWLING IN THE MIDDLE OF THE NIGHT

OBSESSION: SQUEAKY TOYS
FAVORITE TOY: ANYTHING SQUEAKY
FAVORITE FOODS: RICE CAKE AND GREEN BEANS
NAUGHTIEST DEED: DIGGING UP EXPENSIVE ROSES TO GET A MOLE
KNOWN ACCOMPLICES: FRISKY, BOO, OREO, FRECKLES AND SCOOTER
FAVORITE PASTIMES: GREETING WINERY VISITORS AND MOOCHING CRACKERS

ZOE

MARKHAM

OBSESSION: PEOPLE
PET PEEVE: BEING PULLED WHEN HE
DOES NOT WANT TO GO SOMEWHERE
FAVORITE FOOD: ANYTHING WITH BEEF
FAVORITE TOY: HIS FRIEND BABA THE CAT
FAVORITE PASTIME: SLEEPING (WITH OR WITHOUT THE CAT)

OBSESSION: THE UPS MAN
PET PEEVE: BEING LEFT ALONE
KNOWN ACCOMPLICE: HOMER
FAVORITE TOYS: MUDDY TENNIS BALLS
NAUGHTIEST DEED: EAT'ING MICHELLE'S PILLOW
FAVORITE PASTIME: WATCH'ING FOR THE UPS MAN
FAVORITE FOODS: STEAK BONES AND ORANGE SLICES

WINNIE

MADDUX

FAVORITE FOOD: SALMON
PET PEEVE: THINGS THAT BEEP
FAVORITE TOYS: FRISBEES AND TENNIS BALLS
FAVORITE PASTIME: LEADING VINEYARD TOURS
OBSESSION: EXCAVATING TOYS FROM THE VINEYARD
NAUGHTIEST DEED: DROPPING A DEAD RABBIT AT THE FEET
OF VISITING 'NEW YORK TIMES' WINE EDITOR, ERIC ASIMOV
KNOWN ACCOMPLICES: BUBBA, JEWEL, ELI AND SEBASTIAN

OBSESSION: SHOES
FAVORITE FOOD: CAT FOOD
KNOWN ACCOMPLICES: CHIEF AND PRINCESS
NAUGHTIEST DEED: CHEWING THE TELEPHONE CORD
FAVORITE PASTIME: STANDING IN FRONT OF CARS AS THEY
ARRIVE AT THE TASTING ROOM TO KEEP THEM FROM PARKING

QUINCY

AIREE

FAVORITE TOY: PEOPLE
PET PEEVE: BEING LEFT BEHIND
FAVORITE FOOD: AMAZINGLY, DOG FOOD!
KNOWN ACCOMPLICE: THE NINE BARN CATS
NAUGHTIEST DEED: JUMPING INTO THE BACKSEAT AND
ONTO THE LAP OF A VISITOR ON A LOVELY WET OREGON DAY
FAVORITE PASTIME: DIGGING FOR FIELD MOLES AND GOPHERS
OBSESSION: HAVING TO GET UP AND GO TO WORK, RAIN OR SHINE

FAVORITE FOOD: RAW LEG OF LAMB
NAUGHTIEST DEED: EATING UNDERWEAR
FAVORITE TOYS: RED BEAR AND HER CAR TOY
OBSESSIONS: DISEMBOWELING STUFFED ANIMALS,
PREENING KITTENS AND CHASING VOLES
KNOWN ACCOMPLICES: GRACIE AT PATTON VALLEY VINEYARDS,
ERIC AND CARMEN AT NICK'S ITALIAN CAFE
PET PEEVE: NOT GETTING ENOUGH ATTENTION FROM THE HUMANS

BELLA

NICKI

PET PEEVE: BIRDS
FAVORITE FOOD:
KIBBLE WITH OLIVE OIL
FAVORITE TOY: SQUEAKY BALL
OBSESSION: DOSAGE THE CAT
KNOWN ACCOMPLICES:
DONNA, DOSAGE AND SOOTS
NAUGHTIEST DEED: EATING FIREWOOD
AND BRINGING IT INTO THE HOUSE

PET PEEVE: STRANGERS
FAVORITE FOOD: HORSE HOOVES
FAVORITE TOY: CHUCK IT FRISBEE
FAVORITE PASTIME: HERDING COWS
NAUGHTIEST DEED: CHASING CHICKENS
KNOWN ACCOMPLICES: DAISY AND KOOSH
OBSESSIONS: COWS, HORSES AND PUPPIES

RED

CHARGER

OBSESSION: BALLS
FAVORITE FOOD: STEAK
FAVORITE TOY: TENNIS BALLS
PET PEEVE: THE GARDEN HOSE
KNOWN ACCOMPLICES: HAL,
JOHN AND GLEN (THE NEIGHBORS)
NAUGHTIEST DEED: RUNNING OFF
TO VISIT THE NEIGHBORS
FAVORITE PASTIME: CHASING THE BALL

FAVORITE TOY: PINK POODLE
PET PEEVE: MISSING A MEAL
FAVORITE FOOD: FRENCH CHEESE
FAVORITE PASTIME: PLAYING WITH
HER CHEW TOYS, OTIS AND CHARGER
OBSESSION: KRISPY KREME DONUTS
KNOWN ACCOMPLICES: CHARGER AND OTIS
NAUGHTIEST DEED: PEEING ON GUESTS' PILLOWS

LILY

FAVORITE FOOD: LILY'S
OBSESSION: ANY FOOD
PET PEEVE: TOUR BUSES
FAVORITE TOY: TUG OF WAR ROPE
FAVORITE PASTIME: ROAMING THE VINEYARD
NAUGHTIEST DEED: REMOVING
SANDWICHES FROM THE KITCHEN COUNTER
KNOWN ACCOMPLICES: DAISY DUKE AND JOEY

OTIS

PRIVÉ VINEYARD NEWBERG, OR | REDBONE COONHOUND, 3 | OWNER: MARK HAMMOND

PET PEEVE: GOING TO THE VET
OBSESSIONS: FOOD AND SLEEP
KNOWN ACCOMPLICE: GRACIE THE CAT
FAVORITE TOY: KONG FILLED WITH FOOD
FAVORITE FOOD: ANY AND ALL DOG TREATS
FAVORITE PASTIME: BEING THE OFFICIAL TASTER FOR
ALL WINERY FOOD PAIRED WITH BOURASSA WINES
NAUGHTIEST DEED: RAIDING THE FOOD PANTRY THEN BLAMING THE CAT

JASPER

OBSESSION: ROCKS
FAVORITE TOY: ROCKS
FAVORITE PASTIME: BURYING ROCKS
FAVORITE FOOD: WHATEVER FALLS ON THE FLOOR
NAUGHTIEST DEED: BURYING ROCKS IN
CLOTHING THEN CHEWING HOLES TO GET TO THEM
PET PEEVE: NOT BEING ABLE TO REACH THE ROCKS
THAT SHE'S PUSHED UNDER THE LIVING ROOM CHAIR

ELSA

PET PEEVE: HER LITTLE SISTER ELSA
KNOWN ACCOMPLICES: THE MULTIPLE
PERSONALITIES THAT EXIST IN HER HEAD
OBSESSION: FINDING THE MOUSE THAT
MAY OR MAY NOT LIVE IN THE PALLET JACK
NAUGHTIEST DEED: MULTIPLE CAR VS DOG ENCOUNTERS
FAVORITE PASTIMES: PROWLING FOR MICE AND EATING LIZARDS

LUCY

OBSESSION: *RIDING IN THE CAR*
FAVORITE PASTIMES: *RUNNING, JUMPING,*
RUNNING, EATING, RUNNING...
FAVORITE FOODS: *TURKEY AND VEGGIES*
FAVORITE TOYS: *JAY AND KAREN'S SLIPPERS*
NAUGHTIEST DEED: *EATING AN IPOD HEADSET*
PET PEEVE: *ANYTIME JAY AND KAREN LEAVE*
KNOWN ACCOMPLICE: *BOBBY, THE AUSSIE/POINTER*

ELLIE

PET PEEVE: THE UPS GUY
KNOWN ACCOMPLICE: DELA
FAVORITE PASTIME: PASSING WIND
FAVORITE TOYS: ERIKA AND CAMILLE
NAUGHTIEST DEED: SNEAKING UP ON THE DEAF KITTY
FAVORITE FOOD: PEANUT BUTTER COVERED RAWHIDE BONE
OBSESSIONS: RABBITS AND WHINING WHILE RIDING IN THE CAR

HANK

OWNER: ERIKA J. GOTTL | WEIMARANER, 6 | **MERUS** NAPA, CA | 487

PHOEBE

PET PEEVE: TIRES
FAVORITE TOY: THE FUNKY MONKEY
FAVORITE PASTIMES: RUNNING IN THE
VINEYARD AND DIVING INTO THE POND
OBSESSION: CHASING INVISIBLE THINGS
KNOWN ACCOMPLICES: MOSES AND PAZ
NAUGHTIEST DEED: CHASING MIDNITE THE KITTY

FAVORITE TOY: STUFFED DUCK
FAVORITE FOOD: ANY TREAT YOU HAVE
FAVORITE PASTIMES: CHASING ANYTHING
THAT MOVES AND SOMETIMES A GOOD NAP
KNOWN ACCOMPLICES: GUS, JACKSON AND BUDDIE
OBSESSION: ANY KIND OF MOVING OBJECT TO CHASE
PET PEEVE: NOT BEING ALLOWED TO GREET EVERYONE SHE SEES
NAUGHTIEST DEEDS: EATING TRASH AND PAPER AND STEALING CORKS

HANNAH

ZORRO

PET PEEVE: *TAKING A BATH*
FAVORITE FOOD: *MEXICAN FOOD*
FAVORITE PASTIME: *SITTING IN THE SUN*
OBSESSION: *MEETING AND GREETING NEW
PEOPLE THAT COME IN ROBLEDO'S TASTING ROOM*
NAUGHTIEST DEED: *MARKING HIS SPOT
ON EVERY CAR THAT VISITS THE TASTING ROOM*
KNOWN ACCOMPLICES: *BUCK AND MAGNUM*

FAVORITE TOY: FOOTBALL
PET PEEVE: TAKING BATHS
FAVORITE FOOD: NEW YORK STEAK
OBSESSION: DIGGING FOR GOPHERS
NAUGHTIEST DEED: MARKING THE BARRELS
FAVORITE PASTIMES: RUNNING IN THE VINEYARD
AND TRYING TO CATCH JACK RABBITS
KNOWN ACCOMPLICES: ZORRO, MAGNUM AND COCO

BUCK

BAILEY

FAVORITE TOY: BALL WITH BLINKING LIGHT
PET PEEVE: ANIMALS IN THE VINEYARD
NAUGHTIEST DEED: CROTCH SNIFFING
OBSESSION: RIDING IN THE TRUCK
FAVORITE FOOD: ICE CUBES
KNOWN ACCOMPLICE: HANNAH FROM SILENUS VINTNERS
FAVORITE PASTIMES: RUNNING AND GETTING INTO EVERYTHING

FAVORITE TOY: HUGE STICKS
FAVORITE FOODS: CHEESE AND SALAMI
PET PEEVE: OTHER DOGS HAVING A TOY
OBSESSION: ESCAPING FROM GROOMING SESSIONS
KNOWN ACCOMPLICES: MOOSE, WINNIE, DAISY, BERNIE AND WILBUR
FAVORITE PASTIME: ROLLING AROUND ON A WET LAWN IN THE MORNING
NAUGHTIEST DEED: OPENING GATES AND LETTING ALL THE OTHER DOGS OUT

PANZER

PET PEEVE: ROB, THE UPS GUY
FAVORITE TOY: A BIG BONE TO CHEW ON
OBSESSION: CHASING ROB THE UPS GUY
KNOWN ACCOMPLICES: DAISY AND PANZER
FAVORITE PASTIME: HANGING OUT AT THE OFFICE
NAUGHTIEST DEED: BARKING AT ROB THE UPS GUY
FAVORITE FOOD: ALL TREATS – ANYTHING AND EVERYTHING

WINNIE

FAVORITE TOY: PEOPLE
OBSESSION: GETTING ATTENTION
PET PEEVE: DOING WHAT SHE'S TOLD
FAVORITE FOOD: WHATEVER YOU ARE EATING
NAUGHTIEST DEED: SLEEPING ON THE HOODS OF CARS
FAVORITE PASTIMES: GETTING PETTED AND BEGGING FOR TREATS

DAISY

PEACHES

OBSESSION: FOOD
FAVORITE TOY: FOOD
PET PEEVE: PAUCITY OF FOOD
FAVORITE FOOD: A LOT OF ANYTHING
KNOWN ACCOMPLICES: THE NEIGHBORS WHO
PUT OUT BREADCRUMBS FOR THE BIRDS
FAVORITE PASTIMES: EATING AND
SEARCHING FOR, OR BEGGING FOR FOOD
NAUGHTIEST DEED: STEALING A LOAF OF BREAD

FAVORITE FOOD: SYRUP
FAVORITE TOY: BRAD'S CLOTHING
OBSESSION: ANYTHING THAT MOVES
KNOWN ACCOMPLICE: THE 11-MONTH OLD BABY
WHO DROPS FOOD FROM HIS HIGH CHAIR
NAUGHTIEST DEED: JUMPING OUT OF A MOVING CAR TO CHASE A ROLLERBLADER

SYDNEY

OWNERS: KATHLEEN AND BRAD McLEROY | AUSTRALIAN CATTLE DOG, 13 | **AYRES VINEYARD** NEWBERG, OR | 497

BELLA LUNA

FAVORITE FOOD: BIRDS
OBSESSION: THE FULL MOON
KNOWN ACCOMPLICES: THE KIND OF PEOPLE
WHO VISIT THE WINERY AND FEED HER
FAVORITE TOY: WHATEVER THE BABY IS PLAYING WITH
FAVORITE PASTIME: CHECKING THE PERIMETER OF THE VINEYARD

KNOWN ACCOMPLICE: BULLETT
PET PEEVE: ANY TRAINING TOOL
FAVORITE TOY: SMALL STUFFED ANIMALS
NAUGHTIEST DEEDS: DIGGING UP NEW FLOWERS IN
THE GARDEN AND BARKING AT STRANGE MEN
FAVORITE FOOD: HUMAN FOOD WHEN NO ONE'S LOOKING
FAVORITE PASTIMES: PLAYING BALL AND CHASING THE KIDS
OBSESSION: TAKING STUFFED ANIMAL TOYS OUT WITH HER TO USE THE POTTY

MESA

OWNERS: THE REYNOLDS FAMILY | AUSTRALIAN SHEPHERD, 11 MONTHS | REYNOLDS FAMILY WINERY NAPA, CA /99

FAVORITE FOOD: BONES
KNOWN ACCOMPLICE: HOLLY
NAUGHTIEST DEED: STEALING
THE VINEYARD CREW'S LUNCH
FAVORITE TOY: TENNIS BALLS
FAVORITE PASTIME: PLAYING FETCH
OBSESSIONS: FOOD AND SWIMMING
PET PEEVE: NOT GETTING ENOUGH ATTENTION

KODY

VIADER DEER PARK, CA | LABRADOR, 8 | OWNERS: THE VIADER FAMILY

FAVORITE FOOD: BONES
OBSESSION: GOING TO WORK
FAVORITE PASTIME: PLAYING TUG OF WAR
FAVORITE TOY: STUFFED PORCUPINE THAT SQUEAKS A LOT
PET PEEVE: ALAN AND MARIELA NOT GETTING UP TO PLAY AT 6AM
NAUGHTIEST DEED: SLEEPING ON THE BED WHEN NO ONE'S HOME

EMMA

HOLLY

FAVORITE FOOD: BONES
KNOWN ACCOMPLICE: KODY
FAVORITE PASTIME: SLEEPING
OBSESSION: HAVING HER BELLY RUBBED
PET PEEVE: ANYBODY WITH A UTILITY BELT
NAUGHTIEST DEED: GETTING INTO THE
GARBAGE AFTER EVENTS AT THE WINERY
FAVORITE TOY: ROPE WITH A BALL ON THE END OF IT

FAVORITE FOOD: GRAPES
OBSESSION: HUMAN MOM
FAVORITE TOY: TENNIS BALL
FAVORITE PASTIME: SNIFFING
KNOWN ACCOMPLICE: ANYONE WITH A TREAT
NAUGHTIEST DEED: EATING EXPENSIVE SUNGLASSES
PET PEEVES: NOT GOING FOR A WALK OR GETTING ATTENTION

CASH

KONA

OBSESSION: HUMAN MOM
FAVORITE FOOD: LIVERWURST
FAVORITE TOYS: ANY BALL OR CHEW TOY
FAVORITE PASTIMES: BARKING AND EATING
KNOWN ACCOMPLICE: ANYONE WITH A TREAT
PET PEEVES: NOT GOING FOR A WALK OR GETTING ATTENTION

FAVORITE FOOD: LEFTOVERS
NAUGHTIEST DEED: EATING THE COUCH
FAVORITE TOY: ANY BALL OR CHEW TOY
FAVORITE PASTIMES: BARKING AND EATING
PET PEEVES: NOT GOING FOR A WALK OR GETTING ATTENTION

FRITZ

OWNERS: CLAY AND FREDERICKA THOMPSON | WINE DOG, 9 | **CLAIBORNE & CHURCHILL** SAN LUIS OBISPO, CA | 505

PET PEEVE: BAD WINE
OBSESSION: YOGA BALL
FAVORITE TOY: RUBBER CRABBY
FAVORITE FOOD: FRENCH CHEESE
KNOWN ACCOMPLICE: TOFFEE THE SHIH TZU
FAVORITE PASTIME: EATING HUMAN FOOD
NAUGHTIEST DEED: SNEAKING OUTSIDE TO CHASE CATS

COCO

BUEHLER VINEYARDS ST. HELENA, CA | SHIH TZU, 3 | OWNERS: THE BUEHLER FAMILY

PET PEEVE: BANDIT
FAVORITE FOOD: CAT FOOD
KNOWN ACCOMPLICE: PAGE
FAVORITE TOY: THE SIAMESE CAT
FAVORITE PASTIMES: EATING THE CAT'S
FOOD AND SWIMMING IN THE ESTATE POOL
OBSESSIONS: TOURISTS – THE OFFICIAL WINERY GREETER
NAUGHTIEST DEED: PEEING ON BANDIT, THE MINIATURE POODLE

PORTO

CELIA

KNOWN ACCOMPLICE: OLIVE
FAVORITE PASTIME: NAPPING
FAVORITE FOOD: FILET MIGNON
NAUGHTIEST DEED: GOING AWOL
FAVORITE TOY: OLIVE THE BABY SISTER
PET PEEVE: SHARING HER BED WITH OLIVE
OBSESSION: RETRIEVING THE MORNING PAPER

SILVER OAK CELLARS GEYSERVILLE, CA | A-1 MUTT, 7 | OWNERS: TIM AND ROO DUNCAN

PET PEEVE: NAPPING
OBSESSION: CHEWING
KNOWN ACCOMPLICE: CELIA
FAVORITE FOOD: FILET MIGNON
FAVORITE TOY: BIG SISTER CELIA
NAUGHTIEST DEED: CHASING THE CHICKENS
FAVORITE PASTIME: CHEWING ON ANYTHING

OLIVE

FAVORITE TOY: STICKS
OBSESSION: FOX NEWS
KNOWN ACCOMPLICE: NIMITY
NAUGHTIEST DEED: SHAKING
WATER ON WINERY GUESTS
FAVORITE FOOD: ARTISAN CHEESES
PET PEEVE: DAD LEAVING FOR WORK
FAVORITE PASTIMES: SNUGGLING AND TV

PEPPER

FAVORITE TOY: SHOES
PET PEEVE: BEING LEFT ALONE
KNOWN ACCOMPLICE: PEPPER
OBSESSION: ROLLING IN DIRT
NAUGHTIEST DEED: EATING SHOES
FAVORITE FOOD: WHATEVER JOHN'S EATING
FAVORITE PASTIMES: CHASING BIRDS AND SWIMMING

NIMITY

510 | **JORDAN WINERY** HEALDSBURG, CA | LABRADORS, 12 AND 2 | OWNER: JOHN JORDAN

FAVORITE FOOD: GREENIES
FAVORITE TOY: WINE CORKS
KNOWN ACCOMPLICE: SHORTY
PET PEEVE: BEING SCOLDED
FOR CHEWING UP WINE CORKS
NAUGHTIEST DEED: CHEWING UP WINE CORKS
FAVORITE PASTIME: CHEWING UP WINE CORKS
OBSESSION: TAKING CARE OF THE NALLE'S ROAD

PIP

PET PEEVE: BEING SCOLDED
FAVORITE TOY: BASKETBALLS
FAVORITE FOOD: WHITE BREAD
KNOWN ACCOMPLICES: PIP AND SHORTY
FAVORITE PASTIME: SHOPPING FOR LIZARDS AND BUNNIES
OBSESSION: HUNTING FOR MICE AND LIZARDS IN THE VINES
NAUGHTIEST DEED: RIPPING VINES APART TO GET LIZARDS OR MICE

OWNERS: TOM AND TINA MAPLE | 50 POUND MIX 6 | **MAPLE VINEYARDS** HEALDSBURG, CA | 513

FAVORITE TOY: HIS KITTEN MISTY
PET PEEVE: THAT HE CAN'T EAT STEAK DAILY
FAVORITE FOOD: ANYTHING – HE'S A BEAGLE
FAVORITE PASTIME: ROAMING THE VINEYARD HILLS
OBSESSION: FOLLOWING HIS NOSE WHEREVER IT LEADS HIM
NAUGHTIEST DEED: EATING THE STEAKS AT A EMPLOYEE CHRISTMAS BBQ
KNOWN ACCOMPLICE: HIS KITTEN MISTY, COUSIN NALA AND HIS CAT SEABISCUIT

ELVIS

FAVORITE FOOD: PIG EARS
OBSESSION: 4-WHEELER RIDES
FAVORITE PASTIME: LAYING ON THE COUCH
FAVORITE TOYS: "DOG PERIGNON" CHAMPAGNE
BOTTLE TOY AND ROCKIE THE RACCOON
NAUGHTIEST DEED: TRYING TO STEAL ALL
THE FISHERMEN'S CATCHES OF THE DAY
PET PEEVE: HAVING A FINGER POINTED AT HER
KNOWN ACCOMPLICES: NALA, ZOE, SYRAH, ZINNY, MATTIE AND WILLOW

FINA

BACCI

PET PEEVE: THE CATS
FAVORITE TOY: ROCKS
KNOWN ACCOMPLICE: DAG
FAVORITE FOOD: PEOPLE FOOD
OBSESSION: RIDING IN THE ATV
FAVORITE PASTIME: PLAYING BALL
NAUGHTIEST DEED: CHASING THE CATS AND SKUNKS

FAVORITE TOY: BUNGS
PET PEEVE: BIG DOGS
OBSESSION: KAYAKING
KNOWN ACCOMPLICE: BACCI
FAVORITE FOOD: PEOPLE FOOD
FAVORITE PASTIME: CHASING BUNGS AND BALLS
NAUGHTIEST DEED: TRYING TO STEAL BUNGS FROM BARRELS

DAG

PET PEEVE: BEING IGNORED
OBSESSION: HIS SQUEAKY BALL
FAVORITE FOOD: DOGGIE TREATS
FAVORITE TOY: HIS SQUEAKY BALL
NAUGHTIEST DEED: MARKING IN THE HOUSE
FAVORITE PASTIME: PLAYING WITH HIS TOYS
KNOWN ACCOMPLICES: COCOA, GEORGE AND KATY

BUDDY

FAVORITE FOOD: RARE STEAK
FAVORITE PASTIME: SUNBATHING
FAVORITE TOY: CHEWING RAWHIDE
PET PEEVE: STRANGERS AT THE DOOR
KNOWN ACCOMPLICES: BUDDY, GEORGE AND KATY
OBSESSION: BURROWING IN BLANKETS AND CLEAN CLOTHES
NAUGHTIEST DEED: PULLING ORNAMENTS OFF THE CHRISTMAS TREE

COCOA

MOLLY BLUE

FAVORITE TOY: BALLS
OBSESSION: JACK RABBITS
FAVORITE FOOD: AFTER-DINNER COOKIES
PET PEEVE: NOT CATCHING JACK RABBITS
FAVORITE PASTIME: HERDING GOATS
NAUGHTIEST DEED: STEALING A
RUGBY BALL DURING THE GAME

OBSESSION: ATTENTION
FAVORITE FOOD: PEANUT BUTTER
KNOWN ACCOMPLICES: YORKI AND CYRUS
PET PEEVES: FIRE ALARM AND THUNDERSTORMS
NAUGHTIEST DEED: STEALING SOCKS FROM THE LAUNDRY BIN
FAVORITE PASTIMES: SLEEPING ON THE SOFA AND RUNNING IN THE CAVE
FAVORITE TOYS: ANYTHING PLUSH OR STUFFED, OR HER WOOBIE WATER TOY

MEL

SLEY AND JESSICA

JAKE JR

OBSESSION: SUNGLASSES
PET PEEVE: GOING TO THE KENNEL
FAVORITE TOYS: SOFT TOYS, BALLS AND KONGS
KNOWN ACCOMPLICES: BROCK AND AUNT JULIE
FAVORITE PASTIME: RESTING ON BED WITH ALL HIS TOYS
NAUGHTIEST DEED: CHEWING FOUR PAIRS OF MOM'S SUNGLASSES

PET PEEVE: LINDA'S SINGING
FAVORITE TOY: HER LITTLE SISTER, DITTO
FAVORITE FOODS: ICE CUBES AND CASHEWS
KNOWN ACCOMPLICES: MOLLY MALONE, MANDY AND DITTO
FAVORITE PASTIME: MOUTH WRESTLING WITH HER SISTER, DITTO
OBSESSIONS: LOOKING FOR SQUIRRELS AND DIGGING FOR GOPHERS

MINDY

SHELBY

FAVORITE FOOD: APPLE CORES
PET PEEVE: BEING LEFT ALONE
OBSESSION: CHASING SQUIRRELS
FAVORITE TOYS: TOY CHICKEN AND SKATE
NAUGHTIEST DEED: EATING A WHOLE LOAF OF BREAD
KNOWN ACCOMPLICES: MAGGIE #1, MAGGIE #2, CHAMP AND COCOA
FAVORITE PASTIMES: EATING, CHASING SQUIRRELS, WALKS AND SKIING

OBSESSION: BEING FIRST IN LINE
FAVORITE FOODS: SLOW ROASTED BEEF
AND THE KID'S LEFTOVER BACON
NAUGHTIEST DEED: TRYING TO HERD THE
SURLY NEIGHBOR'S CATTLE IN THE POURING RAIN
KNOWN ACCOMPLICES: PYGMY GOATS AND A COYOTE
FAVORITE PASTIME: BEING THE CENTER OF ATTENTION
PET PEEVES: HAVING HIS TAIL TOUCHED AND HIS PAWS TICKLED

RICO

SCOUT

FAVORITE TOY: BONES
FAVORITE FOOD: BACON
OBSESSION: SQUEAKY TOYS
FAVORITE PASTIMES: SLEEPING AND EATING
KNOWN ACCOMPLICE: BEST FRIEND CHOWDER
NAUGHTIEST DEED: RUNNING OFF WITH CHOWDER
AND REQUIRING A HELICOPTER TO BE FOUND
PET PEEVE: NOT GOING TO THE WINERY OFTEN ENOUGH

FAVORITE FOOD: PORK
FAVORITE TOY: HER KONG
OBSESSION: HUNTING
FAVORITE PASTIME: GIVING CHASE
KNOWN ACCOMPLICE: BEST FRIEND SCOUT
NAUGHTIEST DEED: THE 'HELICOPTER' INCIDENT

CHOWDER

MAX AKA SCHMOO

PET PEEVE: FRENCH BULLDOGS
FAVORITE FOOD: BORDELAIS SAUCE
OBSESSION: ANY VARMINT THAT MOVES
NAUGHTIEST DEED: LOVING CATS TO DEATH
FAVORITE TOY: STUFFED CHIRPING BIRD FROM THE AUDUBON SOCIETY
FAVORITE PASTIME: LAYING RIGHT IN FRONT OF THE OVEN IN HIS MOM'S WAY

FAVORITE TOY: BUNG
PET PEEVE: SWIMMING
FAVORITE PASTIME: CHASING COYOTES
KNOWN ACCOMPLICES: MAX, CODY AND GEORGE
NAUGHTIEST DEED: CHEWING UP HER MOM'S BACKPACK
OBSESSION: BEING FED AND PETTED BEFORE HER BROTHER MAX
FAVORITE FOOD: ANYTHING THE VINEYARD CREW GIVE HER, EXCEPT JALAPENOS

LUPE

CURLY

FAVORITE FOOD: BEEF JERKY
FAVORITE PASTIME: RUNNING
KNOWN ACCOMPLICES: HIS FAMILY
OBSESSION: CHASING BIRDS AND RABBITS
FAVORITE TOY: CHARLOTTE'S STUFFED ANIMALS
NAUGHTIEST DEED: WANDERING THE NEIGHBORHOOD
PET PEEVE: NOT BEING ABLE TO CATCH ANY RABBITS

STATS, FACTS
AND MORE LIES...
by Craig McGill

We often get asked questions about the production of our books. So here are some answers relating to Wine Dogs USA 2 *most-asked questions. Stay tuned for our 'Wine Dogs Trivial Pursuit' board game due for release for next Christmas (..not actually true). These answers will give you a much-needed advantage over your fellow players (... probably not).*

- *Number of days of photography: 85*

- *Miles traveled by car: 12,580 miles*

- *Miles traveled by plane: 19,152.6 miles*

- *Number of States visited: 9 (California three times, Oregon twice, Washington, Idaho, Maryland, Virginia, Tennessee, Arkansas and Texas)*

- *Amount of times we got lost: nil*

- *Amount of wrong turns: 3*

- *Flat tires: 1*

- *Most common dog breed: Labrador (107)*

- *Least common breed: Spotted Norwegian elephant hound*

- *Number of wineries featured in this edition: 315*

- *Total number of dogs photographed for this edition: 450*

- *Number of wineries visited worldwide by Wine Dogs: 1,214 (as of April 2008)*

- *Hamburgers consumed by the photographer: 16 (in one sitting: 2)*

- *Number of dogs referred to by the owner as 'gifted' or a 'genius': 33*

- *Number of dogs that couldn't sit when asked: 258*

- *Number of pedigree dogs: 78*

- *Number of rescue dogs: 319*

- *Number of dogs with botox or cosmetic surgery: 3*

- Number of times the photographer was bitten by a dog: nil

- Number of times the photographer was bitten by the owner: 2

- Number of times the photographer bit the dog: 1

- Most common dog name: Bella (9)

- Number of dogs named after grape varieties: 10

- Number of bottle of wines gifted by generous wineries: 324

- Number of wines tasted: 1,260

- Number of dogs with lingerie fetishes: 6

- Number of dogs that drink wine or eat grapes (not recommended for health reasons): 112

- Favorite restaurant: Deborah's Room, Justin Vineyards, Paso Robles CA

- Favorite brewpub: Golden Valley, McMinnville OR

- Favorite bakery: Bouchon Bakery, Yountville CA

- Favorite wine bar: Vintner's Collective, Napa CA

- Favorite café: Nick's Italian Café, McMinnville OR

- Favorite record store: Waterloo, Austin TX

- Most original dog name: The Scheming Beagle ("Duhg") Stone House Vineyard, TX

- Number of dogs that have their own business cards: 3

- Number of dogs that have eaten furniture or electrical appliances: 8

- Number of dogs with only three legs: 3

- Number of dogs "turned-on" by being photographed: 39

ALL PHOTOGRAPHY © CRAIG McGILL 2008

SUSAN ELLIOTT

SYDNEY, NSW

SUSAN IS A MULTI-SKILLED ARTIST WITH A BACKGROUND IN FINE ART, ILLUSTRATION AND PRINTMAKING. AFTER COMPLETING TWO YEARS OF A PSYCHOLOGY DEGREE, SUE CHANGED TO A CAREER IN ART. SHE GRADUATED FROM THE CITY ART INSTITUTE IN 1986, MAJORING IN DRAWING, PRINTMAKING AND PAINTING.

AFTER TWO YEARS LIVING ABROAD, SUE RETURNED TO AUSTRALIA AND EXHIBITED HER GRAPHIC ART AND SCREENPRINTS EXTENSIVELY AROUND SYDNEY, WHILE ALSO WORKING IN A NUMBER OF SMALL DESIGN STUDIOS. SHE HAS DEVELOPED INTO AN AWARD-WINNING GRAPHIC DESIGNER WITH OVER 20 YEARS OF EXPERIENCE IN THE INDUSTRY.

Stella and Sue

SUE JOINED McGILL DESIGN GROUP IN 1999 AS CO-OWNER AND CREATIVE DIRECTOR. SHE IS ALSO CO-FOUNDER AND PRINCIPAL OF THE GIANT DOG PUBLISHING HOUSE, WHICH IS RESPONSIBLE FOR PRODUCING A NUMBER OF BEST-SELLING BOOKS, INCLUDING THE WINE DOGS AND FOOTY DOGS TITLES.

FAVORITE FOOD: NOODLES
FAVORITE PASTIME: WATCHING MOVIES WITH STELLA
NAUGHTIEST DEED: TEASING HUSKIES
KNOWN ACCOMPLICE: CASPER THE GHOST KNIFE FISH
OBSESSIONS: BATH SALTS AND CRYPTIC CROSSWORDS
PET HATES: WHISTLING AND RAISIN TOAST WITH PEEL

SUE'S KNOWLEDGE OF DOGS IS UNPARALLELED, AND IN THE PAST SHE HAS ALSO FOUND TIME TO BE A SUCCESSFUL SIBERIAN HUSKY BREEDER. SHE IS CONSIDERED AMONGST THE PACK TO BE A GREAT OWNER. SUE IS A LOVER OF ALL WHITE WINE AND USUALLY REACHES FOR HER FAVORITE RIESLING WHEN FEELING A LITTLE HUSKY.

GIANT DOG PUBLISHING

GIANT DOG IS A NICHE INDEPENDENT PUBLISHING HOUSE SPECIALISING IN PRODUCING BENCHMARK QUALITY DESIGN AND ART BOOKS. RECENT PUBLICATIONS INCLUDE *WINE DOGS ITALY*, *WINE DOGS AUSTRALIA*, *WINE DOGS NEW ZEALAND*, *WINE DOGS DELUXE EDITION*, *FOOTY DOGS* AND *WINE DOGS: USA EDITION*. www.giantdog.com.au

CRAIG McGILL

SYDNEY, NSW

ORIGINALLY FROM SHEPPARTON, VICTORIA, CRAIG IS A SELF-TAUGHT DESIGNER AND ILLUSTRATOR WHO STARTED HIS OWN DESIGN BUSINESS IN MELBOURNE AT 18 YEARS OF AGE. DURING THAT TIME HE WAS APPOINTED AS A DESIGN CONSULTANT TO THE RESERVE BANK OF AUSTRALIA.

HIS DESIGNS AND ILLUSTRATIONS HAVE GRACED BANKNOTES THROUGHOUT THE WORLD, INCLUDING THE AUSTRALIAN BICENTENARY TEN-DOLLAR NOTE. HIS WORK APPEARS ON THE ORIGINAL AUSTRALIAN $100 NOTE, PAPUA NEW GUINEA KINA, COOK ISLAND DOLLARS AND ENGLISH POUND TRAVELLER'S CHEQUES. CRAIG WAS ALSO INVOLVED IN THE DESIGN AND ILLUSTRATION OF MANY COUNTRIES' SECURITY DOCUMENTS SUCH AS PASSPORTS, BONDS AND TRAVELLER'S CHEQUES.

AT THE AGE OF 23 HE DESIGNED THE ENTIRE SERIES OF THE COOK ISLAND BANKNOTES AND IT IS BELIEVED THAT HE WAS THE WORLD'S YOUNGEST DESIGNER TO DESIGN A COUNTRY'S COMPLETE CURRENCY. IN 1991, CRAIG MOVED TO SYDNEY WHERE HIS ILLUSTRATIONS WERE REGULARLY COMMISSIONED BY AGENCIES AND DESIGNERS BOTH IN AUSTRALIA AND AROUND THE WORLD.

Craig and Tarka

DATE OF BIRTH: DEAD IN DOG YEARS

FAVORITE FOOD: ROAST DUCK AND PINOT NOIR

FAVORITE PASTIMES: VENTRILOQUISM AND BEING A BIG KID

NAUGHTIEST DEED: CHASING HUSKIES WHILE STARK NAKED

OBSESSIONS: BEER, WINE AND COLLECTING USELESS THINGS

KNOWN ACCOMPLICES: THE VOICES IN MY HEAD

PET HATE: UNORIGINAL IDEAS

HE IS NOW WIDELY KNOWN AS AUSTRALIA'S ONLY FREELANCE CURRENCY DESIGNER. CRAIG HAS ALSO DESIGNED AND ILLUSTRATED FIVE STAMPS FOR AUSTRALIA POST.

CRAIG HAS BEEN CREATIVE DIRECTOR OF HIS OWN AGENCY, McGILL DESIGN GROUP, FOR OVER TWENTY-THREE YEARS.

HAVING GROWN UP WITH A SUCCESSION OF BEAGLES, CRAIG IS NOW OWNED BY TWO SIBERIAN HUSKIES. www.realnasty.com.au

McGILL DESIGN GROUP

McGILL DESIGN GROUP WAS FORMED IN 1981 AND SPECIALISES IN PROVIDING A WIDE RANGE OF QUALITY GRAPHIC DESIGN SERVICES. THE STUDIO HAS PRODUCED NUMEROUS FINE WINE LABELS AND PACKAGING AS WELL AS CORPORATE IDENTITIES, ADVERTISING, PUBLICATIONS AND TELEVISION COMMERCIALS. www.mcgilldesigngroup.com

WINERY AND VINEYARD LISTINGS

CALIFORNIA

1. Alpha Omega PAGE 393
1155 Mee Ln, Rutherford CA 94573
Phone: 707 963 9999
Email: info@aowinery.com
Web: www.aowinery.com

2. Ambullneo Vineyards PAGE 408
3100 Rancho Tepesquet Rd,
Santa Maria CA 93454
Phone: 805 934 1516
Email: greg@ambullneovineyards.com
Web: www.ambullneovineyards.com

3. Arger-Martucci PAGE 382
1455 Inglewood Ave,
St. Helena CA 94574
Phone: 707 963 4334
Email: katie@arger-martucci.com
Web: www.arger-martucci.com

4. Arnot-Roberts PAGE 205
6450 First St, Forestville CA 95436
Phone: 707 820 1383
Email: mail@arnotroberts.com
Web: www.arnotroberts.com

5. AronHill Vineyards PAGES 193–195
2500 Vineyard Dr, Templeton CA 93465
Phone: 805 772 8181
Email: info@aronhillvineyards.com
Web: www.aronhillvineyards.com

6. Atalon Winery PAGE 401
3299 Bennett Ln, Calistoga CA 94515
Phone: 707 942 3602
Email: info@atalon.com
Web: www.atalon.com

7. B & E Winery PAGE 135
10000 Criston Rd, Paso Robles CA 93446
Phone: 805 238 4815
Email: bevineyard@aol.com

8. B. R. Cohn Winery PAGE 10
15000 Sonoma Hwy,
Glen Ellen CA 95442
Phone: 800 330 4064
Email: info@brcohn.com
Web: www.brcohn.com

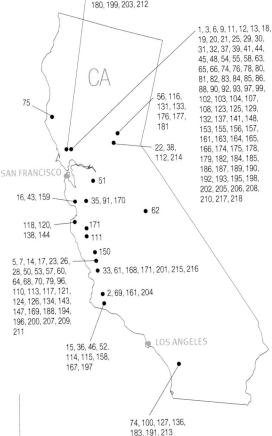

4, 8, 10, 24, 27, 34, 40, 47, 49, 59, 67, 71, 73, 77, 87, 89, 94, 95, 98, 101, 105, 106, 109, 119, 122, 128, 130, 135, 139, 140, 142, 145, 146, 149, 151, 152, 154, 162, 172, 180, 199, 203, 212

CA

1, 3, 6, 9, 11, 12, 13, 18, 19, 20, 21, 25, 29, 30, 31, 32, 37, 39, 41, 44, 45, 48, 54, 55, 58, 63, 65, 66, 74, 76, 78, 80, 81, 82, 83, 84, 85, 86, 88, 90, 92, 93, 97, 99, 102, 103, 104, 107, 108, 123, 125, 129, 132, 137, 141, 148, 153, 155, 156, 157, 161, 163, 164, 165, 166, 174, 175, 178, 179, 182, 184, 185, 186, 187, 189, 190, 192, 193, 195, 198, 202, 205, 206, 208, 210, 217, 218

56, 116, 131, 133, 176, 177, 181

22, 38, 112, 214

75

SAN FRANCISCO

51

16, 43, 159

35, 91, 170

62

118, 120, 138, 144

171

111

150

5, 7, 14, 17, 23, 26, 28, 50, 53, 57, 60, 64, 68, 70, 79, 96, 110, 113, 117, 121, 124, 134, 143, 147, 169, 188, 194, 196, 200, 207, 209, 211

33, 61, 168, 171, 201, 215, 216

2, 69, 161, 204

LOS ANGELES

15, 36, 46, 52, 114, 115, 158, 167, 197

74, 100, 127, 136, 183, 191, 213

9. Baldacci Family Vineyards PAGE 405
6236 Silverado Trail, Napa CA 94558
Phone: 707 944 9261
Email: info@baldaccivineyards.com
Web: www.baldaccivineyards.com

**10. Balletto Vineyards
and Winery** PAGE 223
5700 Occidental Rd, Santa Rosa CA 95401
Phone: 707 568 2455
Email: info@ballettovineyards.com
Web: www.ballettovineyards.com

11. Barnett Vineyards PAGE 482
4070 Spring Mountain Rd,
  St. Helena CA 94574
Phone: 707 963 7075
Web: www.barnettvineyards.com

12. Beaulieu Vineyard PAGE 291
1960 St. Helena Hwy, Rutherford CA 94573
Phone: 707 967 5200
Email: bvinfo@bvwines.com
Web: www.bvwines.com

**13. Behrens & Hitchcock /
  Erna Schein Winery** PAGES 484, 485
4078 Spring Mountain Rd,
  St. Helena CA 94574
Phone: 707 963 1774
Email: info@behrensandhitchcock.com
Web: www.behrensandhitchcock.com

14. Bella Luna Winery PAGES 162, 163
1850 Templeton Rd, Templeton CA 93465
Phone: 805 434 5477
Email: info@bellalunawine.com
Web: www.bellalunawine.com

15. Blair Fox Cellars PAGE 407
PO Box 358, Los Olivos CA 93441
Phone: 805 691 1678
Email: info@blairfoxcellars.com
Web: www.blairfoxcellars.com

16. Bonny Doon Vineyard PAGE 50
328 Ingalls St, Santa Cruz CA 95060
Phone: 831 425 4518
Email: tasting@bonnydoonvineyard.com
Web: www.bonnydoonvineyard.com

17. Booker Vineyard PAGE 79
2640 Antarson Rd, Paso Robles CA 93446
Phone: 805 237 7367
Email: eric@bookerwines.com
Web: www.bookerwines.com

18. Bourassa Vineyards PAGE 481
190 Camino Oruga, Napa CA 94558
Phone: 707 254 4922
Web: www.bourassavineyards.com

19. Boyd Family Vineyard
  PAGES 449–451
4042 Big Ranch Rd, Napa CA 94558
Phone: 707 254 7353
Email: info@boydwine.com
Web: www.boydwine.com

20. Bravante Vineyards PAGE 471
330 Stone Ridge Rd, Angwin CA 94508
Phone: 707 972 1114
Email: michelle@bravantewine.com
Web: www.bravantewine.com

21. Buehler Vineyards PAGES 506, 507
820 Greenfield Rd, St. Helena CA 94574
Phone: 707 963 2155
Email: buehlers@pacbell.net
Web: www.buehlervineyards.com

22. Busby Cellars PAGE 373
6375 Grizzly Flat Rd, Somerset CA 95684
Phone: 530 344 9119
Email: info@busbycellars.com
Web: www.busbycellars.com

23. Calcareous Vineyard PAGE 430
3430 Peachy Canyon Rd, Paso Robles
  CA 93446
Phone: 805 239 0289
Email: bobd@calcareous.com
Web: www.calcareous.com

24. Calluna Vineyards PAGE 115
11450 Brooks Rd, Windsor CA 95492
Phone: 707 239 1325
Email: davidajeffrey@gmail.com
Web: www.callunavineyards.com

25. Castello di Amorosa PAGE 12
4045 North St. Helena Hwy, Calistoga
  CA 94515
Phone: 707 942 8200
Email: info@castellodiamorosa.com
Web: www.castellodiamorosa.com

26. Cayucos Cellars PAGE 192
131 N Ocean Ave, Cayucos CA 93430
Phone: 805 995 3036
Email: cayucoscellars@yahoo.com
Web: www.cayucoscellars.com

27. Chateau Felice Winery PAGE 11
10603 Chalk Hill Rd, Healdsburg CA 95448
Phone: 707 431 9010
Email: info@chateaufelice.com
Web: www.chateaufelice.com

28. Chateau Margene PAGE 272
4385 La Panza Rd, Creston CA 93432
Phone: 805 238 2321
Email: info@chateaumargene.com
Web: www.chateaumargene.com

29. Chateau Montelena PAGE 206
1429 Tubbs Ln, Calistoga CA 94515
Phone: 707 942 1105
Email: customer-service@montelena.com
Web: www.montelena.com

**30. Chateau Potelle Winery /
Gravity Hills Winery** PAGES 295–299
975 Washington St, Napa CA 94559
Phone: 707 265 1282
Email: info@chateaupotelle.com
Web: www.chateaupotelle.com

31. Chiarello Family Vineyards
PAGES 110, 111
PO Box 3596, Yountville CA 94599
Phone: 707 256 0750
Email: wines@chiarellovineyards.com
Web: www.chiarellovineyards.com

32. Chimney Rock Winery PAGE 395
5350 Silverado Trail, Napa CA 94558
Phone: 707 257 2641
Email: tom@chimneyrock.com
Web: www.chimneyrock.com

33. Claiborne & Churchill PAGES 503–505
2649 Carpenter Canyon Rd,
San Luis Obispo CA 93401
Phone: 805 544 4066
Email: info@claibornechurchill.com
Web: www.claibornechurchill.com

34. Clos du Bois PAGE 374
19410 Geyserville Ave, Geyserville
CA 95441
Phone: 707 857 1651
Email: TastingRoom@closdubois.com
Web: www.closdubois.com

35. Clos LaChance Winery PAGES 402–404
1 Hummingbird Ln, San Martin CA 95046
Phone: 408 686 1050
Email: cheryl@clos.com
Web: www.clos.com

36. Clos Pepe Vineyard PAGES 74, 75
4777 East Hwy 246, Lompoc CA 93436
Phone: 805 735 2196
Email: wes@clospepe.com
Web: www.clospepe.com

37. Colgin Cellars PAGES 200–203
PO Box 254, St. Helena CA 94574
Phone: 707 963 0999
Email: info@colgincellars.com
Web: www.colgincellars.com

**38. Colibri Ridge Winery
and Vineyard** PAGES 464, 465
6100 Gray Rock Rd, Fair Play CA 95684
Phone: 530 620 7255
Email: info@colibriridge.com
Web: www.colibriridge.com

**39. CONSTANT-Diamond Mountain
Vineyard** PAGE 359
2121 Diamond Mountain Rd,
Calistoga CA 94515
Phone: 707 942 0707
Email: freddy@constantwine.com
Web: www.constantwine.com

40. Coral Mustang PAGE 43
1136 Palomino Rd, Cloverdale CA 95425
Phone: 707 894 0145
Email: penelope@coralmustang.com
Web: www.coralmustang.com

41. Cosentino Winery PAGES 336, 337
7415 St. Helena Hwy, Yountville CA 94599
Phone: 707 944 1220
Web: www.cosentinowinery.com

42. Coufos Cellars PAGE 461
10065 Rough & Ready Rd,
Rough & Ready CA 95975
Phone: 530 274 2923
Email: coufoscellars@comcast.net

43. Crystal Creek Vineyards PAGE 17
101 Happy Valley Rd, Santa Cruz CA 95065
Phone: 831 457 9362

44. Cuvaison Estate Wines PAGE 486
4515 Silverado Trail, Calistoga CA 94515
Phone: 707 942 2470
Email: info@cuvaison.com
Web: www.cuvaison.com

45. D. R. Stephens PAGE 454
1860 Howell Mountain Rd, St. Helena
CA 94574
Phone: 707 963 2908
Email: info@drstephenswines.com
Web: www.drstephenswines.com

46. D'Alfonso-Curran Wines PAGES 312, 313
4435 Santa Rosa Rd, Lompoc CA 93436
Phone: 805 736 9463
Email: info@curranwines.com
Web: www.curranwines.com

47. DaVero PAGES 228, 229
766 Westside Rd, Healdsburg, CA 95448
Phone: 707 433 2345
Email: webquery@davero.com
Web: www.DaVero.com

48. David Fulton PAGE 325
825 Fulton Ln, St. Helena CA 94574
Phone: 707 967 0719
Email: dink@davidfultonwinery.com
Web: www.davidfultonwinery.com

49. Del Carlo Winery PAGES 56, 57
4939 Dry Creek Rd, Healdsburg CA 95448
Phone: 707 433 1036
Email: lori@delcarlowinery.com
Web: www.delcarlowinery.com

50. Derby Wine Estates PAGE 369
5620 Hwy 46 East, Paso Robles CA 93446
Phone: 800 659 0820
Email: info@derbywineestates.com
Web: www.derbywineestates.com

**51. Diablo Grande Vineyards /
Isom Ranch Winery** PAGE 243
11604 Upper Oak Flat Rd,
Patterson CA 95363
Phone: 209 402 1491
Email: thewinery@diablogrande.com
Web: www.diablogrande.com

52. Dierberg Vineyard PAGE 346
2121 Alisos Ave, Santa Ynez CA 93460
Phone: 805 693 0744
Email: info@dierbergvineyard.com
Web: www.dierbergvineyard.com

53. Doce Robles Winery PAGES 93–95
2023 Twelve Oaks Dr, Paso Robles
CA 93446
Phone: 805 227 4766
Email: sales@docerobles.com
Web: www.docerobles.com

54. Domaine Carneros PAGES 145–153
1240 Duhig Rd, Napa CA 94559
Phone: 707 257 0101
Email: wbruce@domainecarneros.com
Web: www.domainecarneros.com

55. Dominari PAGE 386
PO Box 5060, Napa CA 94581
Phone: 707 226 1600
Email: marieschutz@dominari.com
Web: www.dominari.com

**56. Double Oak Vineyards
and Winery** PAGE 468
14510 Blind Shady Rd,
Nevada City CA 95959
Phone: 530 292 3235
Email: virginia@doubleoakwinery.com
Web: www.doubleoakwinery.com

57. Dover Canyon Winery PAGE 191
4520 Vineyard Dr, Paso Robles CA 93446
Phone: 805 237 0101
Email: dovercanyon@tcsn.net
Web: www.dovercanyon.com

58. Duckhorn Vineyards PAGE 102
1000 Lodi Ln, St. Helena CA 94574
Phone: 888 354 8885 and 707 963 7108
Email: concierge@ duckhorn.com
Web: www.duckhorn.com

59. Dutcher Crossing Winery PAGE 255
8533 Dry Creek Rd, Geyserville CA 95441
Phone: 707 431 2700
Email: info@dutchercrossingwinery.com
Web: www.dutchercrossingwinery.com

60. Eberle Winery PAGES 96, 97
3810 Hwy 46 East, Paso Robles CA 93446
Phone: 805 238 9607
Email: sales@eberlewinery.com
Web: www.eberlewinery.com

61. Edna Valley Vineyard PAGE 215
2585 Biddle Ranch Rd, San Luis Obispo
CA 93401
Phone: 805 544 5855
Email: EVVinfo@ednavalley.com
Web: www.ednavalleyvineyard.com

62. Engelmann Cellars PAGES 174, 175
3275 North Rolinda Ave, Fresno CA 93723
Phone: 559 274 9463
Email: ecellars@aol.com
Web: www.engelmanncellars.com

63. Envy Wines PAGE 339
1170 Tubbs Ln, Calistoga CA 94515
Phone: 707 942 4670
Email: info@envywines.com
Web: www.envywines.com

64. EOS Estate Winery PAGE 166
5625 Hwy 46 East, Paso Robles CA 93446
Phone: 805 239 2562
Email: info@eosvintage.com
Web: www.eosvintage.com

65. Esser Vineyards PAGE 51
Phone: 707 963 1300
Email: info@esservineyards.com
Web: www.esservineyards.com

66. Flora Springs Winery and Vineyards
PAGES 322–324
1978 West Zinfandel Ln, St. Helena
CA 94574
Phone: 707 963 5711
Email: info@florasprings.com
Web: www.florasprings.com

67. Foppiano Winery PAGE 310
12707 Old Redwood Hwy,
Healdsburg CA 95448
Phone: 707 433 7272
Web: www.foppiano.com

68. Four Vines Winery PAGE 8
3750 Hwy 46 West, Templeton CA 93645
Phone: 805 227 0865
Email: sales@fourvines.com
Web: www.fourvines.com

69. Foxen PAGE 420
7200 Foxen Canyon Rd,
Santa Maria CA 93454
Phone: 805 937 4251
Email: info@foxenvineyard.com
Web: www.foxenvineyard.com

70. Garretson Wine Company PAGE 132
2323 Tuley Crt, Suite 110, Paso Robles
CA 93446
Phone: 805 239 2074
Email: info@garretsonwines.com
Web: www.garretsonwines.com

71. Gary Farrell PAGES 100, 101
10701 Westside Rd, Healdsburg CA 95448
Phone: 707 473 2900
Email: concierge@garyfarrellwines.com
Web: www.garyfarrellwines.com

72. Gershon Bachus Vintners PAGE 428
37750 de Portola Rd, Temecula CA 92592
Phone: 951 693 9151
Email: info@gershonbachus.com
Web: www.gershonbachus.com

73. Geyser Peak PAGE 42
22281 Chianti Rd, Geyserville CA 95441
Phone: 800 255 9463
Web: www.geyserpeakwinery.com

74. Girard Winery PAGE 170
6795 Washington St, Yountville CA 94599
Phone: 707 968 9297
Email: sales@girardwinery.com
Web: www.girardwinery.com

75. Goldeneye Winery PAGE 372
9200 Hwy 128, Philo CA 95466
Phone: 800 208 0438
Email: hospitality@goldeneyewinery.com
Web: www.goldeneyewinery.com

76. Graeser Winery PAGE 463
255 Petrified Forest Rd, Calistoga CA 94515
Phone: 707 942 4437
Email: info@graeserwinery.com
Web: www.graeserwinery.com

77. Gundlach Bundschu Winery
PAGES 196–198
2000 Denmark St, Sonoma CA 95476
Phone: 707 938 5277
Email: info@gunbun.com
Web: www.gunbun.com

78. HALL Wines PAGES 344, 345
401 St. Helena Hwy South, St. Helena,
CA 94574
Phone: 707 967 2626
Email: info@hallwines.com
Web: www.hallwines.com

79. Halter Ranch Vineyard PAGE 488
8910 Adelaida Rd, Paso Robles CA 93446
Phone: 805 226 9455
Email: info@halterranch.com
Web: www.halterranch.com

80. Harris Estate Vineyards PAGE 522
225 Franz Valley School Rd, Calistoga
CA 94515
Phone: 707 942 1513
Email: estatecab@harrisestatevineyards.com
Web: www.harrisestatevineyards.com

81. Hartwell Vineyards PAGES 124,125
5795 Silverado Trail, Napa CA 94558
Phone: 707 255 4269
Email: info@hartwellvineyards.com
Web: www.hartwellvineyards.com

82. Heitz Wine Cellars PAGE 130
500 Taplin Rd, St. Helena CA 94574
Phone: 707 963 3542
Email: david@heitzcellar.com
Web: www.heitzcellar.com

83. Hendry PAGE 338
3104 Redwood Rd, Napa CA 94558
Phone: 707 226 8320
Email: info@hendrywines.com
Web: www.hendrywines.com

84. Hermosa Vineyards PAGES 282, 283
1350 Walnut Dr, Oakville CA 94562
Phone: 707 944 2110
Web: www.hermosavineyards.net

85. Hill Family Estate PAGES 24, 25
Tasting Room at Antique Fair:
  6512 Washington St, Yountville
  CA 94599
Phone: 707 944 9580
Email: info@hillfamilyestate.com
Web: www.hillfamilyestate.com

86. Honig Vineyard and Winery
  PAGES 436, 437
850 Rutherford Rd, Rutherford CA 94573
Phone: 707 963 5618
Email: info@honigwine.com
Web: www.honigwine.com

87. Hook & Ladder Winery PAGES 188, 189
2134 Olivet Rd, Santa Rosa CA 95401
Phone: 707 526 2255
Email: t_room@hookandladderwinery.com
Web: www.hookandladderwinery.com

88. Hopper Creek Winery PAGE 78
6204 Washington St, Yountville CA 94599
Phone: 707 944 0675
Email: dan@hoppercreek.com
Web: www.hoppercreek.com

89. J. Rickards Winery PAGES 300–303
24505 Chianti Rd, Cloverdale CA 95425
Phone: 707 758 3441
Email: info@jrwinery.com
Web: www.jrwinery.com

90. Jaffe Estate PAGES 446, 447
1240 Spring St, St. Helena CA 94574
Phone: 707 967 9146
Web: www.jaffeestate.com

91. Jason-Stephens Winery PAGE 414
11775 Watsonville Rd, Gilroy CA 95020
Phone: 408 846 8463
Email: jason@jstephens.com
Web: www.jstephens.com

92. Jax Vineyards PAGE 242
3468 Hwy 128, Calistoga CA 94515
Phone: 707 942 5225
Email: kimberly@jaxvineyards.com
Web: www.jaxvineyards.com

93. Jericho Canyon Vineyard PAGES 516, 517
3322 Old Lawley Toll Rd, Calistoga CA 94515
Phone: 707 942 9665
Web: www.jerichocanyonvineyard.com

94. Jordan Winery PAGE 510
1474 Alexander Valley Rd,
  Healdsburg CA 95448
Phone: 707 431 5250
Web: www.jordanwinery.com

95. Joseph Swan Vineyards PAGE 16
2916 Laguna Rd, Forestville CA 95436
Phone: 707 573 3747
Email: rod@swanwinery.com
Web: www.swanwinery.com

96. Justin Winery PAGES 80–82
11680 Chimney Rock Rd,
  Paso Robles CA 93446
Phone: 805 238 6932
Email: info@justinwine.com
Web: www.justinwine.com

97. Kelham Vineyards PAGES 34, 35
360 Zinfandel Ln, St. Helena CA 94574
Phone: 707 963 2000
Email: info@kelhamvineyards.com
Web: www.kelhamvineyards.com

98. Kendall-Jackson PAGES 104, 105
5007 Fulton Rd, Fulton CA 95439
Phone: 707 571 7500
Email: kjwines@kj.com
Web: www.kj.com

99. Kent Rasmussen Winery PAGE 448
1001 Silverado Trail, St. Helena CA 94574
Phone: 707 963 5667
Email: info@kentrasmussenwinery.com
Web: www.kentrasmussenwinery.com

**100. Keyways Vineyard
and Winery** PAGE 341
37338 De Portola Rd, Temecula CA 92592
Phone: 951 302 7888
Email: info@keywayswine.com
Web: www.keywayswine.com

101. Kokomo Winery PAGES 258, 259
4791 Dry Creek Rd, Healdsburg CA 95448
Phone: 707 433 0200
Email: info@kokomowines.com
Web: www.kokomowines.com

102. La Sirena PAGE 209
PO Box 441, Calistoga CA 94515
Phone: 707 942 1105
Email: winery@lasirenawine.com
Web: www.lasirenawine.com

103. Ladera Vineyards PAGES 76, 77
150 White Cottage Rd South,
Angwin CA 94508
Phone: 707 965 2445
Email: info@laderavineyards.com
Web: www.laderavineyards.com

104. Lail Vineyards PAGES 278–281
320 Stone Ridge Rd, Angwin CA 94508
Phone: 707 968 9900
Email: customerservice@lailvineyards.com
Web: www.lailvineyards.com

105. Lambert Bridge Winery PAGE 250
4085 West Dry Creek Rd,
Healdsburg CA 95448
Phone: 707 431 9600
Email: wines@lambertbridge.com
Web: www.lambertbridge.com

106. Lancaster Estate PAGES 444, 445
15001 Chalk Hill Rd, Healdsburg CA 95448
Phone: 707 433 8178
Email: info@lancaster-estate.com
Web: www.lancaster-estate.com

107. Lang & Reed Wine Company
PAGES 232, 233
1200 Oak Ave, St. Helena CA 94574
Phone: 707 963 7547
Email: info@langandreed.com
Web: www.langandreed.com

108. Larkmead Vineyards PAGE 131
1100 Larkmead Ln, Calistoga CA 94515
Phone: 707 942 0167
Email: info@larkmead.com
Web: www.larkmead.com

109. Larson Family Winery PAGES 424, 425
23355 Millerick Rd, Sonoma CA 95476
Phone: 707 938 3031
Email: tr@larsonfamilywinery.com
Web: www.larsonfamilywinery.com

110. Linne Calodo PAGE 210
3030 Vineyard Dr, Paso Robles CA 93446
Phone: 805 227 0797
Email: info@linnecalodo.com
Web: www.linnecalodo.com

111. Lockwood Vineyard PAGE 103
59020 Paris Valley Rd, San Lucas CA 93954
Phone: 831 382 4430
Email: lgomez@lockwood-wine.com
Web: lockwood-wine.com

112. Lodi Vintners PAGES 378, 379
3750 East Woodbridge, Woodbridge
CA 95820
Phone: 209 368 5338

113. Lone Madrone PAGE 222
2485 Hwy 46 West, Paso Robles CA 93446
Phone: 805 238 0845
Email: info@lonemadrone.com
Web: www.lonemadrone.com

114. Longoria Wines PAGE 409
2935 Grand Ave, Los Olivos CA 93441
Phone: 805 688 0305
Email: info@longoriawine.com
Web: www.longoriawine.com

115. Lucas & Lewellen Vineyards
PAGES 216, 217
1645 Copenhagen Dr, Solvang CA 93463
Phone: 805 686 9336
Email: lisa@llwine.com
Web: www.llwine.com

**116. Lucchesi Vineyards
and Winery** PAGE 380
19698 View Forever Ln, Grass Valley
CA 95945
Phone: 530 273 1596
Email: info@lucchesivineyards.com
Web: www.lucchesivineyards.com

117. Maloy O'Neill Vineyards PAGES 4, 230
5725 Union Rd, Paso Robles CA 93446
Phone: 805 238 7320
Email: winery@maloyoneill.com
Web: www.maloyoneill.com

118. Manzoni Estate Vineyard
PAGES 238, 239
30981 River Rd, Soledad CA 93960
Phone: 831 596 0183
Email: info@manzoniwines.com
Web: www.manzoniwines.com

119. Maple Vineyards PAGES 511–513
PO Box 1546, Healdsburg CA 95448
Phone: 707 431 7171
Email: info@maplezin.com
Web: www.maplezin.com

120. Marilyn Remark PAGE 355
645 River Rd, Salinas CA 93908
Phone: 831 455 9310
Email: joel@remarkwines.com
Web: www.remarkwines.com

121. Martin & Weyrich Winery
PAGES 178–181
2610 Buena Vista Dr, Paso Robles
CA 93446
Phone: 805 238 2520
Email: marketing@martinweyrich.com
Web: www.martinweyrich.com

122. Medlock Ames PAGES 46, 47
13414 Chalk Hill Rd, Healdsburg CA 95448
Phone: 707 431 8845
Email: ames@medlockames.com
Web: www.medlockames.com

123. Merus PAGE 487
PO Box 360, Napa CA 94559
Phone: 707 251 5551
Email: merus@meruswines.com
Web: www.meruswines.com

124. Midlife Crisis Winery PAGES 342, 343
PO Box 4082, Paso Robles CA 93447
Phone: 805 237 8730
Email: info@midlifecrisiswinery.com
Web: www.midlifecrisis.com

125. Miller Wine Works PAGE 370
PO Box 3148, Napa CA 94558
Phone: 707 254 9727
Email: kim@millerwineworks.com
Web: www.millerwineworks.com

126. Minassian-Young Vineyards
PAGES 86, 87
4045 Peachy Canyon Rd, Paso Robles
CA 93446
Phone: 805 238 7571
Email: info@minassianyoung.com
Web: www.minassianyoung.com

127. Miramonte Winery PAGE 366
33410 Rancho California Rd, Temecula
CA 92591
Phone: 951 506 5500
Email: cane@miramontewinery.com
Web: www.miramontewinery.com

128. Mosaic Vineyards and Winery
PAGE 375
2001 Hwy 128, Geyserville CA 95441
Phone: 707 857 2000
Email: discover@mosaicvineyards.com
Web: www.mosaicvineyards.com

129. Mumm Napa PAGE 390
8445 Silverado Trail, Rutherford CA 94573
Phone: 707 967 7700
Email: info@mummnapa.com
Web: www.mummnapa.com

130. Munselle Vineyards PAGE 438
3763 Hwy 128, Geyserville CA 95441
Phone: 707 857 9988
Email: wines@munsellevineyards.com
Web: www.munsellevineyards.com

131. Naggiar Vineyards PAGES 268–271
18125 Rosemary Ln, Grass Valley CA 95949
Phone: 530 268 9059
Email: info@naggiarvineyards.com
Web: www.naggiarvineyards.com

132. Napa River Inn PAGE 398
500 Main St, Napa CA 94559
Phone: 707 251 8500
Email: concierge@napariverinn.com
Web: www.napariverinn.com

133. Nevada City Winery PAGE 381
321 Spring St, Nevada City CA 95959
Phone: 530 265 9463
Email: lori@ncwinery.com
Web: www.nevadacitywinery.com

134. Neveridle Vineyard PAGES 226, 227
3135 Ridge Rd, Templeton CA 93465
Phone: 805 434 1990
Email: neveridle@calinet.com

135. *O'Neel Family Vineyard* PAGE 23
5045 Hall Rd, Santa Rosa CA 95401

136. *Palumbo Family Vineyards*
& Winery PAGES 234, 235
40150 Barksdale Circle, Temecula CA 92592
Phone: 951 676 7900
Email: info@palumbofamilyvineyards.com
Web: www.palumbofamilyvineyards.com

137. *Paradigm Winery* PAGE 387
1277 Dwyer Rd, Oakville CA 94562
Phone: 707 944 1683
Email: info@paradigmwinery.com
Web: www.paradigmwinery.com

138. *Paraiso Vineyards* PAGE 240
38060 Paraiso Springs Rd, Soledad
CA 93960
Phone: 831 678 0300
Email: info@paraisovineyards.com
Web: www.paraisovineyards.com

139. *Pax Wine Cellars* PAGES 40, 41
3352-D Coffey Ln, Santa Rosa CA 95403
Phone: 707 591 0782
Email: mail@paxwines.com
Web: www.paxwines.com

140. *Pedroncelli Winery* PAGE 253
1220 Canyon Rd, Geyserville CA 95441
Phone: 800 836 3894 or 707 857 3531
Email: service@pedroncelli.com
Web: www.pedroncelli.com

141. *Peju Province Winery* PAGES 122, 123
8466 St. Helena Hwy, Rutherford CA 94573
Phone: 707 963 3600
Email: info@peju.com
Web: www.peju.com

142. *Pellegrini Family Vineyards* PAGE 520
4055 West Olivet Rd, Santa Rosa CA 95401
Phone: 707 545 8680
Email: info@pellegrinisonoma.com
Web: www.pellegrinisonoma.com

143. *Penman Springs Vineyard* PAGE 213
1985 Penman Springs Rd, Paso Robles
CA 93446
Phone: 805 237 8960
Email: inquiry@penmansprings.com
Web: www.penmansprings.com

144. *Pessagno Winery* PAGE 399
1645 River Rd, Salinas CA 93908
Phone: 831 675 9463
Email: info@pessagnowines.com
Web: www.pessagnowines.com

145. *Petroni Vineyards* PAGE 288
990 Cavedale Rd, Sonoma CA 94123
Phone: 707 935 8311
Email: wine@petronivineyards.com
Web: www.petronivineyards.com

146. *Pezzi King Vineyards* PAGE 254
412 Hudson St, Healdsburg CA 95448
Phone: 707 473 4310
Email: info@pezziking.com
Web: www.pezziking.com

147. *Pipestone Vineyards* PAGES 306, 307
2040 Niderer Rd, Paso Robles CA 93446
Phone: 805 227 6385
Web: www.pipestonevineyards.com

148. *PlumpJack Winery* PAGES 26, 27
620 Oakville Cross Rd, Oakville CA 94562
Phone: 707 945 1220
Email: winery@plumpjack.com
Web: www.plumpjack.com

149. *Porter Creek Vineyards* PAGES 14, 15
8735 Westside Rd, Healdsburg CA 95448
Phone: 707 433 6321
Email: info@portercreekvineyards.com
Web: www.portercreekvineyards.com

150. *Pretty-Smith Vineyards*
& Winery PAGES 168, 169
13350 River Rd, San Miguel CA 93451
Phone: 805 467 3104
Email: info@prettysmith.com
Web: www.prettysmith.com

151. *Pride Mountain Vineyards* PAGE 53
4026 Spring Mountain Rd, St. Helena
CA 94574
Phone: 707 963 4949
Email: contactus@pridewines.com
Web: www.pridewines.com

152. *Puccioni Vineyards* PAGES 218, 219
22300 Puccioni Rd, Healdsburg CA 95404
Phone: 707 576 8490
Email: info@puccionivineyards.com
Web: www.puccionivineyards.com

153. Ramian Estate PAGE 492
5225 Solano Ave, Napa CA 94558
Phone: 707 287 2721
Email: info@ramianestate.com
Web: www.ramianestate.com

154. Ravenswood Winery PAGE 214
18701 Gehricks Rd, Sonoma CA 95476
Phone: 707 933 2332
Email: cathleen.francisco@ravenswood-wine.com
Web: www.ravenswood-wine.com

155. Regusci Winery PAGES 126, 127
5884 Silverado Trail, Napa CA 94558
Phone: 707 254 0403
Email: info@regusciwinery.com
Web: www.regusciwinery.com

156. Reverie on Diamond Mountain
PAGE 19
1520 Diamond Mountain Rd, Calistoga CA 94515
Phone: 707 942 6800
Email: info@reveriewine.com
Web: www.reveriewine.com

157. Reynolds Family Winery PAGE 499
3266 Silverado Trail, Napa CA 94558
Phone: 707 258 2558
Email: info@reynoldsfamilywinery.com
Web: www.reynoldsfamilywinery.com

158. Rideau Vineyard PAGE 426
1562 Alamo Pintado Rd, Solvang CA 93463
Phone: 805 688 0717
Email: rideauvineyard@verizon.net
Web: www.rideauvineyard.com

159. Ridge Vineyards PAGE 351
17100 Monte Bello Rd, Cupertino CA 95014
Phone: 408 867 3233
Email: wine@ridgewine.com
Web: www.ridgewine.com

160. Riverbench PAGES 364, 365
6020 Foxen Canyon Rd, Santa Maria CA 93454
Phone: 805 937 8340
Email: info@riverbench.com
Web: www.riverbench.com

161. Robert Mondavi Winery PAGE 52
7801 St. Helena Hwy, Oakville CA 94562
Phone: 707 968 2200
Email: info@robertmondaviwinery.com
Web: www.robertmondaviwinery.com

162. Robledo Family Winery PAGES 490, 491
21901 Bonness Rd, Sonoma CA 95476
Phone: 707 939 6903
Email: francisco@robledofamilywinery.com
Web: www.robledofamilywinery.com

163. Rombauer Vineyards PAGE 36
3522 Silverado Trail, St. Helena CA 94574
Phone: 707 963 5170
Email: info@rombauer.com
Web: www.rombauer.com

164. Round Pond Estate Winery
PAGES 493–495
875 Rutherford Rd, Rutherford CA 94573
Phone: 707 302 2575
Email: roundpond@roundpond.com
Web: www.roundpond.com

165. Rubicon Estate PAGES 360, 361
1991 St. Helena Hwy, Rutherford CA 94573
Ph: 707 968 1100
Email: info@rubiconestate.com
Web: www.rubiconestate.com

166. Rudd Winery PAGE 388
500 Oakville Cross Rd, Oakville CA 94562
Phone: 707 944 8577
Email: info@ruddwines.com
Web: www.ruddwines.com

167. Rusack PAGES 421–423
1825 Ballard Canyon Rd, Solvang CA 93463
Phone: 805 688 1278
Email: info@rusackvineyards.com
Web: www.rusack.com

168. Salisbury Vineyards PAGES 184, 185
6985 Ontario Road, San Luis Obispo, CA 93405
Phone: 805 595 9463
Email: harvest@salisburyvineyards.com
Web: www.salisburyvineyards.com

169. San Marcos Creek Vineyard PAGE 363
7750 North Hwy 101, Paso Robles CA 93446
Phone: 805 467 9260
Email: info@sanmarcoscreek.com
Web: www.sanmarcoscreek.com

170. Sarah's Vineyard PAGE 350
4005 Hecker Pass Rd, Gilroy CA 95020
Phone: 408 847 1947
Email: wineclub@sarahsvineyard.com
Web: www.sarahsvineyard.com

171. Saucelito Canyon Vineyard
PAGES 224, 225
3080 Biddle Ranch Rd, San Luis Obispo
CA 93401
Phone: 805 543 2111
Email: info@saucelitocanyon.com
Web: www.saucelitocanyon.com

172. Sbragia Family Vineyards
PAGES 514, 515
9990 Dry Creek Rd, Geyserville CA 95441
Phone: 707 473 2992
Email: info@sbragia.com
Web: www.sbragia.com

173. Scheid Vineyards PAGE 462
1972 Hobson Ave, Greenfield CA 93927
Phone: 831 455 9990
Email: info@scheidvineyards.com
Web: www.scheidvineyards.com

174. Schramsberg Vineyards
PAGES 466, 467
1400 Schramsberg Rd, Calistoga CA 94515
Phone: 707 942 4558
Email: info1@schramsberg.com
Web: www.schramsberg.com

175. Seavey Vineyard PAGES 176, 177
1310 Conn Valley Rd, St. Helena CA 94574
Phone: 707 963 8339
Email: info@seaveyvineyard.com
Web: www.seaveyvineyard.com

**176. Sierra Knolls Vineyard
and Winery** PAGES 442, 443
19635 Kingswood Ct, Grass Valley
CA 95949
Phone: 530 268 9225
Email: sierraknolls@yahoo.com
Web: www.sierraknollswinery.com

177. Sierra Starr PAGES 452, 453
209 West Main St, Grass Valley CA 95945
Phone: 530 477 8282
Email: sierrastarr1@sbcglobal.net
Web: www.sierrastarr.com and
www.sierrastarrwine.com

178. Signorello Vineyards PAGES 434, 435
4500 Silverado Trail, Napa CA 94558
Phone: 800 982 4229
Email: info@signorellovineyards.com
Web: www.signorellovineyards.com

179. Silenus Vintners PAGES 376, 377
5225 Solano Ave, Napa CA 94558
Phone: 707 299 3930
Email: TastingRoom@silenusvintners.com
Web: www.silenusvintners.com

180. Silver Oak Cellars PAGES 508, 509
24625 Chianti Rd, Geyserville CA 95441
Phone: 707 857 3562
Email: info@silveroak.com
Web: www.silveroak.com

181. Smith Vineyard PAGE 431
13577 Dog Bar Rd, Grass Valley CA 95949
Phone: 530 273 7032
Email: christina@smithvineyard.com
Web: www.smithvineyard.com

182. Smith-Madrone PAGE 530
4022 Spring Mountain Rd, St. Helena
CA 94574
Phone: 707 963 2283
Web: www.smithmadrone.com

**183. South Coast Winery
Resort & Spa** PAGE 167
34843 Rancho California Rd, Temecula
CA 92591
Phone: 951 587 9463
Email: wineclub@wineresort.com
Web: www.wineresort.com

184. Spelletich Cellars PAGE 13
880 Vallejo St, Napa CA 94559
Phone: 707 363 5757
Email: info@spellwine.com
Web: www.spellwine.com

185. Spring Mountain Vineyard
PAGES 518, 519
2805 Spring Mountain Rd, St. Helena
CA 94574
Phone: 707 967 4188
Email: office@springmtn.com
Web: www.springmountainvineyard.com

**186. St. Supéry Vineyards
and Winery** PAGES 476, 477
8440 St. Helena Hwy, Rutherford CA 94573
Phone: 707 963 4507
Email: divinecab@stsupery.com
Web: www.stsupery.com

187. Staglin Family Vineyard PAGE 128
1570 Bella Oaks Ln, Rutherford CA 94573
Phone: 707 944 0477
Email: info@staglinfamily.com
Web: www.staglinfamily.com

188. Still Waters Vineyards PAGE 244
2750 Old Grove Ln, Paso Robles CA 93446
Phone: 805 237 9231
Email: winery@stillwatersvineyards.com
Web: www.stillwatersvineyards.com

189. Stonehedge Winery PAGE 290
1004 Clinton St, Napa CA 94559
Phone: 707 257 7400
Email: lisa@stonehedgewinery.com
Web: www.stonehedgewinery.com

190. Storybook Mountain Vineyards
PAGE 470
3835 Hwy 128, Calistoga CA 94515
Phone: 707 942 5310
Email: topzin@storybookwines.com
Web: www.storybookwines.com

191. Stuart Cellars Winery PAGES 334, 335
33515 Rancho California Rd, Temecula
CA 92591
Phone: 888 260 0870
Email: winery@stuartcellars.com
Web: www.stuartcellars.com

192. Summers Estate Wines PAGE 400
1171 Tubbs Ln, Calistoga CA 94515
Phone: 707 942 5508
Email: beth@summerswinery.com
Web: www.summerswinery.com

193. Swanson Vineyards PAGES 318, 319
1271 Manley Ln, Rutherford CA 94573
Phone: 707 967 3500
Email: salon@swansonvineyards.com
Web: www.swansonvineyards.com

194. Tablas Creek Vineyard PAGE 472
9339 Adelaida Rd, Paso Robles CA 93446
Phone: 805 237 1231
Email: info@tablascreek.com
Web: www.tablascreek.com

195. Tench Vineyards PAGES 28, 29
7631 Silverado Trail, Napa CA 94558
Phone: 707 944 2352
Email: rbwtench@tenchvineyards.com

196. Thacher Winery PAGES 68, 69
8355 Vineyard Dr, Paso Robles CA 93446
Phone: 805 237 0087
Email: info@thacherwinery.com
Web: www.thacherwinery.com

197. Three Creek Vineyard PAGES 20–22
1777 Fletcher Way, Santa Ynez CA 93460
Phone: 805 686 1349
Email: info@threecreek.com
Web: www.cimarone.com

198. Three Palms Vineyard PAGES 432, 433
4205 Silverado Trail, North Calistoga
CA 94515
Phone: 707 942 5251
Email: threepalmsvineyard@aol.com

199. Tin Barn Vineyards PAGES 186, 187
21692 Eighth St East, Sonoma CA 95476
Phone: 707 938 5430
Email: wine@tinbarnvineyards.com
Web: www.tinbarnvineyards.com

200. Tobin James Cellars PAGE 212
8950 Union Rd, Paso Robles CA 93446
Phone: 805 239 2204
Email: information@tobinjames.com
Web: www.tobinjames.com

201. Tolosa Winery PAGE 326
4910 Edna Rd, San Luis Obispo CA 93401
Phone: 805 782 0500
Email: info@tolosawinery.com
Web: www.tolosawinery.com

202. Tom Eddy Winery PAGE 385
3870 Hwy 128, Calistoga CA 94515
Phone: 707 942 4267
Email: tom@tomeddywines.com
Web: www.tomeddywines.com

203. Trentadue Winery PAGES 439–441
19170 Geyserville Ave, Geyserville CA 95441
Phone: 707 433 3104
Email: info@trentadue.com
Web: www.trentadue.com

204. Tres Hermanas Winery PAGES 418, 419
9660 Foxen Canyon Rd, Santa Maria
CA 93454
Phone: 805 937 8451
Email: info@treshermanaswinery.com
Web: www.treshermanaswinery.com

205. Tres Sabores PAGES 248, 249
1620 S. Whitehall Ln, St. Helena CA 94574
Phone: 707 967 8027
Email: jaj@tressabores.com
Web: www.tressabores.com

206. Turnbull Wine Cellars PAGE 371
8210 St. Helena Hwy, Oakville CA 94542
Phone: 800 887 6285
Email: info@turnbullwines.com
Web: www.turnbullwines.com

207. Venteux Vineyards PAGE 309
1795 Las Tablas Rd, Templeton CA 93465
Phone: 805 369 0127
Email: bobbi@venteuxvineyards.com
Web: www.venteuxvineyards.com

208. Viader PAGES 500–502
1120 Deer Park Rd, Deer Park CA 94576
Phone: 707 963 3816
Email: inquiries@viader.com
Web: www.viader.com

209. Villa Creek Cellars PAGES 264, 265
5995 Peachy Canyon Rd, Paso Robles
CA 93446
Phone: 805 238 7145
Email: wine@villacreek.com
Web: www.villacreek.com

210. Vineyard 7 & 8 PAGE 521
4028 Spring Mountain Rd, St. Helena
CA 94574
Phone: 707 963 9425
Email: info@vineyard7and8.com
Web: www.vineyard7and8.com

211. Whalebone Winery PAGES 30, 31
8325 Vineyard Dr, Paso Robles CA 93446
Phone: 805 239 9020
Email: jan@whalebonevineyard.com
Web: www.whalebonevineyard.com

212. Wilson Winery PAGE 523
1960 Dry Creek Rd, Healdsburg CA 95448
Phone: 707 433 4355
Email: info@wilsonwinery.com
Web: www.wilsonwinery.com

213. Wilson Creek Winery PAGE 236
35960 Rancho California Rd, Temecula
CA 92591
Phone: 951 699 9463
Email: info@wilsoncreekwinery.com
Web: www.wilsoncreekwinery.com

214. Windwalker Vineyard PAGES 70, 71
7360 Perry Creek Rd, Fair Play CA 95684
Phone: 530 620 4054
Email: windwalker.wineclub@gotsky.com
Web: www.windwalkervineyard.com

215. Wolff Vineyards PAGE 273
6238 Orcutt Rd, San Luis Obispo CA 93401
Phone: 805 781 0448
Email: elke.wolff@wolffvineyards.com
Web: www.wolffvineyards.com

216. Wood Winery PAGE 362
136 Bridge Street, Arroyo Grande CA 93420
Phone: 805 489 9663
Email: info@wildwoodwine.com
Web: www.wildwoodwine.com

217. Yates Family Vineyard PAGES 260–262
4723 Redwood Rd, Napa CA 94558
Phone: 707 226 1800
Email: info@yatesfamilyvineyard.com
Web: www.yatesfamilyvineyard.com

218. Zahtila Vineyards PAGE 469
2250 Lake County Hwy, Calistoga CA 94515
Phone: 707 942 9251
Email: sales@zahtilavineyards.com
Web: www.zahtilavineyards.com

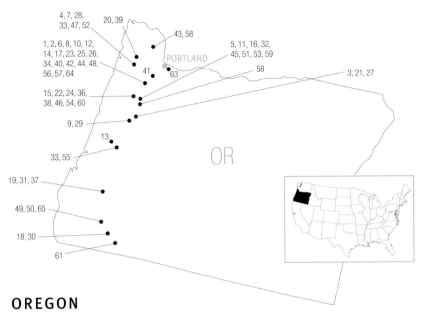

4, 7, 28, 33, 47, 52
20, 39
43, 58
1, 2, 6, 8, 10, 12, 14, 17, 23, 25, 26, 34, 40, 42, 44, 48, 56, 57, 64
5, 11, 16, 32, 45, 51, 53, 59
PORTLAND
41
63
58
3, 21, 27
15, 22, 24, 36, 38, 46, 54, 60
9, 29
13
33, 55
OR
19, 31, 37
49, 50, 65
18, 30
61

OREGON

1. A to Z Wineworks PAGE 109
30835 N Hwy 99W, Newberg OR 97132
Phone: 503 538 0666
Email: info@atozwineworks.com
Web: www.atozwineworks.com

2. Adelsheim Vineyard PAGES 284–287
16800 NE Calkins Ln, Newberg OR 97132
Phone: 503 538 3652
Email: info@adelsheim.com
Web: www.adelsheimvineyard.com

3. Airlie Winery PAGES 66, 67
15305 Dunn Forest Rd, Monmouth OR 97304
Phone: 503 838 6013
Email: airlie@airliewinery.com
Web: www.airliewinery.com

4. Anne Amie Vineyards PAGE 358
6580 NE Mineral Springs Rd,
  Carlton OR 97111
Phone: 503 864 2991
Email: contactus@anneamie.com
Web: www.anneamie.com

5. Archery Summit Winery PAGE 489
18599 NE Archery Summit Rd,
  Dayton OR 97114
Phone: 503 864 4300
Email: info@archerysummit.com
Web: www.archerysummit.com

6. Ayres Vineyard and Winery
PAGES 496–498
17971 NE Lewis Rogers Ln,
  Newberg OR 97132
Phone: 503 538 7450
Email: kathleen@ayresvineyard.com
Web: www.ayresvineyard.com

7. Barking Frog PAGE 392
128 West Main St, Carlton OR 97111
Phone: 503 625 6581
Email: touchsto@hevanet.com
Web: www.barkingfrogwinery.com

8. Beaux Frères PAGE 417
15155 NE North Valley Rd, Newberg OR 97132
Phone: 503 537 1137
Email: info@beauxfreres.com
Web: www.beauxfreres.com

9. Belle Vallee Cellars PAGE 65
804 NW Buchanan Avenue, Corvallis
  OR 97330
Phone: 541 757 9463
Email: info@bellevallee.com
Web: www.bellevallee.com

10. Beran Vineyards PAGE 92
30088 SW Egger Rd, Hillsboro OR 97123
Phone: 503 628 1298
Email: info@beranvineyards.com
Web: www.beranvineyards.com

11. Bethel Heights PAGE 154
6060 Bethel Heights Rd NW, Salem OR 97304
Phone: 503 581 2262
Email: info@bethelheights.com
Web: www.bethelheights.com

12. Brick House Vineyards PAGES 266, 267
18200 Lewis Rogers Ln, Newberg OR 97132
Phone: 503 538 5136
Email: info@brickhousewines.com
Web: www.brickhousewines.com

13. Broadley Vineyards PAGE 64
265 South Sth St, Monroe OR 97456
Phone: 541 847 5934
Email: broadley@peak.org
Web: www.broadleyvineyards.com

14. Chehalem PAGE 18
31190 NE Veritas Ln, Newberg OR 97132
Phone: 503 538 4700
Email: info@chehalemwines.com
Web: www.chehalemwines.com

15. Coleman Vineyard PAGE 391
22734 W Latham Rd, McMinnville OR 97128
Phone: 503 843 2707
Email: kim@colemanwine.com
Web: www.colemanvineyard.com

16. Cristom Vineyards PAGE 526, 527
6905 Spring Valley Rd NW, Salem OR 97304
Phone: 503 375 3068
Email: winery@cristomwines.com
Web: www.cristomwines.com

17. Daedalus Cellars PAGE 368
10505 NE Red Hills Rd, Dundee OR 97115
Phone: 503 537 0727
Email: info@daedaluscellars.com
Web: www.daedaluscellars.com

18. Daisy Creek PAGE 406
675 Shafer Ln, Jacksonville OR 97530
Phone: 541 899 8329
Email: daisycreek@clearwire.net
Web: www.daisycreekwine.com

19. Delfino Vineyards PAGE 317
3829 Colonial Rd, Roseburg OR 97470
Phone: 541 673 7575
Email: delfinos@aol.com
Web: www.delfinovineyards.com

20. Elk Cove Vineyards PAGES 164, 165
27751 NW Olson Rd, Gaston OR 97119
Phone: 503 985 7760
Email: info@elkcove.com
Web: www.elkcove.com

21. Emerson Vineyards PAGE 413
11665 Airlie Rd, Monmouth OR 97361
Phone: 503 838 0944
Email: info@emersonvineyards.com
Web: www.emersonvineyards.com

22. Eyrie Vineyards, The PAGES 44, 45
935 NE 10th Avenue, McMinnville OR 97128
Phone: 888 440 4970
Email: info@eyrievineyards.com
Web: www.eyrievineyards.com

23. Four Graces, The PAGES 120, 121
9605 NE Fox Farm Rd, Dundee OR 97115
Phone: 503 554 8000
Email: anthony@thefourgraces.com
Web: www.thefourgraces.com

24. La Bête Wines PAGE 524
21000 SW Eagle Point Rd, McMinnville
OR 97128
Phone: 503 977 1493
Email: labete@teleport.com
Web: www.labetewines.com

25. Lange Estate Winery PAGES 320, 321
18380 NE Buena Vista Dr, Dundee OR 97115
Phone: 503 538 6476
Email: tastingroom@langewinery.com
Web: www.langewinery.com

26. Laura Volkman Vineyards PAGE 483
14725 NE Quarry Rd, Newberg OR 97132
Phone: 503 806 4047
Email: laura@volkmanvineyards.com
Web: www.volkmanvineyards.com

27. Left Coast Cellars PAGE 353
4225 N Pacific Hwy, Rickreall OR 97371
Phone: 503 831 4916
Email: info@leftcoastcellars.com
Web: www.leftcoastcellars.com

28. Lemelson Vineyards PAGE 460
12020 NE Stag Hollow Rd, Carlton OR 97111
Phone: 503 852 6619
Email: info@lemelsonvineyards.com
Web: www.lemelsonvineyards.com

29. Lumos Wine Company PAGE 525
24000 Carwell Hill Dr, Philomath OR 97370
Phone: 541 929 3519
Email: lumos@lumoswine.com
Web: www.lumoswine.com

30. Madrone Mountain Vineyard PAGE 99
540 Tumbleweed Trail, Jacksonville
  OR 97530
Phone: 541 899 9642
Email: winery@madronemountain.com
Web: www.madronemountain.com

31. Melrose Vineyards PAGES 304, 305
885 Melqua Rd, Roseburg OR 97470
Phone: 541 672 6080
Email: info@melrosevineyards.com
Web: www.melrosevineyards.com

32. Methven Family Vineyards PAGES 32, 33
11400 Westland Ln, Dayton OR 97114
Phone: 503 868 7259
Email: bethany@methvenfamily
  vineyards.com
Web: www.methvenfamilyvineyards.com

33. Monks Gate Vineyard PAGE 474
9500 NE Oak Springs Farm Rd,
  Carlton OR 97111
Phone: 503 852 6521
Email: info@monksgate.com
Web: www.monksgate.com

34. Natalie's Estate Winery PAGE 389
16825 NE Chehalem Dr, Newberg OR 97132
Phone: 503 554 9350
Email: contact@nataliesestatewinery.com
Web: www.nataliesestatewinery.com

35. Noble Estate PAGES 72, 73
29210 Gimpel Hill, Eugene OR 97402
Phone: 541 338 3007
Email: wines@nobleestatevineyard.com
Web: www.nobleestatevineyard.com

36. Oregon Barrel Works PAGE 410
PO Box 748, McMinnville OR 97128
Phone: 505 472 8883
Email: rick@oregonbarrelworks.com
Web: www.oregonbarrelworks.com

37. Palotai Vineyard and Winery PAGE 63
272 Capital Ln, Roseburg OR 97470
Phone: 541 464 0032
Email: gabor@mbol.us
Web: www.palotaiwines.com

38. Panther Creek Cellars PAGES 396, 397
455 NE Irvine St, McMinnville OR 97128
Phone: 503 472 8080
Email: info@panthercreekcellars.com
Web: www.panthercreekcellars.com

39. Patton Valley Vineyard PAGE 354
9449 SW Old Hwy 47, Gaston OR 97119
Phone: 503 985 3445
Email: jerry@pattonvalley.com
Web: www.pattonvalley.com

40. Penner-Ash Wine Cellars PAGE 106
15771 NE Ribbon Ridge Rd,
  Newberg OR 97132
Phone: 503 554 5545
Email: sales@pennerash.com
Web: www.pennerash.com

41. Ponzi Vineyards PAGES 138–141
14665 SW Winery Ln, Beaverton OR 97007
Phone: 503 628 1227
Email: info@ponziwines.com
Web: www.ponziwines.com

42. Privé Vineyard & Winery PAGES 478–480
28155 NE Bell Rd, Newberg OR 97132
Phone: 503 554 0464
Email: privevineyard@privevineyard.com
Web: www.privevineyard.com

43. Purple Cow Vineyards PAGE 473
52720 NW Wilson School Rd,
  Forest Grove OR 97116
Phone: 503 330 0991
Email: wine@purplecowvineyards.com
Web: www.purplecowvineyards.com

44. Raptor Ridge Winery PAGE 412
130 West Monroe, Carlton OR 97111
Phone: 503 887 5595
Email: info@raptoridge.com
Web: www.raptoridge.com

45. Redhawk Winery PAGE 347
2995 Michigan City Rd NW, Salem OR 97304
Phone: 503 362 1596
Email: cellarmaster@redhawkwine.com
Web: www.redhawkwine.com

46. Remy Wines PAGE 475
777 NE 4th St, McMinnville OR 97128
Phone: 503 560 2003
Email: info@remywines.com
Web: www.remywines.com

47. Retour Wines PAGES 54, 55
801 Scott St, Carlton OR 97111
Phone: 971 237 4757
Email: lindsay@retourwines.com
Web: www.retourwines.com

48. Rex Hill Vineyards PAGE 108
30835 N Hwy 99W, Newberg OR 97132
Phone: 503 538 0666
Email: info@rexhill.com
Web: www.rexhill.com

49. Rosella's Vineyard and Winery
PAGE 416
184 Missouri Flat Rd, Grants Pass OR 97527
Phone: 541 846 6372
Email: sandig@peak.org
Web: www.rosellasvineyard.com

50. Slagle Creek Winery PAGE 315
1629 Slagle Creek Rd, Grants Pass OR 97527
Phone: 541 846 6176
Email: slaglecreek@earthlink.net
Web: www.slaglecreek.com

51. Sokol Blosser Winery PAGES 330, 333
5000 NE Sokol Blosser Ln, Dayton OR 97114
Phone: 503 864 2282
Email: info@sokolblosser.com
Web: www.sokolblosser.com

52. Soléna Cellars PAGE 415
213 South Pine St, Carlton OR 97111
Phone: 503 852 0082
Email: info@solenacellars.com
Web: www.solenacellars.com

53. Stoller PAGES 88, 89
16161 NE McDougall Rd, Dayton OR 97114
Phone: 503 864 3404
Email: info@stollervineyards.com
Web: www.stollervineyards.com

54. Stone Wolf Vineyards PAGE 394
2155 NE Lafayette Avenue, McMinnville
OR 97128
Phone: 503 434 9025
Email: stone@stonewolfvineyards.com
Web: www.stonewolfvineyards.com

55. Sweet Cheeks Winery PAGE 411
27007 Briggs Hill Rd, Eugene OR 97405
Phone: 877 309 9463
Email: lorrie@sweetcheekswinery.com
Web: www.sweetcheekswinery.com

56. Terra Vina Wines PAGE 112
33750 SW Ladd Hill Rd, Wilsonville
OR 97070
Phone: 503 925 0712
Email: carole@terravinawines.com
Web: www.terravinawines.com

57. Torii Mor Winery PAGE 293
18325 NE Fairview Dr, Dundee OR 97115
Phone: 503 538 2279
Email: info@torimorwinery.com
Web: www.toriimorwinery.com

58. Tualatin Estate Vineyard PAGE 354
10850 NW Seavey Rd, Forest Grove
OR 97116
Phone: 503 357 5005
Email: Meg.Hursh@wvv.com
Web: www.tualatinestate.com

59. Van Duzer PAGE 316
11975 Smithfield Rd, Dallas OR 97338
Phone: 503 623 6420
Email: kathy@vanduzer.com
Web: www.vanduzer.com

60. Walnut City Wineworks PAGE 114
475 NE 17th St, McMinnville OR 97128
Phone: 503 472 3215
Email: wine@walnutcitywineworks.com
Web: www.walnutcitywineworks,com

61. Weisinger's of Ashland PAGE 91
3150 Siskiyou Blvd, Ashland OR 97520
Phone: 541 488 5989
Email: wine@weisingers.com
Web: www.weisingers.com

62. Willamette Valley Vineyards PAGE 354
8800 Enchanted Way SE, Turner OR 97392
Phone: 503 588 9463
Email: Meg.Hursh@wvv.com
Web: www.willamettevalleyvineyards.com

63. Willamette Valley Wineries
Association PAGES 328, 329
10200 W Eastridge St, Suite 214,
Portland OR 97225
Phone: 503 297 2962
Email: info@willamettewines.com
Web: www.willamettewines.com

64. Wine Country Farm Cellars PAGE 349
6855 NE Breyman Orchard Rd,
Dayton OR 97114
Phone: 503 864 3446
Email: jld@winecountryfarm.com
Web: www.winecountryfarm.com

65. Wooldridge Creek Winery PAGE 367
818 Slagle Creek Rd, Grants Pass OR 97527
Phone: 541 846 6364
Email: admin@wcwinery.com
Web: www.wcwinery.com

WASHINGTON

1. Abeja PAGES 458, 459
2014 Mill Creek Rd, Walla Walla WA 99362
Phone: 509 526 7400
Email: molly@abeja.net
Web: www.abeja.net

2. Dunham Cellars PAGES 83–85
150 East Boeing Ave, Walla Walla WA 99362
Phone: 509 529 4685
Email: info@dunhamcellars.com
Web: www.dunhamcellars.com

3. Dusted Valley PAGE 9
1248 Old Milton Hwy, Walla Walla WA 99362
Phone: 509 525 1337
Email: info@dustedvalley.com
Web: www.dustedvalley.com

4. Glen Fiona PAGE 113
1249 Lyday Ln, Walla Walla WA 99362
Phone: 509 522 2566
Email: syrah@glenfiona.com
Web: www.glenfiona.com

5. Hoodsport Winery PAGE 292
23501 N Hwy 101, Hoodsport WA 98548
Phone: 360 877 9894
Email: wine@hoodsport.com
Web: www.hoodsport.com

6. O. S. Winery PAGES 48, 49
1501 S 92nd Place, Seattle WA 98108
Phone: 206 243 3427
Email: mail@oswinery.com
Web: www.oswinery.com

7. Paradisos del Sol PAGES 142–144
3230 Highland Dr, Zillah WA 98953
Phone: 509 829 9000
Email: info@paradisosdelsol.com
Web: www.paradisosdelsol.com

8. Severino Cellars PAGE 348
1717 1st Ave, Zillah WA 98953
Phone: 509 829 3800
Email: severinocellars@jrone.biz
Web: www.severinocellars.com

9. Silver Lake Winery PAGES 136, 137
1500 Vintage Rd, Zillah WA 98953
Phone: 509 829 6235
Email: tstephas@washingtonwine.com
Web: www.silverlakewinery.com

10. Sleeping Dog Wines PAGE 60
45804 N. Whitmore PR NW,
   Benton City WA 99320
Phone: 509 460 2886
Email: info@sleepingdogwines.com
Web: www.sleepingdogwines.com

11. Tamarack Cellars PAGE 119
700 C St, Walla Walla WA 99362
Phone: 509 526 3533
Email: sandy@tamarackcellars.com
Web: www.tamarackcellars.com

12. Walter Dacon Wines PAGE 352
50 SE Skookum Inlet Rd, Shelton WA 98584
Phone: 360 426 5913
Email: winemaker@walterdaconwines.com
Web: www.walterdaconwines.com

13. Widgeon Hill Winery PAGE 429
121 Widgeon Hill Rd, Chehalis WA 98532
Phone: 360 748 0432
Email: widgeonhill@localaccess.com
Web: www.widgeonhillwinery.com

14. Windy Point Vineyards PAGE 427
420 Windy Point Dr, Wapato WA 98951
Phone: 509 877 6824
Email: winemaker@windypoint
   vineyards.com
Web: www.windypointvineyards.com

15. Zefina Winery PAGES 528, 529
103 Columbia Ridge Rd, Prosser WA 99350
Phone: 509 301 4450
Email: jeanie@pocketinet.com
Web: www.zefina.com

IDAHO

16. Bitner Vineyards PAGE 247
16645 Plum Rd, Caldwell ID 83607
Phone: 208 899 7648
Email: mary@bitnervineyards.com
Web: www.bitnervineyards.com

17. Carmela Vineyards PAGE 308
1289 West Madison, Glenns Ferry ID 83623
Phone: 208 366 2313
Email: carmelavineyards@rtci.net
Web: www.carmelavineyards.com

18. Fraser Vineyard PAGE 327
1004 La Pointe St, Boise ID 83706
Phone: 208 345 9607
Email: fraser@fraservineyard.com
Web: www.fraservineyard.com

19. Hells Canyon Winery PAGE 340
18835 Symms Rd, Caldwell ID 83607
Phone: 208 454 3300
Email: hellwine@yahoo.com
Web: www.hellscanyonwinery.org

20. Parma Ridge Vineyards PAGE 98
24509 Rudd Rd, Parma ID 83660
Phone: 208 722 6885
Email: parmaridge@earthlink.net
Web: www.parmaridge.com

21. Sawtooth Winery PAGE 116
13750 Surrey Ln, Nampa ID 83686
Phone: 208 467 1200
Email: ideboer@sawtooth.com
Web: www.sawtoothwinery.com

**22. Williamson Orchards
   & Vineyards** PAGE 90
19692 Williamson Ln, Caldwell ID 83607
Phone: 208 459 7333
Email: wine@willorch.com
Web: www.willorch.com

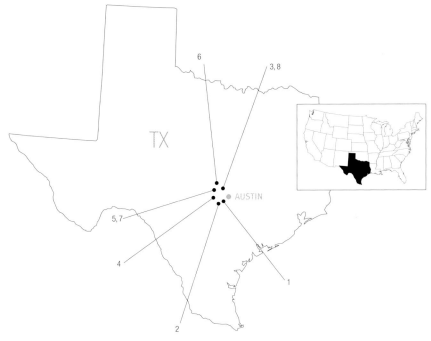

TEXAS

1. Driftwood Vineyards PAGE 182
4001 Elder Hill Rd, Driftwood TX 78619
Phone: 512 692 6229
Email: info@driftwoodvineyards.com
Web: www.driftwoodvineyards.com

2. Dry Comal Creek Vineyards PAGE 204
1741 Herbelin Rd, New Braunfels, TX 78132
Phone: 830 885 4076
Email: xavieramaya@aol.com
Web: www.drycomalcreek.com

3. Flat Creek Estate PAGE 199
24912 Singleton Bend E,
* Marble Falls TX 78654*
Phone: 512 267 6310
Email: wines@flatcreekestate.com
Web: www.flatcreekestate.com

4. Grape Creek Vineyards PAGES 58, 59
10587 East Hwy 290, Fredericksburg
* TX 78624*
Phone: 830 644 2710
Email: relax@grapecreek.com
Web: www.grapecreek.com

5. McReynolds Winery PAGES 220, 221
706 Shovel Mountain Rd, Round Mountain
* TX 78663*
Phone: 830 825 3544
Email: mcreynoldswines@hillcountrytx.net
Web: www.mcreynoldswines.com

6. Pillar Bluff Vineyards PAGE 190
300 Burnet Co. Rd III, Lampasas TX 76550
Phone: 512 556 4078
Email: vineyard@earth-comm.com
Web: www.pillarbluff.com

7. Spicewood Vineyards PAGE 294
1419 Burnet County Rd 409, Spicewood
* TX 78669*
Phone: 830 693 5328
Email: wines@spicewoodvineyards.com
Web: www.spicewoodvineyards.com

8. Stone House Vineyard PAGE 211
24350 Haynie Flat Rd, Spicewood TX 78669
Phone: 512 264 3630
Email: info@stonehousevineyard.com
Web: www.stonehousevineyard.com

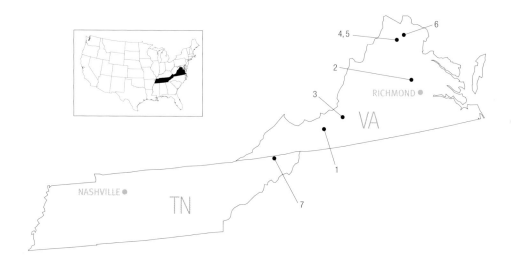

VIRGINIA

1. Chateau Morrisette PAGES 256, 257
Milepost 171.5 Blue Ridge Parkway,
   Meadows of Dan, VA 24120
Phone: 540 593 2865
Email: info@thedogs.com
Web: www.thedogs.com

2. Cooper Vineyards PAGES 159–161
13372 Shannon Hill Rd, Louisa VA 23093
Phone: 540 894 5253
Email: info@coopervineyards.com
Web: www.coopervineyards.com

3. Hickory Hill Vineyards PAGE 263
1722 Hickory Cove Ln, Moneta VA 24121
Phone: 540 296 1393
Email: info@hickoryhillvineyards.com
Web: www.hickoryhillvineyards.com

4. Marterella Winery PAGES 274–277
8278 Falcon Glen Rd, Warrenton VA 20186
Phone: 540 347 1119
Email: kate@marterellawines.com
Web: www.marterellawines.com

5. Miracle Valley Vineyard PAGE 241
3661 Double J Ln, Delaplane VA 20144
Phone: 540 364 0228
Email: joe_and_maryann@
   miraclevalleyvineyard.com
Web: www.miraclevalleyvineyard.com

6. Swedenburg Estate Vineyard
   PAGES 356, 357
23595 Winery Ln, Middleburg VA 20117
Phone: 540 687 5207
Email: info@swedenburgwines.com
Web: www.swedenburgwines.com

TENNESSEE

7. Countryside Vineyards
   & Winery PAGE 183
658 Henry Harr Rd, Blountville TN 37617
Phone: 423 323 1660
Email: csvwinery@wmconnect.com
Web: www.cvwineryandsupply.com

WINE DOGS BREED INDEX

A

Airedale Terrier PAGE 474
Alaskan Husky PAGE 102
Ambullneo Mastiff PAGE 408
American Bulldog PAGE 126
American Eskimo PAGE 227
Anatolian Shepherd PAGE 128
Argentinian Mastiff PAGE 124
Australian Cattle Dog PAGES 148, 149, 216, 217, 497
Australian Shepherd PAGES 53, 68, 112, 205, 212, 218, 291, 296, 297, 303, 309, 342, 343, 349, 353, 381, 387, 448, 473, 477, 486, 499, 511
Australian Shepherd, Miniature PAGES 239, 523
Australian Terrier PAGES 19, 198

B

Basenji PAGE 43
Basset Hound PAGE 82
Beagle PAGES 67, 125, 159, 211, 354, 362, 409, 496, 503, 514
Bedlington Terrier PAGE 130
Belgian Malinois PAGE 131
Belgian Sheepdog PAGE 488
Bernese Mountain Dog PAGES 280, 281
Bichon Frise PAGES 25, 54, 398, 479
Blab PAGE 10
Bloodhound PAGE 195
Blue Heeler PAGE 512
Blue Lacy PAGES 204, 294
Blue Picardy Spaniel PAGE 269
Border Collie PAGES 20, 21, 22, 70, 78, 83, 84, 85, 90, 167, 180, 182, 187, 210, 263, 274, 175, 315, 411, 413, 468, 470, 472
Boston Terrier PAGES 13, 151, 215
Boxer PAGES 50, 178, 369, 382, 417, 476, 515
Brazilian Mastiff PAGE 389
Brittany PAGES 142, 143, 427, 434, 435
Brussels Griffon PAGE 99
Bulldog PAGE 6
Bull-Mastiff PAGES 56, 57
Burgundian Truffle Hound PAGE 451

C

Catahoola Leopard Dog PAGES 243, 307
Cattle Dog X PAGE 153
Cavalier King Charles Spaniel PAGES 290, 344, 345, 446
Chesapeake Bay Retriever PAGES 228, 229, 357
Chihuahua PAGES 44, 144, 259, 339, 401, 419, 490, 519
Chow Chow PAGES 174, 385
Cocker Spaniel PAGE 390
Collie X PAGE 14
Coonhound X PAGES 23, 346, 405
Corgi PAGES 192, 337, 430
Coton de Tulear PAGE 202
Coyote X PAGE 109

D

Dachshund PAGES 51, 378, 421, 428, 484
Dachshund, Miniature PAGES 31, 292, 388, 464
Dalmatian PAGES 75, 299
Doberman PAGES 199, 253

E

English Bull Terrier PAGE 162
English Bulldog PAGES 30, 132, 323, 341, 364
English Cocker Spaniel PAGES 11, 114
English Mastiff PAGES 72, 73, 392
English Setter PAGE 327
English Springer Spaniel PAGES 186, 191, 530

F

Flat-Coated Retriever PAGES 442, 528
Fox Terrier PAGES 138, 478
French Bulldog PAGE 34
French Springer PAGE 214

G

German Shepherd PAGES 12, 93, 94, 95, 100, 160, 188, 312, 313, 316, 325, 441, 444, 461, 482, 489, 493
German Short-Haired Pointer PAGES 98, 244, 302, 367, 373
Golden Retriever PAGES 64, 71, 101, 110, 111, 115, 121, 137, 147, 165, 179, 236, 240, 242, 248, 249, 268, 284, 293, 304, 321, 322, 328, 355, 370, 375, 377, 394, 406, 414, 423, 521
Great Dane X PAGES 235, 463, 492
Great Pyrenees PAGES 15, 119, 400, 460
Greyhound PAGE 74

H

Havanese PAGE 52
Heeler, Red PAGE 86
Heeler X PAGE 8
Hungarian Puli PAGE 407
Hungarian Vizsla PAGES 135, 139, 140, 184, 185, 190
Husky X PAGE 154

I

Irish Setter PAGES 66, 120, 267
Irish Terrier PAGE 46
Irish Wolfhound X PAGES 4, 230, 308

J

Jack Russell Terrier PAGES 40, 41, 58, 59, 116, 164, 170, 176, 198, 241, 247, 443, 485, 516, 517

K

Kerry Blue Terrier PAGE 520
Kelpie X PAGE 372

L

Labradoodle PAGE 76
Labrador PAGES 27, 28, 29, 32, 33, 36, 45, 55, 65, 69, 79, 81, 87, 91, 92, 104, 105, 106, 113, 127, 145, 150, 166, 181, 183, 189, 194, 196, 197, 203, 206, 209, 219, 223, 225, 234, 250, 255, 256, 257, 258, 260, 261, 262, 270, 272, 273, 278, 282, 283, 287, 288, 295, 296, 300, 305, 306, 329, 310, 326, 338, 340, 352, 361, 363, 365, 374, 391, 399, 403, 410, 412, 415, 416, 422, 425, 431, 432, 433, 436, 437, 438, 439, 449, 450, 453, 454, 458, 459, 465, 466, 467, 469, 471, 475, 481, 491, 494, 500, 501, 502, 510, 522, 524, 526
Lhasa Apso PAGES 141, 426

M

Maltese PAGES 271, 335
McNab PAGES 301, 310
Mixed PAGES 77, 175, 213, 220, 266, 356, 380, 498, 505, 508, 509, 513, 527

N

Newfoundland PAGE 366

P

Papillon PAGE 16
Pit Bull Terrier X PAGE 397
Pointer PAGE 529
Pomeranian PAGES 504, 518
Poodle PAGES 96, 97, 161, 169, 333, 334, 495
Portuguese Water Dog PAGES 359, 507
Pug PAGES 88, 89, 445

Q

Queensland Heeler PAGES 17, 42, 163, 264, 265

R

Rat Terrier PAGES 222, 317, 418, 420
Redbone Coonhound PAGES 35, 480
Rhodesian Ridgeback PAGES 47, 379, 383, 402
Rottweiler X PAGES 103, 285, 350, 396, 452

S

Saluki PAGES 232, 233
Samoyed PAGE 351
Schnauzer, Giant PAGE 386
Schnauzer, Miniature PAGES 177, 324
Schnoodle PAGE 9
Scottish Terrier PAGE 254
Setter X PAGE 221
Shar Pei PAGES 49, 358
Shepherd X PAGES 60, 393, 462, 525
Shetland Sheepdog PAGES 108, 320
Shih Tzu PAGES 48, 80, 122, 123, 276, 429, 506
Shorkie PAGE 447
Siberian Husky PAGES 18, 286, 404
South African Boerboel PAGE 368
Springer Spaniel PAGE 26
St. Bernard PAGES 279, 483

T

Terrier X PAGES 63, 326

W

Walker Hound PAGE 193
Weimaraner PAGE 487
West Highland Terrier PAGES 348, 371, 440
Wheaten Terrier, Soft-Coated PAGES 318, 319, 347, 395
Whippet X PAGE 224

Y

Yorkshire Terrier PAGES 201, 226, 238 277

THANK YOU...

Wine Dogs would like to thank the following people who helped us on our journey.

To our wonderful network of friends and family back in Australia whose constant support and enthusiasm has made this book a lot easier to produce. To our four-legged clowns back home – Tarka and Stella for the constant laughs and for still loving us when we returned after 11 weeks away.

Along our travels we were helped and encouraged by many wonderful people including: Roger and Priscilla Higgins at Three Creek Vineyard; Garret Thomas Murphy and Andy Renda at the Vintners Collective Napa Valley; the wonderful Tina Cao and the dynamic Chris Parker from St Supéry; Sue Horstmann at Willamette Valley Wineries Association; Pat and Robert Parker; Patrick Chastain and Tona Kovacevic at Rombaurer Vineyards; Doug Margerum; Paul LaRose at the Bounty Hunter; Wendy Bruce and Kate Bennett at Domaine Carneros; Michele Lytle at Clear Image labels; Cloud 9 in Corvallis Oregon; Xylia Buros at August Cellars; Sloan and Caroline Upton at Three Palms Vineyard; Randy Lemke at Evergreen Aviation Museum; Monty Sander at Monty J Sander Communications; The Lail family for helping Craig on a particularly difficult day; Kristen Spelletich for being a star; Pat Dudley at Bethel Heights for clothing Craig more appropriately for the Oregon winter; Greg Merritt at Citibank Napa; Andy Ward; Richard Hogan from Zoowines distribution in Australia for his continued support; and Buff and the splendid people at Buffalo Shipping Post in Napa. A big thank you to all the very generous wineries that gave us bottles of their fine wine to bring back to Australia. It's a real treat for us Aussies to taste what the other side of the world are drinking.

And we must draw special attention to the wonderful generosity and hospitality offered to us by Robert and Margrit Mondavi. We really appreciate your support and kindness. Like the rest of the wine world, we'll truly miss Robert. It was a pleasure and an honor to know him.

We are extremely grateful to Leah Delyte Di Bernardo and the generous people at The Castle Wine Country Bed & Breakfast. The Castle is based in the heart of Temecula wine country and is the must-stay place to make your Temecula visit all the more interesting. Special thanks to Karen Lindstrom for looking after us and telling lots of great stories.

Thanks also to Deborah and Justin Baldwin and Katelyn Silva at Justin Vineyards for accommodating us during our stay in Paso Robles. The house was fantastic, surrounded by vineyards and we had the privilege of seeing magnificent sunrises and sunsets. It's an experience that we will never forget and Justin Vineyards' wonderful wines made the visit even more enjoyable. Thanks again.

When in Napa Valley, Wine Dogs recommends you stay at the amazing Napa River Inn located in the very heart of Napa town. Stunning rooms and pet-friendly, it's within staggering distance from many fine restaurants and wine bars. Many thanks to Lisa Koester for making our exhausting travels less stressful.

Our visit to Oregon was hilighted by our stay at Joan Davenport's Wine Country Farm in Dayton. Heralded as one of the 1,000 places in the world you must see before you die, this Inn is sensational, and Joan's hospitality seemed like nothing was too much bother. Breathtaking views and Joan's superb breakfasts made it very difficult to move on. Thanks for looking after us, Joan, and we can't wait to come back.

Every wine region in the world needs someone like Diane Naggiar whose wonderful promotion of the Grass Valley appellation led us to discover for ourselves what a beautiful part of the world it is. Everyone should visit this great area. Thanks to Diane and Mike for your tour guidance and hospitality – it's much appreciated.

Much thanks to Ron and Mary Bitner at Bitner Vineyards for their sensational hospitality while we stayed in Idaho. Ron's detailed knowledge of the local area was extremely helpful and made visiting this location a pleasure.

Special thanks too to all our contributors: Robert Parker, Brian Doyle, Elin McCoy, Eric Dunham, Garen Staglin, Heidi Barrett, Jennifer Rosen, John Potter, Kris Curran, Larry Oates, Lori Crantford, Mat Garretson, Susan Sokol Blosser, Zoe Williams, Zar Brooks and Adam Lechmere for their excellently crafted stories and support. Thanks guys.

To Catherine Rendell for her amazing Wine Dogs website work, Melinda McFadden, Lily Li and Vicky Fisher for helping make Wine Dogs great.

Our apologies to the wineries that we didn't get to visit. Please contact us and we'll be sure to get you in the next edition.

WINE DOGS USA 3

If your winery and woofer missed out on appearing in this edition, please contact us at entries@winedogs.com and register for the Wine Dogs USA 3. We'll look forward to hearing from you. Woof!